Mass Murder
in the United States

Mass Murder
in the United States
A History

Grant Duwe

McFarland & Company, Inc., Publishers
Jefferson, North Carolina, and London

LIBRARY OF CONGRESS CATALOGUING-IN-PUBLICATION DATA

Duwe, Grant, 1971–
    Mass murder in the United States : a history / Grant Duwe.
      p.   cm.
    Includes bibliographical references and index.

    ISBN-13: 978-0-7864-3150-2
    softcover : 50# alkaline paper ∞

    1. Mass murder — United States.   2. Criminal psychology —
United States.   3. Criminals — Identification — United States.
4. Mass murder investigation — United States.   I. Title.
HV6529.D89   2007
364.152'30973 — dc22   2007013518

British Library cataloguing data are available

Cover photograph ©2007 Shutterstock

Manufactured in the United States of America

McFarland & Company, Inc., Publishers
  Box 611, Jefferson, North Carolina 28640
   www.mcfarlandpub.com

Table of Contents

To my wife,
Susie

Preface

In the fall of 1991, the United States witnessed a series of highly publicized mass murders in which offenders used guns to kill publicly. In October, Joseph Harris, a postal worker, killed four in New Jersey. Later that same month, George Hennard gunned down 23 at a Luby's cafeteria in Killeen, Texas. The following month, another postal worker, Thomas McIlvane, murdered four co-workers at the post office in Royal Oak, Michigan, while graduate student Gang Lu killed five and wounded one more at the University of Iowa. And in December, Joe Johnson carried out a sniper attack in Missouri that claimed the lives of four victims.

My interest in the topic of mass murder was, to a large extent, precipitated by these widely publicized incidents. Like most, I imagine, I was interested in the "why." Why would an individual go into his workplace and attempt to murder his co-workers? Or why would someone enter a restaurant and try to kill as many people as possible? In short, why do mass murderers commit such senseless acts of extreme violence?

As this book attests, my interest in the topic has shifted over the years. When I began studying mass murder, I quickly discovered that the five aforementioned cases that initially caught my attention were the exception rather than the norm. The most common form of mass murder involves a man who kills his wife and children, often in the privacy of their own home. This observation later led to my interest in the news media's coverage of mass killings and, in particular, the role it has played in the social construction of mass murder. Rather than defining social problems in terms of their objective conditions, the social constructionist perspective views them as the product of claimsmaking activity. Examining what others have claimed about mass murder ultimately led to my interest in its history. Most notably, many have claimed that mass murder is a historically new crime that was virtually non-existent prior to the mid–1960s.

1

Reflecting these interests, this book explores the factors that have influenced the prevalence of mass murder in the U.S. In addition to describing the characteristics of mass murderers and the circumstances surrounding their crimes, this work examines the role of the news media in the social construction of mass murder. But perhaps most important, this book attempts to provide a history of mass murder in the U.S., a history firmly situated within the broader social, political, and economic context of the twentieth century.

Completing this book would not have been possible without the assistance from a number of individuals. Professors Gary Kleck, Ted Chiricos, and Jim Orcutt, all of Florida State University, provided valuable commentary on earlier versions of this research. I want to thank my parents, Richard and Mary Kay, for their support over the years. Last, but certainly not least, my deepest gratitude goes to my wife, Susie. Without her love and encouragement, finishing this book would have been impossible. Truly a blessing in ways too numerous to count, she is my little angel. Despite the help I have received along the way, any errors or omissions in this book are entirely my own.

Grant Duwe
Spring 2007

Introduction

Few mass murders are more notorious than the one committed by Richard Speck in Chicago on July 14, 1966. Shortly before midnight, Speck broke into a row house that served as a dormitory for eight student nurses. His crime ostensibly began as an attempted robbery. It quickly degenerated into wholesale slaughter, however, as he herded the young women into the back bedroom of the dormitory and then, one by one, led them to their deaths in other rooms. But Speck, in his alcohol-induced haze, lost track of how many women were in the back bedroom. A ninth student nurse, Corazon Amurao, survived the ordeal by hiding under a bed until she heard the ring of an alarm clock. Reasoning that Speck had left the premises, Amurao cautiously moved out of the back bedroom whereupon she discovered the bodies of her dead friends. Stumbling over their bloody corpses, Amurao made her way to the balcony, where she screamed hysterically, "They are all dead! They are all dead! My friends are all dead! Oh God, I'm the only one alive."

Though badly traumatized, Amurao was able to provide police with a positive identification of Speck. Two days later, he was found bleeding in a Chicago skid row hotel after he had slashed his wrists in an apparent suicide attempt. He was rushed to a local hospital, where he was apprehended after an emergency room physician recognized Speck from his picture in the newspaper. Convicted a year later, Speck was eventually sentenced to life in prison, where he died in 1991.

Looking back on the rampage twenty-five years later, criminologist Thomas Petee said in a 1991 newspaper article that "the Speck case represents the first truly high-profile multiple murder case that we see" (*Houston Chronicle*, December 6, 1991; Section A, p. 11). While the present study shows there is little truth to this claim, it is clear that his crime attracted an extraordinary amount of attention. It dominated the headlines both at home and abroad. Having taken place near the height of the Cold War, the mass murder was used by the former Soviet Union as a political cudgel to attack the United States. *Red Star*, the Soviet military newspaper, proclaimed, "There is no need to seek the help of computers and other techniques to understand what social evil caused this crime. The reasons lie in the New York slums, the ghettos of Chicago and Los Angeles, in the children's toys, books, and television programs which are raising American youth in the spirit of force" (*New York Times*, July 17, 1966).

The Speck case was a major news event largely because it was widely regarded as one of the worst crimes ever committed in the United States. The mass killing was described by *Time* magazine (July 22, 1966; pp. 19–21) as "one of the most horrifying crimes in U.S. history," whereas the *New York Times* (July 15, 1966; Section A:1) declared that it was "one of the most savage multiple murders in the history of crime." Coroner Andrew Toman, who worked on the case, said, "In my six years as coroner, and in many years as police surgeon, I have never seen anything this bad. This is the crime of the century" (*Time*, July 22, 1966; pp. 19–21). Chicago police superintendent O.W. Wilson called it the most shocking crime since the 1929 St. Valentine's Day Massacre, when seven members of the George "Bugs" Moran gang were lined up against a garage wall in Chicago and mowed down with machine guns (*New York Times*, July 15, 1966; Section A:1).

These comments were based not only on the relatively high body count, but also on the notion that mass murders were exceptionally rare in the U.S. before 1966. In the wave of publicity following Amurao's gruesome discovery, the *New York Times* (July 15, 1966) attempted to place Speck's crime in a historical context by listing previous instances of mass murder. Despite stating that "mass murders abound in history," the *Times* painted a different picture of the American experience — only five cases were mentioned. Among those discussed were infamous cases such as the aforementioned St. Valentine's Day Massacre and the 1949 mass shooting carried out by Howard Unruh in which he killed 13 and wounded 4 during a 12-minute walk along a neighborhood street in Camden, New Jersey. Also mentioned was the 1959 murder of the Herbert Clutter family in Holcomb, Kansas. Although newspapers such as the *New York Times* reported this incident at the time it occurred, it did not become well known until Truman Capote wrote about it in his best-selling 1965 "nonfiction novel," *In Cold Blood*. The apparent paucity of mass killings in the U.S. before 1966 conveyed the impression that the Speck massacre was among the nation's first. Indeed, criminologist James Alan Fox said in 1991 that "mass murder was not something that was in our vocabulary until Richard Speck" (*Houston Chronicle*, December 6, 1991; Section A, p. 11).

The enormous publicity given to this case also stemmed from the fact that it was a gripping, tragic crime, a "Sophoclean horror" fraught with melodrama. As the lone survivor, Corazon Amurao provided the news media the means to deliver a grim but fascinating first-hand account to the public, allowing them to experience vicariously the terror of the event. James Alan Fox speculates, for example, that "America was under the bed with her there. That was what was so heart-wrenching. The idea that one survivor was under the bed and watched as, one by one, her friends were removed from the room" (*Houston Chronicle*, December 6, 1991; Section A, p. 11). Clearly, the massacre in Chicago was an incident with which many people could identify: it could have happened to anyone, for the victims were strangers to Speck, seemingly killed at random for no apparent reason. The poignancy of the crime was further "accentuated by the youth and decency of the victims" (*Time*, July 22, 1966; pp. 19–21). The eight student nurses were pursuing a noble, altruistic calling; they were "Good Samaritans" who planned on helping people for a living. Speck, on the other hand, was a hard-drinking ex-convict who sported a "Born to Raise Hell" tattoo on his arm. In light of this striking contrast, the Chicago mass killing truly epitomized a morality play — a dramatic yet disastrous conflict between good and evil.

With the Speck massacre still fresh in the minds of many Americans, the United States witnessed another catastrophic mass murder a little more than two weeks later on August 1, 1966. This time, the location was the University of Texas at Austin, where 25-year-old student Charles Whitman climbed atop the 307-foot-high campus tower and began shooting at passersby below. Armed with three rifles, a shotgun, and three handguns, the former Marine sharpshooter gunned down 14 and wounded 30 during his sniper attack, hitting some victims from as far as 500 yards away. Ninety-six minutes after he began the shooting spree, Whitman was killed in a hail of gunfire after police had cornered him on the observation deck of the tower. It was later discovered that he had also murdered his wife and mother the night before, which brought the death toll to 16 — or 17, counting Whitman.

Recalling that the Speck massacre was dubbed the "crime of the century," Austin police chief Robert A. Miles observed, "It isn't anymore" (*Time*, August 12, 1966; pp. 14–19). Whitman was believed to be "the perpetrator of the worst mass murder in recent U.S. history" (*Time*, August 12, 1966; p. 14–19). According to Lavergne (1997, p. 258), he "committed what was at the time America's largest mass murder." While the number of victims killed was regarded as unprecedented, the horror and anguish caused by the highly visible, sensational mass killing was heightened further by Whitman's seemingly indiscriminate selection of victims. For some, this was painfully reminiscent of the recent mass murder in Chicago. In discussing the two incidents, *Time* magazine (August 12, 1966; pp. 18–19) noted, "What is ultimately so disturbing about the 23 lives so taken is that nearly all were snuffed out for no reason and at random. In almost every case, they were unnamed and unknown to their killers, the incidental and impersonal casualties of uncharted battlefields that exist only in demented minds. They were sacrifices to the irrational, wherein lies, as it always has for reasoning man, the ultimate terror."

The shooting spree in Austin was also similar to the Speck massacre in another respect: it generated heavy media coverage. Reports of the incident interrupted regular programming throughout the world. In fact, Whitman's sniper attack lasted long enough for major news organizations to cover some of the event live (Lavergne, 1997, p. 223). Again, the former Soviet Union used the mass killing to denounce the United States. Tass, the official Soviet news agency, adduced the crime as evidence that "murders, armed attacks, robbery, and rapes have become common in present-day America" (Lavergne, 1997, p. 239). And a Japanese news agency reported that the incident "resulted from an unbalanced situation because of the increased gap between the rich and poor, some of whom are unwillingly sent to Vietnam" (*New York Times*, August 3, 1966).

In the wake of the UT massacre, there was much scrutiny and debate about what caused Charles Whitman, whom some described as the "all–American boy," to commit such an atrocity. President Lyndon Johnson, a native Texan, personally ordered FBI director J. Edgar Hoover to conduct an investigation of the incident (Lavergne, 1997). Also trying to make sense of the tragedy was Texas governor John Connally, who assembled a fact-finding commission to examine the events and circumstances that led up to the mass shooting. The explanations offered for Whitman's rampage focused on the hatred he held for his domineering, abusive father, his use of illicit drugs, and his military training as a Marine — an explanation that was quite popular at the time due to growing opposition to the Vietnam War (Lavergne, 1997).

Whitman's preoccupation with weaponry and use of guns during his attack was seen by the nascent gun control movement as proof that the nation needed stronger gun laws. Connecticut senator Thomas Dodd argued that his gun bill, which was before Congress at the time, might have prevented the massacre since it would have required Whitman to present identification when he bought a rifle and a shotgun on the morning of the shootings. Even though the bill would not have prohibited Whitman from purchasing the guns, Dodd suggested that the mere fact of having to identify himself might have caused him to hesitate and perhaps change his mind (*New York Times*, August 3, 1966). And President Johnson urged Congress to pass the legislation "to help prevent the wrong persons from obtaining firearms" (*Time*, August 12, 1966; p. 15).

A great deal of attention was also given to the small tumor found in Whitman's brain during the autopsy. What made the finding especially significant was that Whitman had asked for an autopsy in his "suicide note" because he suspected that he suffered from a physical disorder due to the tremendous headaches he had experienced in the past (Lavergne, 1997, p. 93). Whitman's mental health was the topic of further discussion when it was revealed that he had seen a psychiatrist, Dr. Maurice Heatly, four months earlier at the university health center. During his visit, Whitman told Dr. Heatly that he had been "thinking about going up on the tower with a deer rifle and start shooting people" (Lavergne, 1997, p. 233). Although Heatly did not consider Whitman psychotic, some believed that his actions were obviously those of a person who had lost touch with reality. New York senator Robert Kennedy claimed that Whitman would have been acquitted had he lived to face a trial because "he was so clearly insane." The solution prescribed by Kennedy was a law that would require persons to be committed for psychiatric treatment if they were acquitted of a federal crime on the ground of insanity. Likewise, Texas governor Connally suggested that persons should be institutionalized for life when they were acquitted on the basis of insanity for murders and kidnappings (*Time*, August 12, 1966; pp. 14–19).

Together, the Speck and Whitman murders were thought to have had a substantial impact on beliefs and perceptions about crime. These two incidents occurred on the cusp of a turbulent period in American society, as the 1960s brought forth political assassinations, the civil rights movement, urban riots, the war in Vietnam, and the rise of the youth counterculture. It was also a time in which crime rates were increasing dramatically. As two of the most celebrated crimes in recent memory, the Speck and Whitman massacres figured prominently in discussions about the rise in crime and were later cited as examples of the general violence problem in the United States (Jenkins, 1994, p. 40). It was also believed that they had a profound influence on the public's fear of crime. Lavergne (1997, p. 270) argues that Richard Speck shattered people's perceptions of safety in their own homes, whereas Charles Whitman had an equally damaging effect on notions about safety in public places.

The Speck and Whitman killings have also played a significant role in shaping what is known about mass murder. Before the 1980s, the term *mass murder* was widely used as a catchall phrase to refer to all incidents in which a number of persons were killed. In the mid–1970s, however, researchers coined the phrase *serial murder* to describe a string of homicides in which one or more offenders killed a number of persons (at least 3) over a relatively long duration (i.e., days, weeks, months, or even years) with "cooling off" periods between the murders (Busch and Cavanaugh, 1986, p. 6; Egger, 1984, p. 348; Gresswell and Hollin, 1994, p. 3; Holmes and Deburger, 1985, p. 30; Jenkins, 1994, p. 56; Keeney and Heide, 1994, p. 384; Newton, 1988, p. x). The creation of the serial murder concept was notable in that it gave rise to a classification scheme in which *multiple murder* or *multicide* replaced *mass murder* as the umbrella term for homicides involving multiple victims. Under the new typology, multiple murders were distinguished according to the amount of time over which the homicides took place. Whereas serial murders occurred over an extended period of time, mass murders were classified as incidents in which one or more offenders killed a number of victims (at least 3 or 4) over a short period of time (i.e., minutes or hours) (Busch and Cavanaugh, 1986, p. 6; Gresswell and Hollin, 1994, p. 2; Holmes and DeBurger, 1985, p. 30; Holmes and Holmes, 1992, p. 53; Jenkins, 1994, p. 21; Newton, 1988, p. x; Rappaport, 1988, p. 40; Ressler, Burgess, and Douglas, 1988, pp. 138–39).[1]

The shift in terminology narrowed the meaning of the term *mass murder*. Popular use of the new, more limited definition was evident at least as early as 1984 when an article in the *New York Times* (August 27, 1984; p. 1:1) commented on the then-recent McDonald's massacre committed by James Huberty. The newspaper reported, "Mass murderers like Mr. Huberty ... kill groups of people in a single outburst," whereas "serial murderers ... kill many victims over a long period." The restricted parameters within which mass murder was discussed were soon visible in academic research as well. In 1985, Levin and Fox published their ground-breaking work on multiple murder in which they moved beyond the single case study approach, which had theretofore dominated the literature, by examining 42 cases of mass and serial murder. As the authors of a landmark study, Levin and Fox (1985, p. 19) were among the first to emphasize the historical significance of the Speck and Whitman killings, stating that these incidents marked the "onset of the age of mass murder in the United States." This claim was based, in part, on the notion that mass killings were an extremely rare occurrence prior to the 1960s. Indeed, Fox (*Houston Chronicle*, December 6, 1991; Section A, p. 11) has asserted that "there were very few mass murders before 1966." Since that time, however, there has been, according to Levin and Fox, an ever-growing mass murder wave in the U.S.

But Levin and Fox were not the only ones who viewed the Speck and Whitman murders as the bellwether of a sharp upward trend in mass murder activity. After 1985, it became common for those in academia and the news media to regard the mid–1960s as a time in which the mass murder rate began to skyrocket. For example, after the 1986 mass shooting carried out by Patrick Sherrill in which he killed 14 and wounded 6 at an Edmond, Oklahoma, post office, an article in *Time* (1986) declared, "In the past two decades, random mass slayings have become increasingly common in the U.S. It is a phenomenon peculiar to the late 20th century: a single twisted soul slaughtering near or total strangers, acting on a vague, incomprehensible motive." Shortly thereafter, criminologist Jack Levin was quoted in a *People* magazine article (1986) as saying that mass murders "have been on the rise in the U.S. since the mid–60s. Before that the episodes in which four or more people were killed were rare. Lately, there has been a dramatic increase."

In early 1988, after a string of high-profile cases occurred throughout 1987, *U.S. News & World Report* claimed that "the nation suffered its worst mass-murder toll ever in 1987." Similarly, an article in the *New York Times* (January 3, 1988; p. 1:1) reported that mass murder was "on the rise." In the article, James Alan Fox repeated the earlier claim that 1966 was the "onset of the age of mass murder." He also said, "Mass murder is still a rare phenomenon and it's hard to make predictions about the future, but over the decades there has definitely been an increase in this type of crime." Forensic psychiatrist Park Dietz concurred: "I've been resistant to calling it an increase, but I think there's no avoiding the fact there is an increase" (*New York Times*, January 3, 1988; p. 1:1). The following year, criminologist Michael Rustigan declared that the 1980s would be known for its "great proliferation of massacres" (*The Orange County Register*,

January 29, 1989; p. A3). And in 1990 Falk (1990, p. 86) claimed that "mass murders have occurred with ever increasing frequency in the United States over the past several decades," and added, "mass murders have become more frequent as the years and decades go by."

Claims about an unprecedented mass murder wave continued in late 1991 after another series of heavily publicized massacres. For example, the *Houston Chronicle* ("Mass killings: A phenomenon made in America," October 20, 1991) reported that although mass killings have only "been around for several decades," their incidence has grown to the extent that they have become "commonplace." Indeed, an article in *USA Today* (December 16, 1991) reported that "mass murder is horrifyingly common in the United States." According to James Alan Fox (*Houston Chronicle*, October 19, 1991; p. A13), mass murders were not only "becoming more frequent," they were also becoming "more deadly." Fox (*USA Today*, December 16, 1991) also made the dire prediction that "there will be even more mass killings in the coming years ... it's going to be horrible." This opinion was shared by sociologist Richard Hawkins, who said, "The evidence is that these things are going to occur on a more frequent basis" (*Houston Chronicle*, October 20, 1991).

The view that the incidence of mass murder continued to grow in the 1980s was repeated several years later by Chester (1993, p. 238), who claimed that "in the United States, the mass murder rate, which had begun to climb dramatically in the late 1960s and early 1970s, continued its meteoric rise." In a 1996 A&E television program on massacres, *60 Minutes* reporter Mike Wallace, who hosted the program, asserted that mass murder was a new crime, stating, "In the late twentieth century a new phenomenon appeared: attacks, without warning, by men intent on killing as many people as they could." Wallace added, "There can be no doubt that in the latter decades of the twentieth century, the senseless and appalling crime of mass murder has occurred more frequently than ever before in history, and that is a grim legacy that America will take into the next century. Part of what has made that possible is the easy availability of guns." The following year, Petee, Padgett, and York (1997, p. 322) reported, "the acceleration of mass murder incidents ... occurred in the mid–1960s." Meanwhile, in his book on homicide in American history, the noted historian Roger Lane (1997, p. 318) alleged that "mass killings clearly ... have been on the rise since the early 1970s." More recently, Hempel, Meloy, and Richards (1999, p. 213) have noted that "the incidence of mass murder appears to have increased during the past half century."

Based on the above statements, it would seem clear that the history of mass murder in the United States is relatively brief in that it did not begin to fully emerge until the 1960s. Recent research has demonstrated, however, that mass murder has a longer history than previously thought (Duwe, 2004). Although the 1960s marked the beginning of a mass murder wave, it was not unprecedented. Indeed, mass murder was nearly as common during the 1920s and 1930s as it has been since the 1960s.

Overview

This book attempts to provide a history of mass murder in twentieth-century America by examining 909 mass killings that took place in the United States between 1900 and 1999. In Chapter 1, following a brief discussion about the operational definition used here, I delineate the prevalence and patterns of mass murder during the twentieth century. In particular, this chapter depicts the mass murder rates from 1900 through 1999 and places the findings within a broader context by comparing trends in mass murder activity with previous research on homicide and serial murder. In addition, this chapter describes the incident, victim, and offender patterns in mass murder. Because less is known about mass killings before the 1970s, much of the discussion focuses on the characteristics of pre–1970 massacres and on the ways in which mass murder has changed over the twentieth century.

Whereas Chapter 1 gives a broad overview of mass murder, a more detailed portrait is provided in chapters 2 through 4. Prior research suggests there were three distinct periods of mass murder activity during the twentieth century (Duwe, 2004). Mass murder rates were relatively high during the first four decades, were low from 1940 to 1965, and then climbed and stayed high for the last third of the century. Consequently, I break down mass killings according to these three periods, with Chapter 2 covering 1900–1939, Chapter 3 the 1940–1965 period, and Chapter 4 the 1966–1999 period.

In these three chapters, I examine the motives of mass killers and the circumstances surrounding their crimes by presenting brief case studies on more than 100 mass murders. To place the discussion of these cases in a historical context, I consider how the patterns and prevalence of mass murder have been affected by the major social, cultural, political, and economic trends of each period examined. I also attempt to show more clearly the trends identified in Chapter 1 by selecting cases that reflect the dominant themes in mass murder for each period. Again, because more is known about the high-profile cases from the recent past, I try to give more attention to the pre–1970 massacres and to the more recent lower-profile cases that have occurred since that time.

As noted above, research on the prevalence of mass murder from 1900 through 1999 does not support some of the historical claims that have been made about it (Duwe, 2004). In light of this discrepancy, why did journalists, scholars, and other commentators see the mid–1960s as the start of an unprecedented mass murder wave? Just as important, why did they make these claims, despite having no evidence? And why did these claims begin to emerge in the mid–1980s and not sometime earlier in the 1960s or 1970s, for example, at the beginning of the alleged increase?

Drawing upon the social constructionist perspective, I argue that mass murder emerged as a new crime problem not because it was, in fact, historically new, but because key claimsmakers *perceived* it was new and began to make claims about it. This perception was largely based upon an overall increase in news coverage of mass killings and, most notably, a growing prevalence of high-profile cases. In Chapter 5, I present evidence indicating the *New York Times'* coverage of mass murder increased in the late 1960s, both in terms of the average number of stories per incident and the total number of stories per year. I further examine the *Times'* presentation of mass murder from 1900 through 1999 by looking at the characteristics that made a mass killing more newsworthy. In addition, I present findings from a previous study (Duwe, 2000) that analyzed newspaper, network television, and newsweekly magazine coverage of 495 mass murders from 1976 through 1996.

The news media have had a substantial impact on the social construction of mass murder. I address this issue in Chapter 6, examining why it was identified as a new crime problem, how it has been typified, and what policies have been recommended to control it. The findings presented in this chapter reveal that claimsmakers have used high-profile cases not only as indicators of trends in the prevalence of mass killings, but also as typifying examples. As shown in Chapter 5, the high-profile cases are the most unusual and least representative examples of mass murder, which is precisely why they are more newsworthy. Consequently, in using heavily publicized cases as typifying examples, claimsmakers have presented a distorted image of mass murder. This is significant because the popular perceptions of a problem often help shape the policy recommendations to control it. Indeed, the policy proposals to control mass murder have consisted mainly of stronger gun laws, particularly a ban on assault weapons, and efforts to prevent workplace and school violence. The focus on guns and violence in both schools and the workplace, however, is a reflection not only of the most publicized mass killings, but also of the values and interests of claimsmakers themselves.

The measure of success in social problem construction is often whether claimsmakers are able to influence the enactment of legislation or policies they promoted. By this standard, claimsmakers were modestly successful in constructing mass murder, for they used high-profile mass killings to bring about a federal ban on assault weapons and to justify changes in policy concerning workplace and school violence. But not all of the solutions offered were embraced by policymakers.

There are several reasons why mass murder never developed into a full-blown moral panic. First, although claimsmakers asserted that mass murder was on the rise, they correctly noted it was still rare. Second, unlike other social problems such as hate crimes, for example, there has been an absence of an interest group whose *raison d'etre* is mass murder. As a result, the limited success of claimsmakers may be due to the fact that none have had a vested interest in eliminating, or at least controlling, mass murder. Finally, there was already considerable opposition to some of the proposals to control mass murder — namely, calls for more stringent gun laws such as a ban on handguns. In the conclusion, I summarize the findings presented here and offer suggestions for future research.

1

The Patterns and Prevalence of Mass Murder

Defining Mass Murder

According to the literature, it is generally agreed that the definition of mass murder is contingent on the total amount of time over which the murders take place and the number of persons killed (Busch & Cavanaugh, 1986, p. 6; Dietz, 1986, pp. 479–480; Fox & Levin, 1998, p. 432; Gresswell & Hollin, 1994, p. 2; Hempel et al., 1999, p. 214; Holmes & Holmes, 1992, p. 53; Levin & Fox, 1985, p. 41; Petee, Padgett, and York, 1997, p. 334; Ressler, Burgess & Douglas, 1988, p. 138). Other criteria have also been mentioned such as the location of the murder and the geographical distance between murder sites (Holmes & Holmes, 1992, p. 53), offender motive (Rappaport, 1988, p. 40; Hempel et al., 1999, p. 214), offender age (Hempel et al., 1999, p. 214), the type of weapon used (Hempel et al., 1999, p. 214), the number of wounded victims (Dietz, 1986, p. 480), and the number of offenders (Dietz, 1986, p. 480). I do not use these criteria, however, because they are either unduly arbitrary or problematic from an operational standpoint. The definition of mass murder used here also does not include riots, lynchings, and other instances of collective violence. Although there is clearly some justification to classifying such incidents as mass killings, I excluded these cases because it is often difficult to disentangle the victims from the offenders.

Following previous research (Dietz, 1986; Duwe, 2000), I distinguish mass murder from spree and serial murder by limiting the former to incidents that take place within a twenty-four hour period. There is less consensus, however, regarding the minimum number of fatal victims necessary for mass murder classification, as previous studies have used either a three

(Dietz, 1986; Holmes and Holmes, 1992; Petee et al., 1997) or four victim criterion (Duwe, 2000; Fox and Levin, 1998, p. 429; Levin and Fox, 1985, p. 41; 1996, p. 58; Ressler et al., 1988, p. 138). I selected the four-victim threshold because, compared to a three-victim requirement, it minimizes the potential for measurement error in the identification of mass killings.[1]

The Prevalence of Mass Murder

Mass murder is, fortunately, a rare offense. Since 1976, the average annual number of mass murders occurring in the U.S. is 27, or about two per month. Given that approximately 20,000 homicides take place each year, mass murders account for 0.1 percent of all homicide incidents. Due to the greater number of victims per incident, however, victims of mass murders constitute approximately 0.7 percent of all homicide victims each year.

But how common are mass killings compared to other forms of extreme violence such as serial murder? Criminologists often refer to the crimes about which little is known as the dark figure of crime. Compared to mass murder, the dark figure of serial murder is substantial. As noted in the Appendix, the Supplementary Homicide Reports (SHR) are an invaluable source of data on mass murder in that they contain information on nearly every homicide that has occurred in the U.S. since 1976. In particular, the SHR include information on the number of victims killed per incident, month and year of occurrence, and where the homicide took place (i.e. reporting law enforcement agency). Because virtually all mass killings take place in one general location over a short period of time, the SHR can be used to identify when and where mass murders (i.e. homicides involving four or more victims) have occurred.

In contrast, serial murders take place, by definition, over an extended period of time (e.g. months, weeks, or years), often in different locations and sometimes even in different jurisdictions. Due to these temporal and spatial issues, the SHR seldom link homicides that are part of a series and, thus, cannot be used to effectively track the incidence of serial murder. Instead, news media coverage has been the primary source of data used to identify instances of serial murder. But the main problem with using news coverage to track the incidence of serial killings is that not all cases are widely reported, making it difficult to locate every case of serial murder.

Moreover, determining the exact number of victims is even more difficult. Serial killers are frequently suspected of having victims in addition to the ones for which they were convicted. Some offenders, on the other hand, have been known to inflate the number of victims they have murdered.

Despite these problems, there have been quite a few attempts since the 1980s to estimate the prevalence of serial murder. As others have documented (Jenkins, 1988, 1994; Kiger, 1990), the earliest prevalence estimates were grossly exaggerated. Conflating the number of unknown victims recorded by the SHR with the annual number of serial murder victims, initial estimates claimed that serial killers were responsible for approximately 5,000 victims each year (about 25 percent of all homicide victims). Further, the number of serial killers operating at any one time was estimated to be as many as 500 (Norris, 1988).

More recent prevalence estimates, however, have been far more conservative. Examining the major newspaper wire services from 1960 through 1991, the FBI found 357 instances (11 per year) of serial murder involving 3,169 victims (99 per year) (Jenkins, 1994). Using a four-victim criterion, as opposed to the three-victim standard used by the FBI, Fox and Levin (2005) identified 494 serial killings since 1900 that claimed, at a minimum, 3,850 victims. Further, they found that there have been approximately 100 serial killers apprehended per decade since the 1960s, resulting in an average of about 10 each year. Fox and Levin estimate, moreover, that during the peak years in the 1980s, the annual number of serial murder victims ranged between 120 and 180. However, given that their data indicate there were fewer serial murders both before and after the 1980s, the estimated annual number of victims is probably somewhat lower.

In light of these figures, it is reasonable to estimate that there are likely between 10 and 15 serial murderers operating at a time who collectively claim between 100 and 150 victims per year. As noted above, there are, on average, 27 mass murders that take place each year in the U.S. Considering that the average number of victims killed per incident is 5.2, the annual number of mass murder victims is a little more than 140. The prevalence of mass murder is thus roughly comparable to that of serial murder.

Trends in the Prevalence of Mass Murder

Although mass murder, like serial murder, is an infrequent occurrence, what are the trends in its prevalence over time? As shown in the last chapter, mass murder was widely believed to have been virtually non-existent prior to the mid–1960s. Recent evidence indicates, however, that mass murder was far from non-existent before the 1960s (Duwe, 2004). Indeed, from 1900 through 1965, the *New York Times* reported at least 173 mass murder incidents that occurred in the U.S. As shown in Figure 1, which depicts the annual number of mass murders reported by the *Times*, there was a modest increase in the number of mass killings reported by the *Times* during the 1920s and 1930s, followed by a sharp increase beginning in the late 1960s. Throughout the rest of the century, the yearly number of *Times*-reported cases fluctuated wildly but remained relatively high.

Figure 1 also illustrates the extent to which the *Times* underreported mass killings between 1976 and 1999. Of the 649 mass murders that occurred from 1976 through 1999, 290 (45 percent) were reported by the *Times*. During this 24-year period, however, there was a relatively high correlation (r = .74) between the annual number of mass killings and those reported by the *Times*. Because the *Times* is a good indicator of trends in overall mass murder activity from 1976 through 1999, this information was used to forecast or backcast the mass murder rate from 1900 through 1975. Further, to account for changes in the U.S. population over the twentieth century, U.S. census figures from 1900 through 1975 were used to calculate annual rates per 100,000 residents of the population (see the Appendix

Figure 1. Annual Mass Murders, 1900–1999

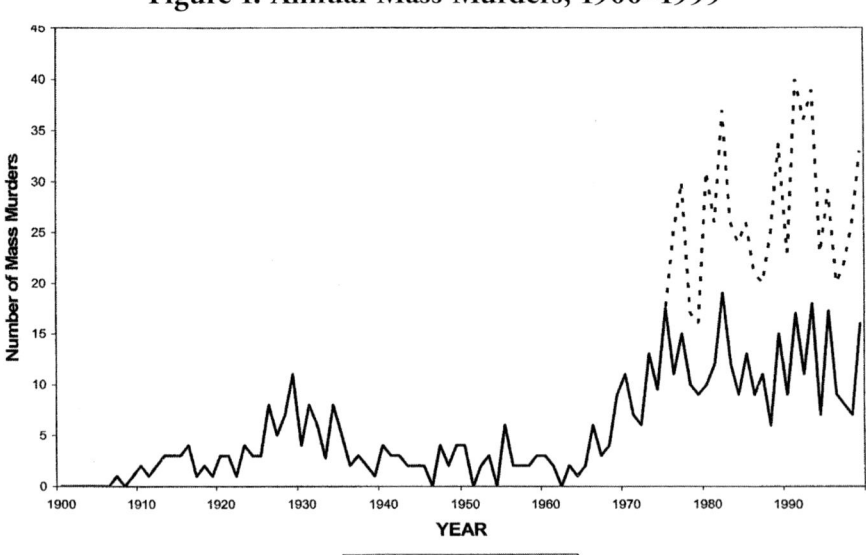

Figure 2. Mass Murder and U.S. Homicide Rates, 1900–1999

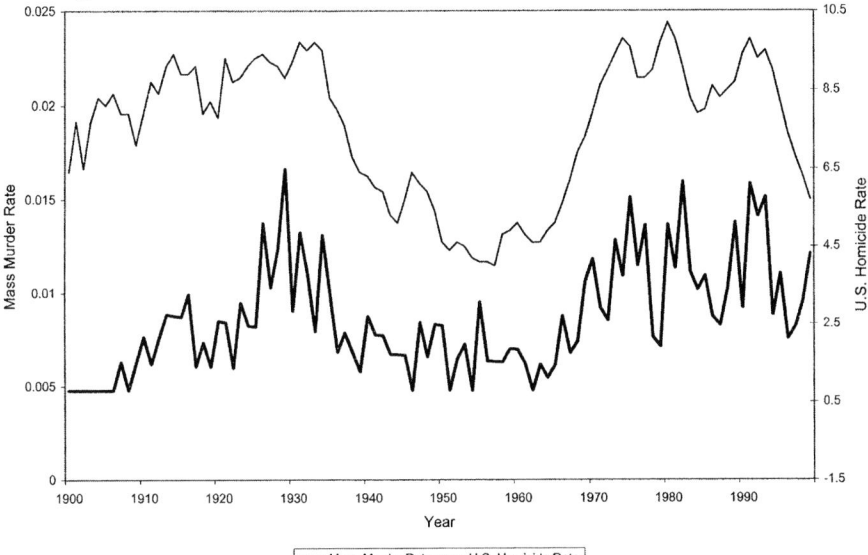

for a more detailed discussion on the methodology used to estimate the mass murder rates from 1900 through 1975).

As shown in Figure 2, mass murder rates were relatively low during the first two decades of the twentieth century. In the mid–1920s, however, the mass murder rate begins to skyrocket, reaching its apogee in 1929, and then starts to fall in the late 1930s. Aside from a brief spike in the mid–1950s, there was a trough in the mass murder rate until the mid–1960s, when it climbed again and stayed relatively high for the rest of the century.

The historical trends in mass murder are generally consistent with previous research on serial murder and ordinary homicide. For example, using extreme cases (i.e. those involving 10 or more victims) as indicators of the overall prevalence of serial murder, Jenkins (1989) suggests that serial killings were fairly common from 1900 through 1940. Following a tranquil period in the 1940s and 1950s, they became much more prevalent beginning in the 1960s. And in his study on U.S. homicide rates, Eckberg (1995) found that rates were relatively high at the start of the twentieth century; in the mid–1930s, they descended and were low until the mid–1960s, when they began to increase dramatically.

As suggested in Figure 2, there is a fairly high correlation (r = .51) between mass murder and U.S. homicide rates for the twentieth century.

This has several implications. First, the factors that affect trends in the mass murder rate may not be that much different from those that influence homicide or even crime in general. Second, the similarity between trends in the mass murder and homicide rates suggests that the pre–1976 estimates may be a fairly accurate representation of the actual prevalence of mass murder. In fact, the correlation between the mass murder and homicide rates for the 1900–1975 period (r = .54) is quite a bit higher than it is for the 1976–1999 period (r = .32).

Nevertheless, despite the similarities, the difference between trends in mass murder and ordinary homicide for the first few decades of the twentieth century may be genuine. But it is also possible that Figure 2 understates the incidence of mass murder prior to the mid–1920s. Evidence presented later in Chapter 5 indicates that before the 1970s the *Times* presented fewer stories per mass killing. This suggests that the *Times* may have considered massacres to be less newsworthy, which would result in a greater proportion of unreported cases. This does not explain, however, why there might be more unreported cases before the mid–1920s.

A more likely explanation is that the estimates are simply not as precise for the beginning years of the twentieth-century. As Eckberg (1995, p. 5) points out, forecasting techniques are typically used to predict values of a variable of a time period close to that in which the equation is estimated. Here, though, there is a 76-year separation between the earliest year (1900) for which I estimated the mass murder rate and the beginning year of the period (1976–1999) in which I estimated the equation on the extent to which the *Times* underreported mass killings. Consequently, estimates from the earlier years of the twentieth century should be viewed with more caution than, say, those from the 1950s or 1960s.

Even if Figure 2 underestimates the mass murder rate prior to the 1920s, the findings still challenge the notion that the mid–1960s marked the beginning of an unprecedented and ever-growing increase in the incidence of mass murder. Although claimsmakers correctly noted that a mass murder wave began in the 1960s, it was neither unprecedented nor did it continue to escalate with each passing year. Rather, Figure 2 suggests that the first mass murder wave in the twentieth century was in the 1920s and 1930s, followed by the one that began in the mid–1960s. As shown later in this chapter, however, these waves were qualitatively different. This finding, together with the tranquility of the 1940s and '50s, may help explain why claimsmakers thought the latter mass murder wave was unprecedented.

The Patterns of Mass Murder

Although previous research has devoted little attention to estimating the prevalence of mass murder, there has been an emphasis on examining the causes and correlates of mass killings. From the 1950s through the early 1980s, research on mass murder consisted entirely of psychological and psychiatric case studies (Banay, 1956; Bruch, 1967; Evseef and Wisniewski, 1972; Gallemore and Panton, 1976; Galvin and Macdonald, 1959; Kahn, 1960; McCully, 1978; Malmquist, 1980). Using data gathered mainly from clinical interviews with just one or, at most, a few offenders, these studies generally focused on the most extreme and atypical mass killings. In 1985, however, Levin and Fox published their landmark study in which they systematically examined 42 cases of multiple murder.

Since Levin and Fox's study, researchers have broadened their approach by attempting to develop descriptive typologies of mass murder. In 1986, Dietz presented a typology in which he classified mass killings into three categories: family annihilators (i.e. paranoid, depressed, and often suicidal individuals who murder their entire families), pseudocommandos (i.e. persons fascinated with weaponry who carry out military-style assaults in public places), and set and run killers (i.e. those who bomb buildings or set fires, usually for the sake of revenge). These categories were retained in the typologies created by Rappaport (1988) and Holmes and Holmes (1992, 1994), although Holmes and Holmes identified two additional types: the disciple (i.e., a young person who follows the dictates of a charismatic leader) and the disgruntled employee (i.e., a fired employee who kills former co-workers or supervisors).

Criticizing these efforts for confounding offender motive and victim-offender relationship, Levin and Fox (1996) created a typology based exclusively on motive, resulting in the following categories: revenge, profit, terrorism, and a warped sense of love. Noting that revenge is the most common motive among mass killers, they further divided these cases on the basis of victim selection into three subcategories: individual-specific, category-specific, and nonspecific. Following Levin and Fox (1996), Petee, Padgett, and York (1997) created a typology based on offender motive, although they limited their focus to mass killings that occurred in public settings. Petee et al. grouped cases into the following nine categories: domestic-related, direct interpersonal conflict, felony-related, gang-motivated, political, nonspecific, and three types of anger-revenge — specific person, specific place, and diffuse target.

The emphasis on creating typologies notwithstanding, several more recent efforts have attempted to describe the offender, victim, and incident characteristics of mass murder in general (Duwe, 2000; 2004; Fox and Levin, 1998; Hempel, Meloy, and Richards, 1999; Levin and Fox, 1996). All but one of these studies focused mainly on mass murders that have occurred since the mid–1970s. The one exception is my study from 2004 (Duwe, 2004), where I delineated the offender, victim, and offender characteristics of 909 mass killings that occurred between 1900 and 1999. The remainder of this chapter discusses the patterns of mass murder and, in particular, notes the extent to which they have changed over the twentieth century.

Offender Demographic Characteristics

The 909 mass killings from 1900 through 1999 involved 1,186 offenders. As shown in Table 1, 93 percent were male and 67 percent were white. The average age was 30, with 42 percent age 30 and above. Thus, compared to ordinary homicide offenders, mass murderers are, on average, slightly older and more likely to be male and white, although blacks are still overrepresented relative to their share of the population. Compared to serial killers, however, mass murderers are slightly younger, more likely to be male, but less likely to be white. For example, of the 558 serial murderers examined by Fox and Levin (2005), 47 percent were above the age of 29, 86 percent were male, and 82 percent were white.

Over the twentieth century, the percentage of male mass killers was consistently high, as there was only one decade where it did not reach at least 90 percent (see Table 2). Prior to the 1970s, however, mass murderers were older and more likely to be white. The greater percentage of white offenders before 1976 is, to be sure, partly a function of the decision to record offenders' race as white when race was not identified in the story presented by the *Times* (see the Appendix for a more detailed discussion). But the decrease in white offenders, along with the concomitant increase in black offenders, since the 1970s may also be attributable to a rise in felony-related cases and, in particular, the emergence of the drug-related massacres, which is discussed in more detail later in this chapter.

Offender Background Characteristics

Research suggests that mass murderers often experience a long history of frustration and failure, both at home and at work (Fox and Levin,

Table 1.
The Patterns of Mass Murder, 1900–1999

Variables	1900–1975	NYT: 1976–1999	1976–1999	Overall: 1900–1999
Average Death Toll	5.82	6.42	5.22	5.39
Average Wounded Count	3.20	8.48	4.31	3.97
Weapon Type				
Gun	63%	68%	69%	67%
Other	31%	17%	17%	21%
Fire	6%	15%	14%	12%
Victim-Offender Relationship				
Stranger	22%	31%	24%	24%
Family	52%	37%	40%	44%
Acquaintance	26%	32%	36%	32%
Public Location	29%	40%	27%	28%
Assault Weapon	0%	4%	3%	2%
Workplace	5%	10%	5%	5%
Felony-Related	15%	19%	25%	22%
Interracial	4%	14%	9%	8%
White Offenders	85%	65%	61%	67%
Average Offender Age	33.56	29.52	29.19	30.12
Percent Offender Age 30–49	40%	41%	36%	37%
Percent Offender Age ≥ 50	8%	5%	4%	5%
Male Offenders	91%	95%	94%	93%
Suicidal Offenders	42%	31%	24%	29%
Average Offender Count	1.24	1.30	1.30	1.28
White Victims	91%	78%	72%	78%
Average Victim Age	25.68	29.90	28.02	27.51
Victims Age <16 or > 40	53%	61%	56%	55%
Male Victims	56%	54%	55%	55%
Region				
Midwest	31%	22%	26%	27%
East	33%	33%	23%	26%
South	17%	22%	29%	26%
West	19%	23%	22%	21%
N	260	290	649	909

1998, p. 438; Levin and Fox, 1996, p. 69). According to Fox and Levin (1998, p. 439), this helps explain the older age of mass killers: it takes a long-term accumulation of failure and disappointment to produce the level of frustration necessary for mass murder. But mass murderers do not accept responsibility for their problems; rather, they hold others accountable, placing blame on spouses, relatives, co-workers, or society in general (Fox

Table 2.
Trends in Mass Murder, 1900–1999

Variables	1900–19	1920–29	1930–39	1940–49	1950–59	1960–69	1970–79	1980–89	1990–99
Avg. Death Toll	5.96	6.95	5.03	4.88	6.25	6.85	4.93	5.11	5.46
Avg. Wounded Ct.	4.00	6.18	1.62	0.62	1.17	3.59	2.60	2.23	6.69
Weapon Type									
Gun	29%	50%	67%	73%	52%	66%	71%	65%	74%
Other	67%	44%	28%	23%	44%	20%	19%	19%	14%
Fire	4%	6%	5%	4%	4%	14%	10%	16%	12%
Vic.-Off. Relat.									
Stranger	25%	9%	14%	19%	21%	31%	31%	24%	24%
Family	28%	72%	42%	51%	62%	51%	42%	42%	39%
Acquaintance	47%	19%	44%	30%	17%	18%	27%	34%	37%
Public Location	33%	17%	35%	46%	25%	31%	28%	24%	29%
Public Shooting	8%	4%	17%	23%	4%	16%	9%	12%	15%
Workplace	8%	6%	7%	8%	0%	6%	4%	2%	6%
Felony-Related	8%	4%	26%	8%	8%	16%	26%	22%	25%
Interracial	8%	6%	6%	2%	0%	3%	7%	8%	11%
White Offenders	75%	93%	94%	93%	100%	92%	66%	62%	58%
Avg. Off. Age	38.00	40.65	43.76	31.12	32.25	30.29	29.04	29.62	28.93
Pct. Off. 30–49	29%	52%	46%	26%	50%	46%	31%	36%	36%
Pct. Off. ≥ 50	4%	10%	17%	12%	0%	9%	2%	4%	5%
Male Offenders	94%	91%	92%	90%	92%	87%	93%	93%	95%
Suicidal Offenders	43%	60%	36%	39%	54%	41%	19%	26%	27%
Avg. Offender Ct.	1.04	1.23	1.29	1.15	1.08	1.16	1.39	1.22	1.36
White Victims	86%	97%	98%	93%	100%	87%	76%	73%	70%
Avg. Victim Age	29.10	19.32	27.24	29.65	26.52	23.46	28.03	27.55	28.45
Pct.Vics. <16 or >40	36%	56%	57%	64%	56%	56%	54%	56%	55%
Male Victims	68%	62%	56%	57%	55%	42%	54%	54%	55%
Region									
Midwest	46%	45%	35%	35%	24%	40%	27%	32%	20%
East	33%	19%	31%	27%	38%	34%	37%	24%	21%
South	4%	21%	19%	19%	21%	13%	22%	27%	33%
West	17%	15%	15%	19%	17%	13%	24%	17%	26%
N	24	48	42	26	24	32	152	270	291

and Levin, 1998, p. 439; Levin and Fox, 1996, p. 71). Perhaps as a consequence of their tendency to view others as the cause of their discontent, mass murderers are frequently described as "loners" (Hempel, Meloy, and Richards, 1999, p. 214). As a result, they often lack a strong social support system, which inhibits their ability to cope with the difficulties they face (Fox and Levin, 1998, p. 441; Levin and Fox, 1996, p. 72).

For many mass murderers, who are already angry, despondent, and feeling persecuted, a divorce or termination of employment is the final straw. Indeed, previous research indicates that mass killings are usually triggered by the loss of a relationship or a job (Fox and Levin, 1998, p. 439; Hempel et al., 1999, p. 216; Levin and Fox, 1996, p. 71). Fox and Levin (1998, p. 440) suggest that the prevalence of these precipitating events may help account for why men are heavily overrepresented among mass killers, even more than among ordinary homicide offenders. Men are more likely to suffer from relationship or employment problems, they argue, because men are generally the ones who are ousted from the home following a divorce or separation and are more likely to define their self-worth by their occupation.

Victim Selection

Like other forms of interpersonal violence, mass murderers are much more likely to kill someone they know. Indeed, of the 909 mass killings from 1900 through 1999, only 24 percent involved offenders who did not know their victims. That mass killers usually target people they know helps explain why mass murder is, like ordinary homicide, largely an intraracial offense. For example, only 9 percent of the 909 cases involved offenders who killed at least one victim outside of their own race.

Because the most common mass murder involves the male head of the household who kills his wife and children, family members are the most frequent victims, followed by acquaintances (Duwe, 2000; Fox and Levin, 1998, p. 436). Prior to the mid–1970s, however, familicides were even more common, constituting 52 percent of the mass killings that occurred between 1900 and 1975 (see Table 1). In fact, aside from the 1900–1919 period, family members were the most frequent victims of mass murder in every decade (see Table 2).

The predominance of familicides among mass killings, particularly before the 1970s, has a notable impact on several characteristics. Because familicides often involve the senior head of the household, offenders were, on average, older prior to the mid–1970s. Moreover, given that the typical victims in a familicide are the offender's wife and children, mass murder victims are younger and more likely to be female than victims of ordinary homicide. The impact of familicides is particularly evident with respect to victim age. For example, during the 1920s, when 72 percent of the incidents were familicides, the average victim age was 19, eight years younger than the overall average from 1900 through 1999.

Weapon Use

When mass murderers commit their attacks, they clearly prefer to use guns. The level of gun use, however, is not significantly greater in mass killings than in ordinary homicides. Instead, the main difference in weapon use between ordinary homicide and mass murder is that the former are more likely to use personal, hands-on type weapons, whereas the latter are more likely to use fire. Indeed, from 1976 through 1999, mass murders were 13 times more likely than ordinary homicides to involve the use of fire.

Because assault weapons have semiautomatic capability, can accept large ammunition clips, and have been used in several high-profile massacres, they have been referred to as "weapons for crime and mass murder" ("Roberti Joins Lobby," 1994, p. A20) and as "the weapons of choice of mass murderers" (Ackerman, 1989, p. A7). However, assault weapons were used in only 4 percent of the gun-related mass killings from 1976–1999. Further, the prevalence of their use is not significantly greater in mass murders than in ordinary homicides, for the available evidence shows that 0 to 4 percent of 911 gun-related homicides involve the use of assault weapons (Kleck, 1997, pp. 141–142).

Gun use was noticeably less common before the 1930s than it was in the decades that followed, when firearms were clearly the weapons of choice. Arguing that guns are most effective means of mass destruction, Fox and Levin (1994) have linked the rise in mass murder since the mid–1960s with the use of firearms. Prior to the 1970s, however, there does not appear to be a strong positive association between the mass murder rate and levels of gun use. For example, the mass murder rate was high during the 1920s, but the percentage of gun use (50 percent) was low; conversely, the mass murder rate was low during the 1940s, yet the level of gun use (73 percent) was fairly high (see Table 2). Further, national surveys indicate no change in the percent of U.S. households reporting a gun, between the earliest survey in 1959 and the surveys in the early 1980s when the mass murder rate peaked. Thus, gun availability apparently did not increase during the period when mass murder rates increased (Kleck, 1997, p. 98).

Lethality of Mass Murders

Fox and Levin (1994) have also suggested that guns have made mass killings more deadly in recent decades, given that seven of the ten worst massacres have taken place since 1980. As shown in Table 2, however, mass murders have not become more lethal in the last few decades. These findings should be interpreted cautiously, though, since the data on cases that occurred during 1900–1975 are derived from the *Times*, which was more likely to report mass killings with larger body counts.

In addition, Table 3 indicates that although 14 of the 25 worst mass murders have occurred since 1980, the increase in high body-count massacres is not necessarily due to gun use. For example, only four of the top 11 cases involved the use of firearms, and the percentage of gun use for the 25 cases (52 percent) is quite a bit lower than for mass murders in general (67 percent). What is clear from Table 3 (as well as from Table 17 shown later) is that although bombs and fire are not used as often as guns in mass killings, they do tend to produce more fatalities.

Location

As shown in Table 2, the 909 mass killings were distributed fairly evenly across the four major geographic regions. At 29 percent, the South had the highest percentage of incidents in 1976–1999. Before 1976, however, 33 percent of the mass killings took place in the East, which is likely due to the *Times'* preference for reporting locally-occurring cases.

Several researchers have asserted that when mass murders take place, they are more likely to occur in a public location (Kelleher, 1997; Palermo, 1997). Only 27 percent of the 909 cases, however, involved mass murderers who killed publicly. Instead, most occurred in a residential setting, which is mainly attributable to the large proportion of familicides among mass killings.

Mass Public Shootings

The mass murders that often capture the public's imagination are those in which an offender publicly guns down victims for no apparent rhyme or reason. Of the 250 incidents that took place in a public location from 1900 through 1999, 191 involved offenders who used firearms. Excluding those that occurred in connection with criminal activity such as robbery, drug dealing, and organized crime, there were 116 mass public shootings during the twentieth century.

The frequency with which mass public shootings have occurred has accelerated since the 1960s. For example, from 1900 through 1965, there were 21 mass public shootings that took place. But from 1966 through 1999, there were 95. The increase in mass public shootings has been most apparent since 1980, for over half (N = 60) took place during the last two decades of the twentieth century.

Table 3.
Twenty-five Deadliest Mass Murders
in 20th-Century America

Death Toll	Date	Location	Offenders	Weapon
1. 168	4/19/1995	Oklahoma City, OK	Timothy McVeigh	
			Terry Nichols	Bomb
2. 87	3/26/1990	New York, NY	Julio Gonzalez	Fire
3. 44	11/01/1955	Denver, CO	John Gilbert Graham	Bomb
4. 43	5/18/1927	Bath, MI	Andrew Kehoe	Bomb
4. 43	5/08/1964	San Francisco, CA	Frank Gonzalez	Gun*
6. 42	12/07/1987	San Luis Obispo, CA	David Burke	Gun*
7. 40	9/16/1920	New York (Wall St.)	Unknown	Bomb
8. 24	9/04/1982	Los Angeles, CA	Humberto de la Torre	Fire
9. 23	10/16/1991	Killeen, TX	George Hennard	Gun
10. 21	10/01/1910	Los Angeles, CA	James McNamara	Bomb
10. 21	7/18/1984	San Ysidro, CA	James Huberty	Gun
12. 20	6/22/1922	Herrin, IL	Unknown	Gun
13. 16	8/01/1966	Austin, TX	Charles Whitman	Gun
13. 16	12/22/1987	Pope County, AR	R. Gene Simmons	Gun
15. 15	7/07/1984	Beverly, MA	James Carver	Fire
16. 14	7/05/1982	Waterbury, CT	Israel Madera Flores	Fire
16. 14	8/20/1986	Edmond, OK	Patrick Sherrill	Gun
18. 13	6/09/1932	Cleveland, OH	L.J. Kamins	
			Sam Nieman	
			Paul Childs	
			Ben Hirsch	
			Ray Turk	Fire
18. 13	9/06/1949	Camden, NJ	Howard Unruh	Gun
18. 13	12/11/1965	Chicago, IL	Robert Lee Lassiter	Fire
18. 13	9/25/1982	Wilkes-Barre, PA	George Banks	Gun
18. 13	2/18/1983	Seattle, WA	Benjamin Ng	
			Willie Mak	
			Tony Ng	Gun
18. 12	4/20/1999	Littleton, CO	Eric Harris	
			Dylan Klebold	Gun
24. 12	6/09/1969	Parkersburg, WV	Susan Bailey	
			Roger Bailey	Fire
24. 12	7/29/1999	Atlanta, GA	Mark Barton	Gun

*Used a gun to shoot the pilot, forcing the plane to crash and kill all the passengers on board.

Workplace Violence

Perhaps the best known type of mass public shooting over the last few decades has been the workplace massacre. Indeed, some have claimed that shootings carried out by disgruntled customers, employees, and former employees have figured prominently in mass murder. For example, in discussing the alleged rise in workplace violence since the mid–1980s, a *Washington Post* article ("Berserk!" October 1, 1989; p. D1) proclaimed that "mass murder seized the workplace with unprecedented fury." Moreover, Kelleher (1997, p. 6) has claimed that the workplace mass killer "has become the most common and prolific mass murderer in American history."

Workplace massacres are quite rare, however. From 1900 through 1999, these incidents made up only 5 percent of the mass murders that occurred. Contrary to the claim by Kelleher (1997), workplace massacres did not emerge in the 1980s to represent a "new strain" in mass murder. Rather, these incidents were nearly as common before the 1980s as they have been since that time.

Felony-Related Massacres

If there was a new type of mass murder that emerged during the twentieth-century, it was the drug-related massacre. Before the 1970s, the only drug-related massacre to take place in the U.S. was the infamous St. Valentine's Day Massacre in 1929. This is somewhat surprising, for the Prohibition Era is notorious for precipitating the rise of organized crime and for spawning violence related to bootlegging. Nevertheless, drug-related massacres started to become commonplace in the early 1970s, as violence grew with the burgeoning drug trade. And the incidence of these cases began to accelerate in the late 1970s and early 1980s, especially in places like South Florida.

It is important to note, however, that the emergence of drug-related massacres was part of a larger trend in mass murder. Aside from a brief spike in the 1930s, massacres committed in connection with criminal activities such as robbery or burglary were a relatively infrequent occurrence until the 1960s, when they began to increase. From 1900 through 1975, felony-related massacres accounted for 15 percent of the 260 incidents reported by the *New York Times*. But during the last 24 years of the twentieth century, these cases constituted 25 percent of the 649 mass killings.

Felony-related massacres are different from other mass murders in a number of ways. For example, as shown later, they usually involve a small group of young black males who gun down slightly older acquaintance or stranger victims. In most mass killings, the violence is expressive because the offenders kill for the sake of revenge or, in some cases of familicide, out of a warped form of love, a belief that the wife and children are "better off dead." With most felony-related massacres, however, the violence is instrumental in that it is a means to an end, i.e., killing an eyewitness to a robbery seemingly offers a greater chance of evading detection. Perhaps as a consequence of this relative absence of emotion, those who commit felony-related massacres are much less likely to engage in suicidal behavior than other mass murderers.

The surge in felony-related massacres since the 1960s has had an impact on the overall patterns in mass murder. For instance, in the last several decades, mass murderers have become younger and less suicidal. The evidence also suggests that since the 1970s they are less likely to be white; as noted in the Appendix, however, the data on offender race are badly flawed before 1976, so it is difficult to draw any definite conclusions about this issue. The rise in felony-related cases has also led to an increase in mass murders involving multiple offenders. Between 1900 and 1975, multiple-offender cases accounted for 12 percent of the mass killings. During the last quarter of the century, though, these cases made up 19 percent of the incidents.

Suicidal Tendencies

Much attention has been given to the suicidal tendencies of mass killers. Despite having no evidence, a number of scholars have asserted that most mass killers die at the scene of the crime, either by their own hand or by police gunfire (Hempel et al., 1999; Holmes and Holmes, 1992; Levin and Fox, 1996; Palermo, 1997; Palermo and Ross, 1999). The majority of mass murderers do not exhibit suicidal behavior, however, as only 22 percent of the offenders from 1900 through 1999 committed suicide, 4 percent attempted suicide, and another 3 percent forced others (e.g., the police) to shoot them. Still, there is some validity to the overemphasis placed on the suicidal tendencies of mass killers in that they are least 5 times more likely to commit suicide than ordinary homicide offenders (Duwe, 2000; also see Stack, 1997).

Prior to 1976, however, mass murderers were far more suicidal than they have been since that time. For example, 42 percent of the offenders from 1900 through 1975 displayed suicidal tendencies compared to 24 percent from 1976 through 1999. The greater prevalence of suicidal behavior before the mid–1970s is likely due to the greater proportion of familicides during the 1900–1975 period. As discussed later in more detail, those who commit familicides often kill themselves afterwards. Meanwhile, the recent drop in suicidal behavior is, as noted above, likely associated with the rise in felony-related massacres.

Summary

Contrary to the claims of academics, journalists and other commentators, there were more than a few mass killings that occurred before the mid–1960s. In fact, mass murder was nearly as common during the 1920s and '30s as it has been over the last forty years. The first mass murder wave was qualitatively different, however, in that it was composed mainly of familicides and felony-related massacres. As shown later, these are two of the least newsworthy types of mass killings.

The second mass murder wave, on the other hand, has contained a far greater number of mass public shootings. The increase in these incidents has not had a substantial impact, however, on the overall patterns in mass murder. After all, despite becoming more prevalent, mass public shootings still comprised only 13 percent of the mass killings from 1966 through 1999. The rise in mass public shootings is nevertheless significant, however, because, as demonstrated in Chapter 5, these are the most newsworthy mass murders. And the growing number of high-profile cases since the 1960s has played an important role in the identification of mass murder as a new crime problem.

But before examining the social construction of mass murder, we will take a closer look at the patterns of mass killings in the next three chapters. In these chapters, brief cases studies are presented on more than 100 mass murders in order to provide a more detailed understanding of these offenders and the circumstances surrounding their crimes. Further, to highlight the findings presented in this chapter, cases are selected that reflect the major trends in mass murder for each of the three periods examined.

2

The First Mass Murder Wave, 1900–1939

At the turn of the twentieth century, the United States was nearing the end of the Gilded Age and entering the Progressive era. The Gilded Age was marked by political scandal and corruption, Reconstruction and racial violence, the end of the Indian wars and the closing of the Frontier. The Industrial Revolution exploded during the late nineteenth century, which helped foment both labor unrest and waves of immigrants to the U.S. in search of employment and opportunities. Indeed, by 1900, the percentage of foreign-born citizens stood at 15 percent, the highest percentage during the entire twentieth century. The Gilded Age was also marked by the rise of corporations and monopoly capitalism. In fact, the Sherman Antitrust Act was created in 1890 to break up the monopolies, although capitalists later used it to thwart the efforts of the labor movement.

Reform was the zeitgeist of the Progressive era, which was, in large measure, a response to the excesses of the Gilded Age. Politicians attempted to reform the political system by introducing initiatives, referenda, and recalls. The muckraking journalistic exposes of 1902–1907, most notably Upton Sinclair's *The Jungle*, stimulated reform in the food and drug industry, resulting in the creation of the Food and Drug Agency. Reform in the railroad and banking industries was established with the creation of the 1906 Hepburn Act and the 1913 Federal Reserve Act, respectively. And the labor movement scored major victories with the enactment of worker's compensation laws and the Clayton Antitrust Act in 1914, which supplanted the largely ineffectual Sherman Antitrust Act.

The reforms achieved during the Progressive Era came to an abrupt halt, however, with the outbreak of World War I in Europe in 1914, and

U.S. involvement three years later. Entry into the war brought about a number of profound changes in American society, including an acceleration of the Great Black Migration to the North (Cooper, 1990). From 1900 to 1909, roughly 200,000 blacks moved North, and this figure grew to over 300,000 during the following decade. One of the consequences of this migration was heightened racial hostility.

After the end of the Civil War in 1865, violence was a popular method by which Southern white hegemony was preserved. Indeed, during Reconstruction from 1865 to 1877, at least ten deadly race riots took place in the South, claiming hundreds of black lives. Yet the toll that these riots inflicted on blacks, at least in terms of the number of victims killed, was relatively minor compared to the carnage wrought by lynchings. Although lynchings undoubtedly began after the surrender at Appomattox, there is not an accurate record of these events until the early 1880s. Nevertheless, in their masterful study of Southern lynchings from 1882 through 1930, Tolnay and Beck (1995) estimate that nearly 2,500 blacks were killed by lynchings during this time.

To escape the social, psychological, and economic oppression caused by violence and Jim Crow laws, more blacks began to move North, especially after World War I. But the violence that blacks encountered in the South followed them to the North. Beginning in 1917, the U.S. experienced a wave of race riots that lasted until 1923. For example, 39 blacks were killed in East St. Louis on July 2, 1917; 13 black soldiers were hanged after they killed 17 whites in Houston in 1917; at least 25 blacks were killed in Elaine, Arkansas, in 1919; 23 blacks and 15 whites died during a week of rioting in Chicago in 1919; 23 blacks were killed in Tulsa in 1921; and at least 40 blacks were massacred in Rosewood, Florida, in 1923 (Goldberg, 1999).

Whereas blacks were, by and large, the victims in these race riots, the *New York Times* reported a number of mass murders committed by "crazed Negroes." On July 3, 1914, Sholl Mannings, a "negro," killed eight other "Negroes" in Texas who had accused him of stealing horses (*New York Times*, July 4, 1914; p. 2:6). He had been arrested twice that week for horse theft, and had broken out of jail both times. After escaping the second time, he started looking for his accusers to exact vengeance. At the time the article was reported, Mannings had escaped again, and a posse was looking for him.

A little more than a month later, Julian Carlston, a 30-year-old chef employed by famed architect Frank Lloyd Wright, used a hatchet to kill six and wound four at the cottage where he worked (*New York Times*, August 16, 1914; p. 12:5). Carlston came to the U.S. from Cuba, and lived in the "Black Belt" on the south side of Chicago. One of Carlston's victims, Mamah Borthwick and formerly Mrs. E.H. Cheney, had an affair with Frank Lloyd Wright, which ultimately led to her divorce. When the victims returned at noon for lunch, Carlston locked the doors and started a fire under the dining room window. According to the *Times*, Carlston "suddenly went mad" and used the hatchet to slash his victims. He and his wife then fled across a cornfield to some woods 16 miles away, where bloodhounds tracked him down and police arrested him.

The following year, William Arthur Steele, a 35-year-old "Negro" employee at the Newton Inn in Danbury, Connecticut, used an axe to kill his wife, brother-in-law, stepson, and stepdaughter (*New York Times*, December 30, 1915; p. 22:2). He killed himself by swallowing a bottle of carbolic acid. And in the summer of 1916, Henry J. McIntyre, a "crazed negro," murdered four and wounded three in Chicago (*New York Times*, July 16, 1916; p. 3:3). Described as "heavy and very black," McIntyre had been regarded as "queer" for years. He harbored a grudge against the police, and told neighbors that he would never be taken alive when they threatened him with arrest for offending behavior.

On the night of the killings, McIntyre wrote two letters, which stated that he was a prophet who had to die in order to take his report to God. McIntyre and his wife then armed themselves, Henry with a pistol and rifle, and his wife, Hattie, with a rifle. They started shooting at neighbors, killing three, until the police showed up. The police burst into the house, whereupon McIntyre killed one officer and wounded two others. Retreating to wait for reinforcements, the police fired hundreds of rounds into the house, with little effect. They then dynamited the house and, after a lull, an officer went inside to find Hattie McIntyre dead and her husband, Henry, barely breathing. McIntyre turned at the presence of the officer, who then shot him dead.

Terrorism: Anarchists, Wobblies and Wall Street

The start of World War I prompted much discussion over whether the U.S. should get involved. Aside from the fact that most Americans thought that the war did not concern them because it was "over there," reluctance to get involved stemmed from a number of reasons. For example, Democrats and Progressives were concerned that increased military spending would attenuate money allocated for domestic reform. Many wanted to appear neutral so as not to stir up the emotions and passions of the different ethnic groups in the U.S. In addition, there were concerns that those encouraging military preparedness, such as munitions manufacturers and Wall Street financiers, were the same ones who stood to gain from the war. Also, by 1915, many Americans were acutely aware of the horrific stalemate that had developed along the Western Front, which involved trench warfare, aerial bombing, and the use of poison gas.

But the war that was "over there" hit home on May 7, 1915, when a German submarine sank the *Lusitania*, killing nearly 1,200, of whom 128 were Americans. Still, the horrors of war prevented a wellspring of support for going to war. Yet the sinking of the *Lusitania* helped ratchet up debate over military preparedness. To marshal support for preparedness, employers in San Francisco organized a parade that was held on July 22, 1916. But at 1:50 P.M., a bomb exploded, killing 10 and wounding 40 more. Witnesses later claimed that two dark-skinned men, perhaps Mexicans, planted a suitcase at the site of the explosion. After all, since the end of 1915, dissident Mexican leader Pancho Villa had tried to provoke American intervention in order to strengthen his hand at home by carrying out attacks against Americans. In January 1916, Villa and his men killed 16 Americans in northern Mexico and 10 more two months later in Columbus, New Mexico.

Nevertheless, police immediately focused their attention on two men who had been actively involved in the labor movement: 34-year-old Thomas Mooney and 23-year-old Warren Billings. A member of the Socialist Party, Mooney was well known in the labor movement. He was convicted of illegal possession of explosives in 1913 and sentenced to two years at Folsom Penitentiary. After his release in 1914, he worked full-time as a union organizer, eventually becoming one of the leaders of the California Federation of Labor. Billings, too, was a member of the Socialist Party, which is where he met Mooney. Barred from employment in the shoe manufacturing industry on account of his participation in a strike, Billings found work with the Ford assembly plant. The police also arrested Mooney's wife and Israel Weinberg. After a hastily conducted trial, Mooney and Billings were convicted, while Mooney's wife and Weinberg were found not guilty. For their roles in the crime, Mooney received the death penalty while Billings was given a life sentence.

Shortly after they were sentenced, however, evidence began to surface that the convictions were based largely on false and perjured testimony. And the man who allegedly orchestrated the frame-up was Charles Frickert, the district attorney. John McDonald, whose testimony helped convict both men, later admitted police forced him to lie about seeing Mooney and Billings plant the bomb. And two witnesses came forth to attest that Frank Oxman, who provided incriminating testimony against Mooney, was 200 miles away from San Francisco when the bomb exploded and, thus, was unable to see what he claimed to have witnessed.

Due to the well-publicized problems with the case, Mooney's sentence was commuted to life in 1918, two weeks before he was to be executed. The case aroused international interest and the campaign for a new trial attracted the involvement of luminaries such as H.L. Mencken, George Bernard Shaw, and Carl Sandburg. Over the next few decades, however, pleas for a new trial fell largely on deaf ears, including those of Franklin Delano Roosevelt during his first term in office as president. In 1939, however, newly-elected Governor Culbert Olson released both men. With failing health, however, Mooney died three years later. Billings, meanwhile, went on to become a watchmaker after his release, and later received a pardon in 1961.

The bomb in San Francisco was followed by several other acts of terrorism, both of which were ascribed to anarchists. In 1917, a bomb was planted outside a church in Milwaukee. After discovering the bomb, a local youth took it to the police station, where it later exploded, killing nine policemen. Although no one was ever charged with the crime, it was believed that anarchists targeted the church because its pastor had openly criticized the anarchist riots that had taken place in Milwaukee several months earlier.

Three years later, an even deadlier bomb exploded on Wall Street in New York City. Although the end of World War I brought about a much-welcomed peace, America's involvement in the war marked the beginning of one of the most repressive periods in U.S. history. The 1917 Bolshevik Revolution heightened fears that communism would spread to the United States. Business magnates such as John D. Rockefeller and J.P. Morgan were targets of a nationwide parcel-bomb campaign in 1919, and Attorney General A. Mitchell Palmer narrowly escaped injury from a mail bomb sent to his home. And there were violent labor strikes in the fall of 1919. The confluence of these factors produced a great deal of hysteria, which ultimately found expression in the first Red Scare. On November 7, 1919, U.S. authorities rounded up about 250 suspected communists across the country in what came to be known as the Palmer Raids. On January 2, 1920, Palmer, whose young deputy was J. Edgar Hoover, directed another mass raid on suspected communists, apprehending over 4,000 people in 33 cities. The violation of legal procedures and general heavy-handed nature of these raids aroused widespread opposition. On Labor Day 1920, strikers from several labor unions clashed with police in New York City (*Daily News [New York]*), April 16, 1998; p. 39).

It was against this backdrop that a bomb exploded on Wall Street, killing 40 and wounding more than 200. On September 16, 1920, a horse-drawn wagon, filled with explosives and heavy window weights to serve as shrapnel, was parked outside the headquarters of J.P. Morgan & Company, in the heart of the financial district in Manhattan. At around noon, a tremendous blast rocked nearby buildings, shattered windows, overturned vehicles, and sent bodies flying through the air. Shrapnel from the blast traveled at least 30 stories high and was found as far as five blocks away. In the aftermath, suspicion was immediately focused upon anarchists and Bolshevists at home and abroad, especially from Italy, Germany, and Russia. A dragnet was placed over the country, as police questioned hundreds of suspects. By 1922, the reward money for information was up to $80,000, but no one was ever charged with the crime (*New York Times*, March 14, 1993; Section 10, p. 7:1).

The bombs in San Francisco, Milwaukee, and New York were terrorist acts in which the real culprits were never apprehended. The 1910 bombing of the *Los Angeles Times* building, however, provides an instance in which the terrorists were caught and convicted. Moreover, this bombing, which killed 21 and wounded 19, erupted out of a longstanding labor dispute. The owner and publisher of the *Los Angeles Times*, H.G. Otis, was a staunch opponent of organized labor; in 1891, for example, he turned back an attempt to unionize the *Times*. In June of 1910, when metal workers in Los Angeles went on strike, Otis was determined once again to defeat the efforts of organized labor. The strike, which sparked violent riots, was faltering by the time the *LA Times* building was bombed on October 1 because workers had been unemployed for four months and only two employers had acquiesced to union demands (*New York Times*, December 2, 1911; p. 4:1).

From 1906 to 1910, the National Erectors' Association (NEA), a trade association, and the International Association of Bridge and Structural Iron Workers (IABSIW), a labor union, had been involved in a heated, and sometimes violent, labor dispute. Indeed, NEA property had been bombed over 100 times during the preceding five years. The similarity between these bombs and the one used in the *LA Times* building explosion led investigators to 28-year-old James B. McNamara. McNamara and his 33-year-old brother, John (or J.J.), were both involved in the labor movement; for example, J.J. McNamara was elected secretary-treasurer of the IABSIW in 1904 (*New York Times*, December 2, 1911; p. 1:4). But in their fight for organized labor, the McNamara brothers used bombs to scare and intimidate their adversaries. Indeed, this was the reasoning offered by James McNamara when he confessed to the bombing of the *LA Times* building.

The arrest of the McNamara brothers was a cause celebre among union sympathizers and activists. Lincoln Steffens lobbied the authorities for their release, American Federation of Labor president Samuel Gompers initially called their arrest a "frame-up," and noted trial attorney Clarence Darrow represented them in court. James McNamara eventually confessed to the crime in exchange for a lesser charge against his brother. He was sentenced to life in prison, whereas his brother, J.J., received a 15-year sentence for pleading guilty to another crime — the bombing of property belonging to Llewelyn Iron Works (*New York Times*, December 6, 1911; p. 1:6).

Violence in the Labor Movement: Ludlow and Herrin

Although catastrophic, the *LA Times* mass murder represents but one link in the chain of the long and bloody struggle between capital and labor. The American labor movement traces its history to the earliest days of the republic, but it did not begin to grow significantly until the post–Civil War period when the U.S. made the transition from an agrarian to an industrial economy. The American labor force was dramatically affected by the Industrial Revolution, nearly tripling in size during the last few decades of the nineteenth century. Due in large part to the increased employment opportunities, waves of immigrants, mostly from Southern and Eastern Europe, flooded the U.S. in the late 1800s and early 1900s.

But despite the immense job growth during the late nineteenth and early twentieth centuries, the nation's wealth became increasingly concentrated among the richest 1 percent. This was, after all, the era of monopoly capitalism in which "robber barons" like J.P. Morgan, John D. Rockefeller, and Andrew Carnegie amassed great fortunes. But it was often at the expense of the common laborer, who usually worked long hours for low wages in dangerous and unhealthy conditions. To improve their circumstances, workers attempted to form unions, a movement that expanded dramatically during the late 1800s. For example, in 1886, twenty years after the creation of the first national labor union, the American Federation of Labor (AFL) was formed. Headed by Samuel Gompers, the AFL consolidated labor groups for the sake of promoting advances for individual trades and crafts.

At the time the AFL was established in December 1886, one of the labor movement's main initiatives was the universal adoption of the eight-hour workday. Earlier that year, however, the campaign for the eight-hour workday suffered a serious setback when seven policemen were killed in Chicago during the Haymarket Square Riot. Eight anarchists were tried and convicted for the crime, despite the fact that the state failed to present any physical evidence linking them to the bomb. Later recognizing the miscarriage of justice, Illinois governor John Altgeld pardoned three of the men in 1893. By that time, however, the other five had already died, four by execution and one by suicide.

The Haymarket Square Riot stands as one of the most infamous examples of the violence associated with the labor movement. But many of the most dramatic and violent confrontations between capital and labor occurred in the coal mining industry. During the 1870s, for example, the Molly Maguires attained notoriety when ten Irish immigrants were arrested, convicted, and hanged for the murders they committed that arose out of a labor dispute in Pennsylvania. In 1885, 28 Chinese coal miners were killed and 15 more were wounded by their fellow miners, who were white, for refusing to join a strike at Rock Spring, Wyoming. During the 1890s, the Homestead Riot claimed 18 lives in 1892, 19 miners were killed and 17 more were wounded in the 1897 Lattimer massacre in Pennsylvania, and 11 were killed in the 1898 Virden massacre in Illinois.

In almost all of these incidents, the violence was precipitated by a strike. The conditions under which miners operated were dangerous. For example, between 1880 and 1910, over 42,000 miners died on the job in the United States. Moreover, miners were low paid and, at the turn of the century, were forced to work 10-hour days. Because leaders in the coal mining industry — John D. Rockefeller Jr. in particular — were fiercely resistant to unionization, workers struck for better pay, shorter workdays, and safer and healthier work conditions. To make matters worse, however, employers often resisted attempts to unionize by hiring strikebreakers or scabs to take the place of the union workers; in addition, they sometimes paid security forces to intimidate the strikers and to enforce order so that the strikebreakers could work.

On September 23, 1914, between 9,000 and 12,000 miners struck against the Colorado Fuel and Iron Company, owned by Rockefeller. Before the strike, CF&I dominated the lives of its employees by operating the stores, schools and churches; serving as town and county officials; and by providing housing. Thus, when miners struck, they and their families were evicted from the company-owned homes and forced to set up a tent colony. Home to nearly 1,000, Ludlow was the largest of the tent colonies.

In response to the miners' efforts to prevent strikebreakers from working, CF&I hired Baldwin-Felts security guards to intimidate the miners and to impose order. After a series of violent incidents, however, the mine operators appealed to Colorado governor Elias Ammons, who sent in the National Guard. This was not the first time that the state would act on behalf of, or favor, the interests of the powerful — the capitalists. Nor would it be the last, as evidenced by the 1937 Memorial Day massacre in Chicago when police killed 10 union members during a Republic Steel strike.

On the morning of April 20, 1914, the National Guard opened fire on the Ludlow camp, and set off two dynamite bombs to signal militia and guards in nearby camps. After a day-long gun battle, the National Guard looted and burned the camp after taking control of it. Because, in the preceding months, the National Guard would frequently spray the camp with gunfire, miners dug pits in the tent floor for protection. As a result, two women and 11 children were killed when the National Guard set fire to the camp. Seven miners also lost their lives that day, bringing the death toll of the Ludlow massacre to 20.

The massacre set off a 10-day battle that would not be quelled until President Woodrow Wilson called in federal troops. The Ludlow massacre shocked the nation, stimulated congressional hearings, and further sullied the reputation of the Rockefeller family. Although the Rockefellers later rebuilt their reputation through skillful public relations and generous philanthropy, the miners' strike failed. And to add insult to injury, no charges were ever brought for the murders committed.

Whereas miners were the victims in the Ludlow massacre, and in most of the other mass killings produced by the coal wars, they were the aggressors in the 1922 Herrin, Illinois, massacre. Located in "Bloody

Williamson" County, Herrin had, since the discovery of coal in southern Illinois in the late 1800s, been chiefly a mining town. By the early 1920s, all of the local mining companies employed workers who belonged to unions. The unionization of the local mines did not come without a cost, however, as there were a number of strikes, along with the usual complement of violence, around the turn of the century.

Therefore, when the Southern Illinois Coal Company (SICC) tried to replace all of its union workers with non-union miners in June of 1922, the local mining community saw it as an attempt to take away what they had fought so hard to achieve. Although the UMWA went on a nationwide strike in April of 1922, the SICC worked out a deal with the UMWA that allowed them to remove coal as long as they did not ship it. But after two months of soaring coal prices, the SICC reneged on its agreement by bringing in strikebreakers to ship out the coal.

After arriving at the mines near Herrin, the strikebreakers quickly came under attack from the union workers, who had surrounded the mines. The strikebreakers eventually agreed to surrender. But when they were being led back to Herrin, they were gunned down by the union miners. The mass murder, which claimed the lives of 20 strikebreakers, shocked and outraged the nation. The shock and outrage only intensified, however, after six miners were tried for the murders, but not a single defendant was convicted.

Workplace Violence: "I told those fellows ... I was coming out to get them, and I did"

Many of the improvements in wages and working conditions since the late nineteenth century can be traced back to the labor movement. Although violence was all too common, especially around the turn of the twentieth century, organized labor attempted to address the ruthless and exploitative practices of capitalists through mostly legitimate, peaceful means like collective bargaining. During the twentieth century, however, there were a number of instances in which individuals attempted to wage their own private battle against what they considered to be mistreatment at the workplace. But the means these men (and they were all men) used were hardly peaceful or legitimate; rather, they avenged their mistreatment — whether real or imagined — by killing those whom they deemed responsible.

Although some have suggested that workplace massacres are a relatively new phenomenon, the results in Chapter 1 showed that these incidents were just as common prior to the 1980s as they have been since that time. During the 1900–1939 period, workplace massacres made up 7 percent of the incidents (see Table 4). One of these cases occurred on June 5, 1909, when John Murphy, a 50-year-old butcher at the North Packing and Provision Company slaughterhouse, used a fifteen-inch razor-edged knife to kill five co-workers and wound four others in Somerville, Massachusetts (*New York Times*, June 6, 1909; p. 1:4). Murphy had lived in Iowa before he moved to Somerville nine years before. In the weeks before the massacre, Murphy

Table 4.
Characteristics of Mass Murders, 1900–1939

Variables	Avg/Percent
Average Death Toll	6.04
Average Wounded Count	4.05
Weapon Type	
Gun	53%
Other	42%
Fire	5%
Victim-Offender Relationship	
Stranger	13%
Family	54%
Acquaintance	33%
Public Location	27%
Workplace	7%
Felony-Related	13%
Interracial	6%
White Offenders	91%
Average Offender Age	41.65
Percent Offenders 30–49	45%
Percent Offenders ≥ 50	11%
Male Offenders	92%
Suicidal Offenders	47%
Average Offender Count	1.21
White Victims	95%
Average Victim Age	23.56
Victims Age <16 or >40	52%
Male Victims	62%
Region	
Midwest	26%
East	42%
South	17%
West	15%
N	114

had been acting strangely. A co-worker had given him a bulldog, which died shortly thereafter. Murphy began to ask him constantly for a replacement, and became very insistent. Co-workers also said that he had been paying particular attention to his slaughtering knife of late, and that he would sharpen it at every opportunity.

On the day of the killings, shortly after 2 P.M., Murphy uttered a shriek and stabbed Dr. Daniel Hayes, a government inspector, in the neck and chest. A veterinarian at the plant saw the attack, and Hayes urged him to find a doctor. Murphy blocked the veterinarian's path, but then a sudden change came over him, as he stepped to the side, said, "Hello, doctor," and allowed him to pass. He then resumed his rampage, attempting to slash everyone in sight as employees rushed for the exits to the plant. One worker, an "Italian," struck Murphy with a heavy iron bar. Knocked down momentarily, Murphy continued his attack until he was hit on the head again and the knife was wrested away from his hand. Murphy took a "fearful beating" until police were able to take him to the police station.

Murphy's attack was unusual, however, in that he used a knife to commit the killings. As seen in Table 5, 93 percent of the workplace massacres from 1900 through 1999 involved the use of a gun. Murphy was similar to other mass killers, however, in that he was an older male who targeted victims he knew. Indeed, 83 percent of workplace mass killers were over the age of 29, and 80 percent of the victims in these cases were acquaintances. As the next case illustrates, workplace mass killers usually exact revenge against current or former employers, co-workers, or clients for a real or imagined injustice, which they perceive has ruined their lives. Perhaps as a consequence of their hopelessness, a relatively high percentage (63 percent) commit suicide afterwards or, in the case of Monroe Phillips, they force others to kill them.

On March 6, 1915, Monroe Phillips used an automatic shotgun to kill six and wound 32 in Brunswick, Georgia (*New York Times*, March 8, 1915; p. 3:2). Phillips, a real estate dealer and prominent businessman, had been a resident of Brunswick for about 12 years. He had recently become involved in litigation in the local courts after losing a considerable amount of money in real estate transactions. He had had a number of dealings with Harry Dunwoody, a prominent attorney and local politician, who was mayor of Brunswick at one time and had served in the Georgia Legislature as a representative and as a senator.

Blaming Dunwoody for his financial losses, Phillips began his attack at noon by killing Dunwoody in his office. Phillips then went into the street

Table 5.
Characteristics of Workplace Massacres, 1900–1999

Variables	Avg/Percent
Average Death Toll	7.27
Average Wounded Count	5.85
Weapon Type	
Gun	93%
Other	7%
Fire	0%
Victim-Offender Relationship	
Stranger	20%
Family	0%
Acquaintance	80%
Public Location	95%
City > 250,000	29%
Assault Weapon	7%
Interracial	37%
White Offenders	59%
Average Offender Age	40.08
Percent Offender 30–49	68%
Percent Offender ≥ 50	15%
Male Offenders	100%
Suicidal Offenders	63%
Average Offender Count	1.00
White Victims	91%
Average Victim Age	37.55
Victims Age <16 or >40	55%
Male Victims	72%
Region	
Midwest	17%
East	29%
South	27%
West	27%
N	41

and began to shoot at the crowd that gathered in response to the initial shotgun blasts. A few people were hit with stray bullets a couple of blocks away. A policeman came upon the scene and wounded Phillips before Phillips killed him. After getting shot once, E.C. Butts, an attorney, went to a hardware store, grabbed a pistol, and started firing at Phillips. Nearly 30 minutes after Phillips had started his rampage, Butts hit him with a lethal shot (*New York Times*, March 7, 1915; p. 1:5). While defensive gun use probably prevented a number of incidents from becoming mass murders over the twentieth century, this case marked the first of three times in which a mass murder was cut short by a civilian with a gun. The other two instances of defensive gun use (the 1931 massacre committed by Marco Demofonti and the 1982 mass shooting carried out by Carl Brown) are discussed later.

Workplace mass murderers often make threats before they carry out their attacks, which is illustrated by the mass murder committed by Charles Layman in Los Angeles on December 16, 1935 (*New York Times*, December 17, 1935; p. 1:4). The 44-year-old Layman was employed by the Works Progress Administration (WPA), which was part of the New Deal launched by Franklin Delano Roosevelt in an effort to provide employment for those who were struggling to find work during the Depression. Layman had been a WPA employee for about a year, and was involved in constructing the big WPA sewer in Los Angeles.

On the Friday before the attack, Layman's supervisor, Jack McCarthy, fired him due to his inability to handle the water buckets. But those who commit workplace massacres are often paranoid and blame others for their employment troubles. McCarthy had noted, for example, that Layman had accused practically every employee of keeping him from his job. When he was later apprehended by police, Layman said, "I told those fellows last Friday that I was coming out to get them, and I did. They have been persecuting me for a year and that foreman wouldn't let me work on that job. But I fixed them up all right. If you only understood the whole thing, you wouldn't blame me for what I did. I know them all and I was going to clean them out."

At 2 P.M. on the day of the shootings, Layman hid in the bushes alongside the workers, armed with a .30–30-caliber rifle, 30 rounds of ammunition, a .32-caliber revolver and 22 shells. Layman rose from his concealed position and fired his first shot at McCarthy, but missed. Recognizing Layman, and remembering that he had made threats to "kill everyone on the job," McCarthy ordered the workers to take cover in a trench. After five minutes of shooting, in which he killed four and wounded three, Layman gave himself up to police. He was then taken away, after a crowd of 200 WPA men, armed with shovels, picks, hammers, saws, and clubs, started yelling, "Lynch him! Lynch him!"

Mass Public Killings: Lunatics and Politics

The incident involving Charles Layman marked the last in a series of mass killings committed in public locations during the first half of the

1930s. On July 23, 1931, Marco Demofonti, a 45-year-old miner, used a shotgun, revolver, and butcher knife to kill five and wound three in Mercer, Pennsylvania (*New York Times*, July 24, 1931; p. 6:6). Demofonti claimed that someone had put poison into his drink several weeks before, which made him suffer from spells of insanity. His strange behavior prompted a visit the day before the killings from a local doctor, who advised that he should be taken to an institution. Unable to sleep that night, Demofonti became obsessed with the idea that he should kill everyone at the Number 2 Mine near the village.

At 7:30 A.M. Demofonti took a shotgun and killed his wife and sister-in-law, while two of his seven children looked on. Taking his revolver and butcher knife, he ran to the street and set fire to the house next door, where he shot at two children and missed. He then shot and killed two people in the street and broke into a home, where he stabbed a mother and daughter. He broke into another home, and shot a woman and her son. Responding to a call for help, several men from the company store rushed to confront Demofonti, who tried to shoot at one of them but his gun jammed. One of the men, George Masters, shot Demofonti in the hip, and the men subdued him until the state police arrived.

The mass murder committed by Julian Marcelino in November of the following year provides one of the rare instances in which an offender used a hands-on weapon to kill publicly. Using two knives fashioned from a bolo, Marcelino, who was described as a 30-year-old "crazed Filipino," killed six and wounded 15 in the streets of Seattle (*New York Times*, November 25, 1932; p. 6:5). Marcelino was stabbing and slashing people in the street when an employee from a nearby hotel called the police. Off-duty patrolman George Jensen, who was returning from a football game, happened to drive by when he saw the massacre taking place. Marcelino was eventually overpowered by Jensen (and others), who said of Marcelino: "He fought like a mad wolf. He had more than human strength."

The next month, James Abernathy, a "Negro" army private, "ran amuck" with a .32-caliber revolver, killing four and wounding one at the Fort Huachuca army base in Arizona (*New York Times*, December 30, 1932). Abernathy served in the Tenth Calvary, which was an all-black outfit, for these were the days when the military was largely segregated. Abernathy was working at the post service station, pumping gas for Captain Joseph Wessely, when he fatally shot Wessely, jumped in Wessely's car and drove to the officer's residence, where he killed his wife, Mrs. Wessely. Abernathy then drove to the home of Captain and Mrs. David Palmer, where he shot both dead. After this, Abernathy began searching for Lieutenant Harvie Matthews, whom he wounded by shooting him four times. The shooting spree ended when Abernathy was killed by the post guard.

The overwhelming majority of mass public shootings involve a lone gunman who targets specific individuals (e.g., former co-workers) or an amorphous group of people (e.g., "Uncle Tom" blacks or society in general) for the sake of revenge. The 1934 shooting in Kelayres, Pennsylvania, was different, however, in that it erupted out of a conflict between two political factions (*New York Times*, November 6, 1934; p. 1:1). On election eve, November 5, a Democratic Party parade marched through the mining village of Kelayres. At 9 P.M., as the parade of 200 passed by the home of Joseph Bruno, a Schuylkill County detective and leader of the local Republican Party, shots rang out. Screaming in terror, paraders scurried to find the nearest shelter. A total of 30 people were shot, five of them fatally.

State police quickly arrived on the scene, and were told by witnesses that the gunfire came from the home of Joseph Bruno. Police entered Bruno's home and found an arsenal of revolvers, shotguns, rifles, pistols, and 100 empty cartridges fired from the guns. All fourteen of the people in Bruno's house at the time, most of whom were family and Republican Party members, were arrested. Friends of Bruno insisted that the Democrats provoked the shooting by stoning the first floor of the house. Denying this claim, paraders said that a few warning shots were fired, which were followed by a fusillade of bullets aimed at the marchers. After Bruno and his followers had been taken into custody, angry marchers threatened to blow up Bruno's house with dynamite, but were prevented from doing so by state police, who had formed a barricade around Bruno's home.

The murders were the culmination of a long-running feud between the leaders of the two political parties. In November of 1933, the Democratic Party, headed by George McAloose, broke the hold that Bruno and the Republicans had on local politics by electing school directors and township officers by a plurality of 100 votes. The Bruno faction challenged the election in court, and a recount gave the Republicans the victory. This did not settle the dispute, however. The start of school was delayed, and additional legal proceedings were still pending at the time of the shootings. The murders had a dramatic effect on the voters of Kelayres the next day. Whereas the Bruno organization had dominated in the past, 90 percent of the votes were cast for the Democratic ticket (*New York Times*, November 7, 1934, p. 14:1).

Celebrated Cases: The Dynamite Farmer

The heavy volume of immigration to the U.S. during the late nineteenth and early twentieth centuries engendered much consternation among native-born Americans about the direction in which the country was headed. The largely white Protestant nativists were concerned about the values and customs the recent immigrants, who were mostly Catholics from Southern and Eastern Europe, brought with them to the U.S., especially the use of alcohol. Although the Temperance Movement can be traced back to the 1820s, the drive for national Prohibition did not become the main focus until nativists felt threatened about losing their way of life.

In a triumph of symbolic politics, the Temperance Movement reaffirmed the importance of rural Protestant society with the passage of the Volstead Act in 1919. But since it did little to attenuate the demand for alcohol, Prohibition created a huge black market for the sale and distribution of alcohol, of which organized crime syndicates took advantage. The violence resulting from the illicit alcohol trade is legendary, but it produced only one mass murder, or at least only one reported by the *New York Times*. Prior to the Speck and Whitman mass killings in the summer of 1966, the St. Valentine's Day Massacre was perhaps the most infamous mass murder in American history.

But it was not the only celebrated mass killing that took place during the 1920s. On May 18, 1927, Andrew Kehoe, a 55-year-old school board treasurer, blew up the school in Bath, Michigan, killing 44, including himself, and wounding 95 (*New York Times*, May 19, 1927; p. 1:8). In June 1926, Kehoe was notified that the mortgage on his farm would be foreclosed the following May, a week before the massacre. Kehoe believed that the school taxes were inordinately high, which made it impossible for him to lift the mortgage. An experienced electrician, he was believed to have planted the explosives in November of 1926, for that was when the school board hired him to make some repairs on the school lighting system. In April of 1927, he was seen wiring the buildings on his farm and was evasive when asked what he was doing. Kehoe was said to have an "ungovernable temper," and that he had developed a "mania" for killing things, such as his horse, which he beat to death that spring. Because he was continually blowing up stumps and rocks on his farm, he was known as a "dynamite farmer."

On the morning of the massacre, Kehoe killed his wife, tied her to a milk cart, and then set her on fire (*New York Times*, May 20, 1927; p. 3:1).

Kehoe then drove to the school in Bath where he set off the dynamite explosives, which were placed under every room of the school. At 9:40 A.M., with 260 students in the building, Kehoe used a coil to fire the explosives from his car, which was parked outside. The north wing of the school collapsed from the force of the explosion.

Witnesses stated that Kehoe sat in his car and "gloated" as he watched the bodies of children hurled through the air. After the debris settled, Kehoe used a shotgun to set off dynamite he had placed in his car. The blast killed him and three others. A total of 37 children were killed; a lot more would have been killed, however, had the explosives gone off in the south wing. Shortly after the bomb at the school, a utility company road crew saw the flames coming from Kehoe's farm. Stopping to investigate, they were told by a passerby that the school had been blown up. As they were getting ready to leave the farm, an explosive from one of the buildings went off. None were hurt in this blast.

Familicides: "All that saves you boys is no more shells"

As shown in Table 4, familicides were the most common mass killings from 1900–1939, constituting 54 percent of the cases. During the Progressive era, most of the cases involved families that were murdered on farms. There were at least seven cases during the 1910–1919 period, and all except two took place in the Midwest. On December 10, 1910, the bodies of Emeline Bernhard, her son, a trapper, and a hired hand were found on her farm in Olathe, Kansas (*New York Times*, December 11, 1910; Part 3, p. 1:2). John Feagle, a trapper, was arrested and later released (*New York Times*, December 18, 1910; Part 2, p. 10:6). Dan Okane, his wife, father, and four children were killed on their farm in Lawton, Oklahoma, on March 16, 1916 (*New York Times*, March 7, 1916; p. 6:4). A razor, hammer, and small caliber rifle were used to carry out the murders. And on December 21, 1919, Adam Shank, his wife, and four children were gunned down at their farm in Cilcrest, Colorado (*New York Times*, December 22, 1919; p. 2:4).

Perhaps the best known of these incidents involves the murder of the Josiah Moore family in Villisca, Iowa. On the night of June 9, 1912, Moore, his wife, four children, and two girls were bludgeoned with an axe on their farm (*New York Times*, June 11, 1912; p. 20:4). The two girls, Lena and Ina Stillinger, were staying there because flooding on the Nodaway River prevented them from returning home. An itinerant preacher, Lyn George Jacklin Kelly, was tried twice for the crimes in 1917 but was acquitted both times (*Omaha World-Herald*, June 11, 2000; p. 1B).

Josiah Moore's brother hired James Newton Wilkerson, a detective, to reopen the case. Wilkerson alleged that Frank F. Jones, a local business-man and politician who later became a state senator, hired someone to kill Moore because the two were bitter business rivals who had a long-run-ning dispute. Rumors also spread in town that Moore was having an affair with Jones' daughter-in-law. Jones later sued Wilkerson for slander, but lost the case, not to mention his reputation.

Wilkerson even arrested William Mansfield, the person Wilkerson thought was paid to carry out the killings. But Mansfield had an alibi — he had been working in Illinois at the time. He later won a lawsuit against Wilkerson for battery after Wilkerson and his assistants held him over a bridge and demanded a confession. However, Mansfield's wife, daughter, and parents-in-law were later killed in the Blue Island mass murder in 1914. On July 5, 1914, Jacob Neslesia, his wife, daughter (William Mansfield's wife), and granddaughter were killed with an axe in their home in Blue Island, Illinois (*New York Times*, July 7, 1914; p. 2:4). This mass murder was later solved. The one in Villisca, however, remains unsolved to this day.

Although the 1920s were, in general, a prosperous decade, they were not "roaring" for everyone. Farmers suffered greatly due to an agricultural depression caused by overproduction and an inability to export food to European countries, both consequences of World War I (McElvaine, 1993). There was an ever-widening gap between the rich and poor, and divorce was becoming more common, rising significantly since 1900 (Stevens, 1991). These factors may have had an impact on mass murder, for the 1920s were clearly the decade of the familicide.

Almost three-fourths of the massacres from 1920 through 1929 were those in which the offender wiped out his family. Most of these cases were instances of parental familicide, wherein the offender killed his or her spouse, children, relatives, or a combination of these. As seen in Table 6, these offenders are usually highly suicidal white males in their 30s. Fur-ther, because the victims in parental familicides typically include the offender's wife and children, the victims in these incidents are younger and more likely to be female.

The increase in familicides dovetails with the agricultural depression during this time, for many of the incidents took place in rural areas on

Table 6.
Characteristics of Parental Familicides, 1900–1999

Variables	Avg/Percent
Average Death Toll	4.67
Average Wounded Count	0.45
Weapon Type	
Gun	62%
Other	29%
Fire	9%
Public Location	8%
City > 250,000	29%
Assault Weapon	1%
Interracial	2%
White Offenders	78%
Average Offender Age	35.24
Percent Offenders 30–49	62%
Percent Offenders ≥ 50	6%
Male Offenders	87%
Suicidal Offenders	64%
Average Offender Count	1.04
White Victims	80%
Average Victim Age	17.42
Victims Age <16 or >40	68%
Male Victims	41%
Region	
Midwest	30%
East	29%
South	21%
West	20%
N	271

farms. In these cases, the father was despondent because he could not provide for his family. And viewing the fate of his family as inextricably linked to that of his own, he would kill his wife and kids, rationalizing that they, like him, would be "better off dead." On March 14, 1925, Maurice Gibson became depressed after failing to meet his expenses that winter in Prather Hill, Missouri (*New York Times*, March 15, 1925; p. 20:2). Using an axe, he killed his four children, who ranged in age from 1½ to 7 years old. After the killings, he ran to his sister-in-law's house one hundred yards away, where he hacked himself with an axe and then slashed his wrist. Gibson recovered once he was brought to a hospital.

On December 25, 1929, C.D. Lawson, a 43-year-old farmer from Walnut Cove, North Carolina, killed his wife and six children (*New York Times*, December 26, 1929; p. 2:4). He committed suicide by turning the shotgun on himself. And just a few days later, J.H. Haggard, a 56-year-old tenant farmer, killed his five children, whose ages ranged from 6 to 18 in Vernon, Texas (*New York Times*, December 30, 1929; p. 8:3). The children were killed as they slept, and then he turned the gun on himself. Poverty was the only motive advanced for the killings; they lived in a poverty-stricken home, and there was no trace of Christmas presents. He left a note that said, "All died. I had ruther be ded. Look in zellar."

Poverty also figured prominently in the familicide committed by Guy Taylor on February 18, 1927, in Utica, New York (*New York Times*, February 19, 1927; p. 2:4). Taylor, a 36-year-old unemployed teamster, used a large knife or razor to slit the throats of his wife and five children, ranging in age from 3 to 16. He then committed suicide by slashing his jugular vein. Taylor had been out of work for two weeks, and he allegedly killed his family to prevent them from starving. They lived in what was described as a "squalid home," and the interior reflected their desperate circumstances.

The surge in familicides also coincides with the rise in divorce rates during the 1920s. Although divorce rates had been climbing steadily since 1900, the 71 percent increase during the 1920s represents the second-largest jump during the twentieth century. Only the 1970s, with a 92 percent increase, had a greater percentage increase in divorce rates. In contrast to familicides precipitated by financial troubles, wherein the motive is often altruistic, the motive in familicides triggered by a divorce, or threat of a divorce, is usually revenge. On November 22, 1922, Ben Burchfield, a 41-year-old restaurant employee, murdered his wife, her son, her aunt and uncle, and her niece in Bristol, Tennessee (*New York Times*, November 27, 1922; p. 1:5). Delline Burchfield (his wife) had been married once before and her son was by this previous marriage. The family had lived in West Virginia and Johnson City, Tennessee, before they moved to Bristol two months before. Burchfield had been separated from his wife, and she had recently been contemplating a divorce. Enraged, he went to the police to complain, stating that he would rather see her dead than to have anyone else have her. He used an axe to kill the five and then burned the house in an attempt to conceal the evidence. When he was arrested, Burchfield proclaimed his innocence, but officers observed that his shirt and pants were covered with blood.

The following year in Cooper's Mills, Maine, John Snow, a 25-year-old recent immigrant from Poland, murdered his wife, who was from Maine, her grandmother, her aunt, and the wife (Mrs. Frank Jewett) and son (Kenneth Jewett) of the local deputy sheriff (*New York Times*,

December 23, 1923; p. 1:4). His wife's mother had given him money on several occasions to get him established in various lines of business, all of which were unsuccessful. He was known for having a violent temper, and his in-laws had confided to neighbors that they were afraid of him. Four months before, Snow was arrested after beating his wife and threatening to kill a man if he mowed grass on a field belonging to his wife's grandmother. Snow had been separated from his wife and their child for some time.

On the morning of the killings, he tearfully told his neighbors he wanted his wife and child to live with him again. He asked to borrow the Jewetts' car so he could drive to see his wife. After being refused use of the car, Snow used a revolver to kill Mrs. Jewett and her 15-year-old son. He then drove to Cooper's Mills, where he killed his wife, her grandmother, and her aunt. Snow committed suicide after turning the revolver on himself. Because local residents would not allow Snow's body to rest in a Christian cemetery, he was buried on a remote part of the farm owned by his wife's grandmother. Three days later on Christmas morning, however, they exhumed John Snow's body, dragged it over the snow to the house where he committed the murders, and built a funeral pyre by setting the house ablaze (*New York Times*, December 26, 1923; p. 1:2).

On January 8, 1926, in New York City, Thomas King, an unemployed 28-year-old chauffeur and mechanic, used a baseball bat to kill his wife and three children (*New York Times*, January 9, 1926; p. 19:4). He then used a razor to cut his throat, but not deeply enough, so he asphyxiated himself by breathing through a gas tube. His wife had filed for divorce shortly before the killings. She had obtained a legal separation several months prior, but reconciled on his promise to behave. He was a heavy drinker who frequently beat his wife, often forcing her to take shelter outside the home. They had a boarder, whose weekly payments were at times the only money with which the mother could buy food. This made King jealous. After the crime, Mrs. King's brother, a policeman, said, "My sister was unable to put up with his brutality any longer and had engaged counsel to start an action against him." King pleaded with her to drop the action and, "it was her refusal to drop it that caused him to do this terrible thing" (*New York Times*, January 10, 1926; p. 3:4).

Familicides were again a prominent theme in mass murder during the 1930s. On June 21, 1930, Raymond C. Spang, a 35-year-old World War I veteran and former schoolteacher and filing clerk, killed his wife and four children by hurling them over the face of West Rock, a 400-foot cliff in

New Haven, Connecticut (*New York Times*, June 22, 1930; p. 1:3). Spang then committed suicide by diving headfirst from the cliff. Nearly two months before the killings, Spang was admitted to the Naval Hospital in Flushing, New York. Deemed "acutely insane," he was promptly transferred to the Veterans' Bureau Hospital in the Bronx, New York. There, Spang was diagnosed with "manic depressive insanity." Spang stayed there until June 20, when he escaped from the hospital, which did not confine Spang because he was admitted voluntarily, and hitchhiked to New Haven, where his family was. That night, Spang had dinner with a friend and then rejoined his wife.

The next day, in celebration of their "reunion," Spang took his family on a picnic to West Rock Park. They found a spot near the edge of the cliff and, once his wife was out of sight, Spang tossed his youngest son, four-year-old Donald, over the cliff. Spang then grabbed his oldest child, ten-year-old Helen, and threw her over the cliff as well. Hearing Helen's screams, Spang's wife, Gertrude, rushed to the edge of the cliff. But Spang managed to overpower his wife and throw his seven-year-old daughter, Lorraine, to her death. By this time, hundreds of onlookers had gathered below and saw Gertrude battling Spang to save herself and their five-year-old son, Raymond. Spang was too strong, however. He threw both his son and wife over the cliff.

Seeing that two of his children had lodged in clefts halfway down the cliff and were possibly still alive, he made the descent to where their bodies were. Police had arrived on the scene and fired a few shots at Spang, but missed. He dislodged both children one at a time, held them up over his head, and heaved them out as far as he could. Spang then threw stones, dirt, and roots at those who tried to help the victims. A fireman tried to reach Spang to talk to him. Spang responded by throwing everything he had at the fireman — a knife, his wallet, his coat, and his waistcoat. Spang then stood up, bent his knees, and dove headfirst over the ledge. His head hit a jutting rock on the way down, and then his body bounced from ledge to ledge until it settled at the base below.

The next day, thousands of people gathered at the cliff to get a look at where the tragedy took place (*New York Times*, June 23, 1930; p. 10:4). The hospital caught a lot of criticism in the wake of the killings. Senator Hiram Bingham announced that he would form a governmental investigation to look into Spang's escape from the hospital. And the local head of the American Legion claimed that the hospital was negligent for failing to notify local police (Ansonia) of Spang's escape (*New York Times*, June 24, 1930; p. 4:3).

As noted earlier, parental familicides are usually committed by the male head of the household. During the 1930s, however, there were a relatively large number of cases involving female offenders. Compared to their male counterparts, female mass murderers are much more likely to kill family members and much less likely to use guns or to be involved in felony-related massacres (see Table 7). Women are also more suicidal, which may be partly due to the large percentage who commit familicide. The younger average age of victims killed by female mass murderers reflects the fact that, compared to men, women are less likely to kill their spouses

Table 7.
Patterns of Mass Murder by Offender Sex, 1900–1999

Variable	Female Offenders	Male Offenders
Average Death Toll	4.94	5.50
Average Wounded Count	1.33	4.18
Weapon Type		
Gun	37%	69%
Other	28%	20%
Fire	35%	11%
Victim-Offender Relationship		
Stranger	10%	24%
Family	67%	43%
Acquaintance	23%	33%
Public Location	14%	29%
City > 250,000	40%	35%
Assault Weapon	0%	2%
Workplace	0%	6%
Felony-Related	7%	20%
Interracial	5%	10%
White Offenders	72%	67%
Average Offender Age	31.55	30.07
Offenders Age 30–49	44%	42%
Offender Age ≥ 50	5%	6%
Suicidal Offenders	51%	32%
Average Offender Count	1.21	1.32
White Victims	75%	78%
Average Victim Age	23.77	27.52
Victims Age <16 or >40	80%	56%
Male Victims	48%	54%
Region		
Midwest	31%	29%
East	30%	25%
South	12%	27%
West	27%	19%
N	59	738

when they commit familicide. Rather, as the cases below illustrate, their violence is often directed exclusively towards their children.

On May 6, 1930, 44-year-old Ethel Geller fatally shot seven of her eleven children and then attempted to commit suicide in Columbus, Ohio (*New York Times*, May 7, 1930; p. 5:6). After her first husband died, Geller married Darby Yelden, who was sentenced in 1926 to serve 7 to 10 years in the Ohio Penitentiary. Since Yelden had been incarcerated, Geller started selling newspapers to try to support her children. Yet, she was "despondent over her losing battle against poverty." An hour before the massacre, she took the children to a photographer to have a group picture taken. With four of the children away at jobs or on errands, she tucked the other seven children into their beds, and then proceeded to gun them down.

Believing that her entire family was stricken with cancer, 38-year-old Elizabeth Fiederer decided to kill herself, her husband, and their three children in January of 1936 (*New York Times*, January 28, 1936; p. 40:7). During the two months prior to the killings, Fiederer went to the Passaic (New Jersey) General Hospital every day with her youngest daughter, insisting that they both had cancer. When doctors told her that they were fine, she refused to believe them. Fiederer then decided that killing her family would be the only way to alleviate their pain and suffering. She turned on the gas in their home, and watched her family die. She, too, would have died, had neighbors not broken into the home and rushed her to the hospital. After days of barely hanging on, she recovered. When told that her family had died, she asked, "Why did you let me live?" She eventually confessed to the crime, chanting, "I did it. I did it." During her stay in the hospital, physicians concluded she was psychotic.

The following year, Mrs. James Walkup used an ice pick to stab three of her children in the heart, strangled her other child, and then used a gun to kill herself in Flagstaff, Arizona (*New York Times*, November 1, 1937; p. 9:1). Walkup had been sick for some time, and was despondent because she feared her children would contract her ailment. On the night of the killings, Walkup called her physician and told him that although she did not need his assistance at the moment, she needed him to call the next morning. After Walkup had put her four children to bed, she crept into their room and used an ice pick to stab three of them in the heart. Her fourth child, 8-year-old Rose Marie, began to struggle when she awoke, so Walkup strangled her. Walkup then walked to a nearby golf course and shot herself. Walkup left a note addressed to her husband that read: "Because of my lack of discipline the children are happier to go this way.

Only grief would come to them. You are strong in faith, never doubting — mercy, mercy to my people. I loved you and I have failed."

Later the same year, there were two familicides committed by women in Iowa. On August 24, Elsie Noland, 30 years old, attached a washing machine hose to the family car outside, ran the hose through the bedroom window of their farm house, and then started the car (*New York Times*, August 30, 1937; p. 3:7). The deadly exhaust gas killed Noland and her six children. Her husband, Albert, discovered the bodies at 2 A.M. Noland left a 15-page suicide note in which she mentioned marital trouble and "grief" as reasons for her actions.

On October 30, Mrs. G.R. McAninch, 35 years old, used a shotgun to kill five of her seven children and herself (*New York Times*, July 24, 1937; p. 30:5). McAninch's husband was in jail in Des Moines (about 10 miles away from Norwalk) at the time, having been arrested earlier in the day for breaking and entering. That evening, her sons Ray, 15, and Gail, 11, had left to attend a Halloween celebration. When they returned home, they found a burning oil lamp, an opened Bible, and a note, written by Mrs. G.R. McAninch, that read: "You will find us dead this morning. Don't get excited ... I have stood all I can take, and best to take the kids along. All that saves you boys is no more shells." The two boys then found the bodies of their mother and five siblings.

Felony-Related Massacres: It's All About the Benjamins

The stock market crash on October 29, 1929, was, in essence, the beginning of the Depression. The U.S. witnessed a wave of bank failures the next year and the unemployment rate, which had been between 5 and 6 percent during the '20s, rose to 9 percent in 1930 and peaked at 24 percent in 1932. For the remainder of the decade, the unemployment rate hovered between 16 and 20 percent (McElvaine, 1993). With much of the blame for the economic crisis being placed squarely on the shoulders of Herbert Hoover, Franklin Delano Roosevelt won in a landslide in the 1932 election, becoming the thirty-second president of the United States. Shortly after Roosevelt took office, Prohibition was repealed and the federal government was expanded dramatically through the New Deal. During the 1930s, radio became more accessible, of which Roosevelt made great use in his "fireside chats."

Perhaps as a consequence of the rising unemployment rates, and resultant increases in robbery, felony-related massacres became more prevalent during the 1930s. On April 1, 1932, three bandits, posing as officers hunting for stolen cattle, entered the home of Melquiades Espinosa, a dairy farmer in Berino, New Mexico, and asked for papers on his herd (*New York Times*, April 3, 1932; p. 29:1). After stating that the papers seemed legitimate, the bandits asked Espinosa for $5,000. When he responded that he didn't have the money, the bandits starting shooting. Espinosa was wounded in the cheek, but his wife and six children were all killed.

The next year, Ben Cannon, his brother, and two nephews were gunned down on their farm in Lacrosse, Virginia (*New York Times*, April 2, 1933; Part II, p 2:2). An estimated $35,000 was stolen from the safe in their home, which had been cracked. The home had been ransacked, as the mattresses were ripped and the furniture was left in disarray. Neighbors said that someone who pretended to want to purchase meat had lured Ben Cannon to his smokehouse. Police officers stated that one or more persons familiar with the Cannons' habits probably committed the crime.

On March 28, 1934, Frank Fielder, his wife, a housemaid, a neighbor, and two others were bound, gagged, and shot to death in the Fielder home in Bremerton, Washington (*New York Times*, April 1, 1934; p. 29:4). Robbery was the presumed motive for the slayings, since the home had been badly ransacked and Mrs. Fielder was known to have several diamonds and other valuable items in the home.

Robbery was one of the motives advanced for the mass murder that occurred in Savannah, Georgia, on December 21, 1938 (*New York Times*, December 22, 1938; p. 2:7). Described as "the most brutal murder in the history of Chatham County," by county police chief W.F. Chapman, J.S. Tillman, his wife, and their two girls, ages 6 and 8, were bludgeoned with an iron pipe. Another man, Tom Chester, was killed by a shotgun blast less than 100 yards away in a filling station where he slept. Police were not sure whether the killings were incidental to the robbery. Three vending machines were taken from the filling station and broken open at a nearby welding shop.

3

The Trough Between
the Waves, 1940–1965

For the United States, World War II began when the Japanese bombed Pearl Harbor on December 7, 1941. The start of the war essentially brought an end to the Depression. Whereas the average unemployment rate during the Great Depression was 16.68, it dropped to only 4.35 for the 1941–1960 period. By 1945, with much of Europe crippled by the war, the U.S. emerged victorious and poised to become a superpower.

Upon returning home, many veterans were eager to get married and start families. During the postwar period from 1945 through 1960, marriage and birth rates increased by 13 and 22 percent, respectively. The baby boom would later have an impact on many aspects of American society, including crime. The postwar period was also marked by a 58 percent increase in college enrollment, as scores of veterans began attending college with the help of the GI Bill. Moreover, the abundance of jobs enabled veterans to buy homes, especially in the suburbs. While suburbs existed prior to the war, they grew by 47 percent during the 1950s.

The unprecedented affluence of the postwar period facilitated "white flight" from the cities and provided more Americans with the opportunity to enjoy a higher standard of living. In 1928, for example, only 31 percent of Americans had what could be described as a "middle-class" standard of living. By the mid-'50s, however, this figure rose to almost 60 percent (Reeves, 2000). And by the end of the decade, most families owned an automobile, washing machine, and television set. The advent of television had a significant cultural impact, as Americans began spending less time at movie theaters, dance halls, and skating rinks. And Americans also had a renewed interest in religion, as evidenced by an increase in church construction and membership during the 1940s and '50s (Reeves, 2000).

Due to the prosperity and concomitant rise in the overall quality of life, some have depicted the postwar period as a halcyon time in American history. Although nostalgia often distorts the past, it is certainly true that during the twentieth century, the 1940s and '50s produced the lowest rates for crime, violence and, as shown in Chapter 1, mass murder. Previous historical research on murder in the U.S. suggests that homicide rates were just as high, and possibly even higher, during the nineteenth century. Although nineteenth-century urban homicide rates were relatively low in cities like Philadelphia and New York (Lane, 1979; Monkkonen, 2001), violence levels were exceptionally high on the American frontier (McGrath, 1984; McKanna, 1997). In his excellent study on the history of violence in America, David Courtwright (1996) attributes the high rate of frontier violence to a bachelor subculture. Violence was common to the frontier, Courtwright argues, because it was an anomic society populated mainly by young, uprooted, single males who were sensitive to insults, indifferent to religion, armed with weapons, and were avid consumers of alcohol and other vices such as prostitution and gambling.

Because trends in the mass murder rate tend to parallel those for homicide during the twentieth century, it is reasonable to infer that the same social forces are responsible for long-term changes in the prevalence of both mass killings and ordinary homicides. It is reasonable to infer, moreover, that mass murder rates, too, may have been as high or higher prior to 1900. This is quite plausible because, as discussed in Chapter 7, there were a fairly large number of nineteenth-century massacres that occurred in connection with the Indian wars, the labor movement, and the racial terrorism in the post–Civil War South. If true, the precipitous drop in mass murder rates during the 1940s and '50s truly represents a historical anomaly. But even if it is not true, the reduction in mass murder activity still warrants some attention.

Although the data presented here do not permit formal hypothesis testing, it is possible to speculate that the trough in the mass murder rate during the 1940s and '50s may have been due to the upsurge of the aforementioned pro-social indicators — marriage, family, jobs, college attendance, home ownership, church attendance, and an overall higher standard of living. Because mass killings are generally committed by vengeful, frustrated, and frequently suicidal males who have had difficulty holding on to their spouse or their job, anomie or strain theory provides a useful starting point in explaining long-term changes in the mass murder rate. Yet, because the postwar period was marked by a rise in conformity and respect for authority, I also borrow from control theory.

The origins of both theories can be traced directly to the work of the French sociologist, Emile Durkheim. In his classic 1897 study of suicide, Durkheim postulated that because human nature is plagued by unlimited desires, society must regulate these desires externally. In times of rapid social change, however, society loses its ability to control the aspirations of individuals, resulting in a state of normlessness or anomie. The breakdown of society's regulatory power, Durkheim contended, gave rise to a host of social problems, including suicide.

In 1938, Robert Merton extended Durkheim's analysis, arguing that anomie is a relatively permanent feature of American society. According to Merton, Americans are socialized to believe that the acquisition and accumulation of wealth is available to every member of society. But the opportunities to legitimately obtain monetary success and social rewards are not distributed equally throughout society, and are especially scarce for the underclass. The social structure, then, is incapable of delivering what culture has promised — the American Dream. The dissociation between the culturally-approved goal of material success and the availability of socially-prescribed means to attain this goal produces an intense pressure or strain to deviate. Frustrated by blocked access to legitimate means for achieving success, many "innovate" by using illegitimate means such as robbery or fraud, or they "retreat" by becoming addicted to drugs or alcohol. The American Dream is, therefore, a paradox: although it has led to economic growth and technological innovation, it has also exacted a heavy cost in the form of high rates of crime and violence. As Merton put it, "A cardinal American virtue, 'ambition,' promotes a cardinal American vice, 'deviant behavior.'"

Others have since elaborated on Merton's theory of anomie. In 1959, one of Merton's students, Richard Cloward, noted that, like legitimate means, there are variations in the accessibility of illegitimate means. Whether an individual commits crime or becomes addicted to drugs depends, in large measure, on which one is more readily available. More recently, Robert Agnew (1985, 1992) developed a general strain theory of crime in which he identified three types of deviance-producing strain. The first type, the failure to achieve positively-valued stimuli, is similar to Merton's conception except that in addition to monetary success, Agnew includes status and autonomy as goals towards which individuals strive. The strain resulting from the failure to achieve these goals stems from a disjunction between aspirations and expectations, between expectations and actual achievement, or when the outcome is perceived as unfair. The second type, the removal of positively-valued stimuli, is especially germane to the present discussion considering that many mass killings are committed following the loss of a job or a significant relationship such as a marriage. The third type of deviance-producing strain is the presentation of negative stimuli such as child abuse, neglect, or homelessness.

In 1994, Messner and Rosenfeld presented an institutional strain theory in which they, like Merton, argued that American culture is characterized by a strong emphasis on the goal of monetary success and a weak emphasis on the importance of legitimate means to pursue success. This combination of pressures to succeed monetarily and weak restraints on the selection of means is intrinsic to the dominant cultural ethos: the American Dream. Messner and Rosenfeld posited that the American Dream promotes and sustains the dominance of one institution — the economy — over all others — education, the family, and the political system. The result of this institutional imbalance is an anomic society that produces high levels of crime due to weak social controls.

Emile Durkheim's work has also had a significant influence on control theorists. As noted above, Durkheim believed that deviance could be expected when society could not sufficiently control the infinite desires of individuals. Therefore, whereas most theories of crime attempt to explain why crime occurs, control theory assumes deviance is natural and, instead, asks why individuals conform. In what is perhaps the most influential formulation of control theory, Travis Hirschi argued in *Causes of Delinquency* (1969) that conformity is more likely to occur when an individual establishes a bond to conventional society. The bond, Hirschi continued, is made up of four elements: attachment, commitment, involvement, and belief. Attachment is the affection and sensitivity that one feels for others, which is essential for internalizing the values and norms of society. Commitment, meanwhile, signifies the extent to which individuals have built up an investment in conventionality or a "stake in conformity." Based on the notion that "idle hands are the devil's workshop," involvement in conventional activities like work or school fosters conformity by reducing opportunities for deviant behavior. Finally, belief refers to one's endorsement of general conventional values and norms.

Utilizing the insights from both strain and control theories, it is possible to offer at least a tentative explanation for the drop in the mass murder rate during the 1940s and '50s. As noted above, the postwar era represented a time of unprecedented economic prosperity. The social structure in the U.S. thus delivered on the cultural promise of the American

Dream to a greater extent than perhaps at any time in the nation's history. The rise in employment and educational opportunities made it increasingly possible for more Americans to legitimately attain material and social rewards. These opportunities also enabled more Americans to develop, in the words of control theory, a stronger bond with society. More men working or going to school meant they were establishing a stake in conformity and were involved in conventional activities.

The rise in church attendance also signified a greater commitment to, and involvement in, socially-responsible behavior. Since the 1969 study by Travis Hirschi and Rodney Stark, criminologists have produced mixed evidence as to whether religiosity has a deterrent effect on crime. Recent studies, however, by Byron Johnson and colleagues, which have used stronger methodology and more refined measures of religiosity, have consistently shown that religious commitment has a significant negative effect on crime and deviance (Jang and Johnson, 2001; Johnson, Jang, Larson, and Li, 2001; Johnson, Jang, Li, and Larson, 2000; Johnson, Larson, Li, and Jang, 2000). Church teachings generally proscribe violent, criminal behavior. Moreover, as an institution of social control, churches act as a buffer against crime and deviance by fostering the development of social bonds, providing opportunities for involvement in conventional activities, and helping vitiate the harmful effects of social disorganization. The increased church participation during the postwar era, then, may have kept some individuals from not only committing crime, but perhaps even mass murder, too.

Mass murderers have frequently been depicted as loners in both the popular and professional literature. The growing prevalence of marriage and family during the postwar period may have curbed the deleterious effects of social isolation. The beneficial impact of marriage and family has its limitations, however, considering that the most common mass killing — familicide — generally involves an offender who is married with children. Although more women continued to enter the workforce after World War II, this was still an era in which the male was the sole breadwinner in the vast majority of households. After the 1960s, this arrangement became increasingly less common due to a range of social, economic, and cultural changes that swept the country. During the postwar era, however, the abundance of jobs and the rise in the standard of living made it possible for more men (they are, after all, the ones who commit the vast majority of mass killings and, in particular, familicides) to provide for their families.

As we will see later in this chapter, the rise of these pro-social indicators did not deter everyone from committing mass murder, but it may have dissuaded those at the margins. That is, there may have been a number of individuals who might have committed mass murder under worse economic and social conditions. For example, a married father of three struggling to make ends meet may have decided that killing his family and himself was the only solution to his problems. A paranoid loner having difficulty holding on to a job in a weak economy may have decided to exact revenge against his former co-workers. Or a small group of young males might have committed mass murder in connection with a drug deal that went bad. However, due to the increased efficiency of the social structure to deliver on the cultural promise of success, more Americans were able to develop a stronger bond to society.

The drop in mass murder activity during the 1940s and '50s may have also been due to the absence of a thriving illicit drug trade, which itself may have been a by-product of the improving economic and social conditions. During the twentieth century, flourishing illegal drug markets have been associated with high levels of violent crime, especially homicide (Zahn and McCall, 1999). During Prohibition, for example, murder rates increased as organized crime syndicates waged war for control over the sale and distribution of alcohol. And since the 1960s, the trafficking of drugs like heroin, cocaine, and crack have undoubtedly contributed to the historic growth in the nation's homicide rate. The illicit drug trade certainly existed in the 1940s and '50s, but it was not vibrant like it was during Prohibition with alcohol and like it has been since the 1960s with harder drugs.

For the men of the silent generation, a wife, a family, a steady job, and a home in the suburbs largely fulfilled their vision of the American Dream. While the overall quality of life improved dramatically during the postwar era, it is worth emphasizing that this was a generation whose formative experiences were the Great Depression and World War II. The hardships they faced may have tempered their aspirations and expectations of success. As a result, there may have been greater harmony — and, thus, less strain — between their expectations and their actual achievements than at any time prior to that in the twentieth century. To paraphrase Durkheim, society effectively, albeit unintentionally, regulated the desires of individuals.

Yet, as Durkheim also observed, "overweening ambition" is intrinsic to human nature. Because success is a relative goal, what is considered

3. The Trough Between the Waves, 1940–1965

successful in one era may not be in another. For baby boomers, who grew up in relative peace and prosperity, the American Dream itself may have changed as marriage, family, and a house in the suburbs may no longer have been seen as the epitome of happiness and success. To be sure, the American Dream may have been less accessible after the 1960s due to changing social and economic conditions. But many boomers rejected the overconformity, respect for authority, and relentless pursuit of material success that characterized the postwar era. Instead, they sought to reform society, which they considered sexist, racist, and materialistic, by infusing it with equality, justice, and love.

The social, political and cultural upheavals of the 1960s were, to some extent, a response to the developments of the 1940s and '50s. Despite the many social and economic improvements, there were still several major eyesores that dotted the postwar landscape. During the early 1950s, for example, the United States saw the emergence of the second Red Scare in the twentieth century. Capitalizing on the tension engendered by the Cold War, Wisconsin senator Joseph McCarthy played a central role in the communist witch-hunt that ruined untold lives. Some women chafed under the rigid stereotypes of the postwar era, which later gave rise to the modern feminist movement. And despite the Supreme Court's 1954 decision in *Brown v. Board of Education*, which ruled that segregation in public schools was unconstitutional, blacks still struggled to gain fair and equal treatment under the law. The nascent civil rights movement was galvanized the following year when the arrest of Rosa Parks led to the boycott of city buses in Montgomery, Alabama.

Workplace Violence: "I'll get them all"

Whatever the reasons for the drop in the mass murder rate from 1940–1965, we still see some of the same themes discussed in the previous chapter (see Table 8). For example, on May 6, 1940, Verling Spencer committed a workplace massacre in South Pasadena, California (*New York Times*, May 7, 1940; p. 1:3). Spencer, 38-year-old principal of the South Pasadena Junior High School, fatally shot 5 co-workers, wounded another, and then attempted to commit suicide by shooting himself in the neck. Spencer first went to work at South Pasadena Junior High School in 1933 as vice principal. When C. Derwood Baker stepped down as principal in 1938, Spencer took over. A year later, however, Spencer took a leave of

Table 8.
Characteristics of Mass Murders, 1940–1965

Variables	Avg/Percent
Average Death Toll	6.12
Average Wounded Count	1.43
Weapon Type	
Gun	63%
Other	30%
Fire	7%
Victim-Offender Relationship	
Stranger	24%
Family	53%
Acquaintance	23%
Public Location	38%
Workplace	3%
Felony-Related	12%
Interracial	3%
White Offenders	94%
Average Offender Age	32.72
Percent Offenders 30–49	40%
Percent Offenders ≥ 50	7%
Male Offenders	90%
Suicidal Offenders	45%
Average Offender Count	1.12
White Victims	91%
Average Victim Age	29.33
Victims Age <16 or >40	61%
Male Victims	54%
Region	
Midwest	32%
East	30%
South	20%
West	18%
N	60

absence due to what was described as a "nervous breakdown." He resumed his duties the following school year, but was reported to be gripped by a persecution complex. He believed that the faculty was conspiring against him in an effort to undermine his administration.

Due to his behavior, a meeting was held at Pasadena High School in which the school board refused to renew Spencer's contract. Spencer, an expert marksman and gun enthusiast who owned a large collection of firearms, responded to his termination by gunning down the three members of the school board who were at the meeting. Spencer then ran out of the building, yelling, "I'll get them all!" He drove the three blocks to

South Pasadena Junior High School, where he encountered Ruth Sturgeon, who was one of his main targets of suspicion. Spencer killed her and shot two others before the police arrived. Cornered, Spencer attempted to commit suicide by shooting himself in the neck. Spencer was granted parole 30 years later in 1970. He was scheduled to work with a social service agency for ex-convicts in Hawaii (*New York Times*, June 23, 1970; p. 39:1).

Another workplace mass killing occurred three years later in Philadelphia. On November 29, William Harrison, a 55-year-old real estate salesman, killed two co-workers and two women who worked at the Y.M.C.A where he lived before he committed suicide (*New York Times*, November 30, 1943; p. 46:6). Harrison, a "negro," was described by those who knew him at the "Y" as a "chronic grouch" who dabbled in astrology. Harrison believed that his two employers, who were partners in a realty company, had slighted him a few weeks before.

To exact revenge, Harrison showed up at his workplace, the George H. White Realty and Development Company, armed with a .32-caliber revolver. Harrison first encountered David Fink, one of the partners, and gunned him down. The second partner, Samuel Clokey, was on the phone when this took place. Herbert Silver, who had called the company on business, heard Clokey plead, "No! No! Don't! Don't!" Harrison then shot Clokey in the abdomen as he tried to escape. Harrison went back to his room at the Y.M.C.A., where he encountered two women, both "negroes," who worked as maids at the "Y." Harrison shot them both and then committed suicide by shooting himself.

Mass Public Shootings: Veterans Run Amok

While many veterans were able to make a smooth transition from military to civilian life, there were others who did not. On April 17, 1949, George McIntyre gunned down four and wounded three in Pullman, Washington (*New York Times*, April 18, 1949; p. 1:6). McIntyre was a 24-year-old owner of an electric supplies store who was a Boy Scout troop leader and father of two. In addition, he had served in the European theater of World War II and won several marksmanship medals. The previous fall, McIntyre had been convicted of resisting arrest. While driving through the residential district of Washington State University, three students jumped on the running board of his car because they thought he had been driving too fast. McIntyre pushed the students off the running board and drove home. Officer Ross Claar, who investigated the incident, testified that McIntyre threatened him with a gun and resisted arrest. McIntyre was found guilty and placed on probation after a jury recommended leniency.

On the day of the killings, McIntyre got into a fight with W.H. Kershaw at the Milky Way Dairy, and cut Kershaw with a knife. Officer Claar was called, once again, to investigate. Claar encountered McIntyre at a service station and told him he was being placed under arrest. McIntyre resisted and, as Claar went back to his car to get his nightstick, shot him with a .22-caliber pistol. As Claar lay dying, McIntyre took his gun and nightstick, and beat him with it. A posse was soon formed to apprehend McIntyre, who had fled to his home. McIntyre saw them coming, however, and was able to kill three and wound two before he was killed by police.

McIntyre was not the only World War II veteran to commit mass murder in 1949. On September 6, Howard Unruh went on a shooting spree in which he killed thirteen and wounded four in Camden, New Jersey (*New York* Times, September 7, 1949; p. 1:1). Unruh was born in Haddonfield, New Jersey, in 1921, and was known as a quiet and moody youth. After graduating from high school in 1939, he began working for the naval base at Philadelphia, where he enlisted in 1942. Unruh served three years in the European theater as an artilleryman, and won marksmanship and sharpshooters' ratings in the service. However, after Unruh's honorable discharge from the Army in 1945, his life started to unravel.

He began a GI course in pharmacy at Temple University, but withdrew after only three months. Always a devout churchgoer and avid reader of the Bible, Unruh stopped going to church in the spring of 1948. In the months leading up to the shooting spree, he had been unemployed, and had not even bothered to look for a job. And Unruh's brother noticed that he seemed nervous and distracted. Perhaps this was because Unruh believed that people in his neighborhood had been making derogatory remarks about him.

Tormented by these thoughts, Unruh exacted revenge against those who, in his mind, had persecuted him. At 9:30 A.M. on September 6, Unruh began a 12-minute walk down his neighborhood street in which he killed thirteen and wounded four. After running out of ammunition, he returned to his home, where he surrendered to police. Diagnosed as a paranoid schizophrenic, Unruh was later adjudged insane.

Aside from the 1929 St. Valentine's Day Massacre, the shooting spree carried out by Howard Unruh may have been the most well-known mass murder in twentieth-century America prior to the occurrence of the Speck and Whitman massacres in the bloody summer of 1966. Following Unruh's massacre, though, there were a number of celebrated mass killings during the 1950s. One of these occurred on March 5, 1950, when William "Willie" Jones, a 19-year-old recently released from a hospital for the criminally insane, stabbed seven persons in Brooklyn, killing four and wounding three (*New York Times*, March 6, 1950; p. 1:6). Three years before, Jones was arrested for purse snatching and sent to the Elmira Reformatory. While at the reformatory, Jones contracted tuberculosis and was sent to the Dannemora Prison Hospital and then to the Coxsackle Reformatory. At Coxsackle, Jones became "irrational" when he went on a hunger strike after being turned down for parole. In December of 1948, he was transferred to the Matteawan State Hospital for the Criminal Insane. Jones was released from Matteawan at the end of his prison term on March 1, 1950, and Dr. J.F. McNeil, superintendent of Matteawan, said, "There seemed to be nothing wrong with him. Our doctors found him emotionally upset and unstable, but suffering from no grave psychosis. He responded rapidly to treatment. For the past few months he had acted like any normal prisoner."

On Sunday afternoon, March 5, just several days after his release, Jones got into a fight and suffered a cut to his forehead. At 3:45 P.M., Jones stepped into the Gold Star Restaurant, grabbed the bread knife from behind the counter, and ran out of the restaurant. Moving at a slow trot in the quiet Brooklyn neighborhood, Jones encountered 25-year-old Joseph Bondolato, who was waiting to board the bus. Jones stabbed Bondolato in the back and, holding the knife aloft, headed up the street. Jones next encountered Kenneth Kennedy, with his 5-month-old son, and James Culhane, with his 15-month-old daughter. Jones asked them, "Do you know me?" Before they could reply, Jones plunged the knife into Kennedy's chest twice. Jones took a few steps up the street but, remembering that the knife was still stuck in Kennedy's chest, went back to retrieve it. Still jogging at a slow pace, Jones came upon 46-year-old Frank St. George, and fatally stabbed him in the chest. Jones then stabbed 18-year-old James Yearns, a friend, who had tried to plead with Jones before he was attacked. Jones continued his deadly jog by fatally stabbing three men, all over the age of 50. By this time, police had been called and eight patrol cars converged on Jones. He "fought back savagely" before he was subdued and taken to the police station.

At his arraignment, Jones expressed the desire "to go to the electric chair." While awaiting trial, Jones attempted to act out this desire by twice trying to commit suicide (*New York Times*, March 8, 1950; p. 28:3). The first time, he soaked his body and clothing with water, removed the bulb from the overhead light fixture, and attempted to stick his finger into the socket. Although a guard managed to pull Jones away, he struggled violently, shouting, "Why don't you let me do it? I want to die, I want to eat my last supper and go to the electric chair" (*New York Times*, March 9, 1950; p. 54:2). About six weeks later, Jones used a shard from a broken plate to inflict a five-inch gash to his throat. The cut, however, was superficial and physicians described his condition as "not serious" (*New York Times*, April 20, 1950; p. 30:5). On May 2, 1950, Jones was adjudged insane and sent to the Matteawan State Hospital for the Criminal Insane (*New York Times*, May 3, 1950; p. 32:7). Before he was sentenced, a psychiatrist noted that he was "in a disturbed mental condition," and added, "His assaultive behavior is attributed to the influence of delusions and hallucinations. He is dangerous to the welfare of others, and further hospitalization is necessary."

In response to the massacre, City Councilman Alcysius J. Maickel introduced a resolution that called for an investigation of the parole and release system in place at Matteawan. And three years later, the widow of Frank St. George received $40,712 from the state after a judge ruled that hospital officials were negligent in releasing Jones on the basis of an erroneous diagnosis just a few days before his release (*New York Times*, February 5, 1953; p. 32:7). Hospital records from Matteawan indicated that Jones had frequently been classified as a "disturbed patient" who had been put in a straitjacket on a number of occasions. Judge George Sylvester noted, "The inference is inescapable from the record that the prison psychiatrists were never actually aware of the extent and nature of Jones' assaultive and disturbed behavior and that, consequently, no substantial effort was made at any time to ascertain the delusional motivation for his assaultive conduct." Sylvester cited patient overcrowding, staff shortage, and inadequate supervision as reasons for Jones' discharge.

John Gilbert Graham committed one of the deadliest mass murders in U.S. history on November 1, 1955, when the bomb he planted in his mother's briefcase exploded on a United Air Lines plane as it flew over Colorado; the blast killed all 44 people on board the flight, including his mother (*New York Times*, November 15, 1955; p. 1:2). In fact, the 23-year-old Graham, who was married and the father of two children, had bought

$37,500 worth of vending-machine insurance policies on his mother's life before he placed the bomb in his mother's luggage. As it turned out, Graham would not have been able to collect the insurance money since the policies required his mother's signature. Convicted of the mass murder, he was sentenced to death and later executed in 1959.

Six years later, Frank Gonzalez killed 43 people and himself when he caused a Pacific Air Lines F-27 propjet to crash after he shot the pilot and co-pilot (*New York Times*, May 9, 1964; p. 1:8). Gonzalez, a 27-year-old warehouseman in a department store, grew up in the Philippines, and represented his country in the 1960 Olympics as a yachtsman (*New York Times*, May 10, 1964; p. 1:7). He decided to make San Francisco his home, however, after he saw the city on his way back from the Olympics. Gonzalez was married and had a young son, but two months before the plane crash, his wife left him. His wife, Patricia, had described him as a man with "funny habits ... but nothing really strange. He was outgoing, a good mixer who enjoyed being with people. But he really didn't have any close friends." She also noted that Gonzalez was unhappy over their separation. Gonzalez may have also been unhappy over his financial troubles, as he was deep in debt.

Before he left on the flight, Gonzalez bought a .357 revolver and ammunition, showed it to numerous friends, and told them he was going to kill himself on May 6 or 7. On May 6, Gonzalez boarded a flight to Reno to do some gambling. His brother recalled that Gonzalez had a penchant for gambling, and would sometimes go to Reno without telling his family. After a night of gambling, Gonzalez went to the airport, where he bought insurance policies totaling $105,000. Gonzalez boarded the plane and, when they were about 50 miles from San Francisco, shot the pilot and co-pilot, causing the plane to crash into a hill near Dublin, California (*New York Times*, November 3, 1964; p. 33:8).

Felony-Related Massacres: The Clutter Murders

On November 16, 1959, the *New York Times* presented a story on the murder of the Herbert Clutter family in Holcomb, Kansas. Intrigued by the article, Truman Capote went to Holcomb and began conducting interviews. After spending six years researching and writing the book, Capote published *In Cold Blood* in 1965. It quickly became a best-seller, and later won much critical acclaim. It also provides a vivid illustration of the felony-related massacre, which, as noted earlier, became more common beginning in the late 1960s.

Compared to other mass killings, felony-related massacres are much more likely to take place in a large urban area (see Table 9). Moreover, whereas mass killings tend to be committed by white males in their late 20s and early 30s who act alone, these incidents are more likely to be carried out by young black males operating in small groups of two, three or four. Finally, offenders who commit felony-related massacres are much less likely to engage in suicidal behavior than other mass murderers; in fact, the percentage of suicidal behavior in these incidents is similar to that seen for ordinary homicide.

Although the Clutter family mass murder took place in a rural area, it still, in many ways, provides a fairly representative example of a felony-related massacre.[1] The seeds for this massacre were planted at the Kansas State Penitentiary in Lansing. In June of 1959, Richard "Dick" Hickock shared a cell with Floyd Wells, who had just started serving a three- to five-year sentence for breaking into an appliance store. One day, the two cellmates began talking about previous jobs they had had, and Wells mentioned that he had worked for Herbert Clutter ten years before. He told Hickock that Clutter was a wealthy farmer who, at times, spent $10,000 a week to run his operation. He also recalled that Clutter kept a safe in his home. Suddenly interested, Hickock began asking questions about the Clutter family and the layout of their house. He told Wells that he and Perry Smith, a former cellmate at Lansing, were going to rob and kill the Clutters so as to leave no witnesses, and described in detail how they were going to do it.

Hickock wanted Perry Smith to be his accomplice because he thought Smith was a "natural killer," for Smith had told Hickock about the time he killed a black man in Las Vegas simply for "the hell of it." Although this story turned out to be apocryphal, Perry Smith was known for his violent tendencies. He was the youngest of four children born to Tex John Smith and Flo Buckskin, who met while touring on the Western rodeo circuit. After ailments forced both to retire from the rodeo, the family settled in Reno, Nevada. There, life was far from ideal for Perry Smith. His mother, a promiscuous woman who abused alcohol, fought often with his father. When Perry Smith was 6, his mother left his father and took the children to San Francisco. Allowed to roam free due to his mother's neglect, Smith began stealing and running away from home, which led to numerous stays in detention homes. At the age of nine, Smith went to live

Table 9.
Characteristics of Felony-Related Massacres, 1900–1999

Variables	Avg/Percent
Average Death Toll	4.58
Average Wounded Count	0.51
Weapon Type	
Gun	83%
Other	13%
Fire	4%
Victim-Offender Relationship	
Stranger	49%
Family	6%
Acquaintance	45%
Public Location	40%
City > 250,000 a	50%
Assault Weapon	1%
Interracial	13%
White Offenders	47%
Average Offender Age	26.05
Percent Offender 30–49	21%
Percent Offender ≥ 50	2%
Male Offenders	97%
Suicidal Offenders	5%
Average Offender Count	1.83
White Victims	65%
Average Victim Age	30.71
Victims Age <16 or >40	42%
Male Victims	66%
Region	
Midwest	19%
East	22%
South	34%
West	25%
N	194

with his father and completed the third grade, which was his last year of schooling.

Although Smith felt he was supremely intelligent, his lack of education would later arouse feelings of inferiority and hatred towards his father, whom he blamed for forcing him to drop out. Smith lived and worked with his father until the age of 16, when he joined the Merchant Marines. In 1948, he began a four-year stint in the Army, which included time served in the Korean War. After his discharge from the Army in 1952, Smith was involved in a serious motorcycle accident, and spent six months in a hospital in Washington and another six months on crutches. For the next several years, Smith drifted around the country, and was eventually arrested for burglarizing a store in Phillipsburg, Kansas. He escaped from the jail where he was being held, but was later recaptured in New York. Convicted of grand larceny, burglary and escaping jail, Smith started serving a 5- to 10-year sentence in 1956 at the Kansas State Penitentiary in Lansing. And it was there that Smith would soon meet Dick Hickock.

Dick Hickock was born in 1928, and grew up in what he described as a "normal" home. Although he had above-average intelligence — he scored 130 on an IQ test administered to him in prison — he did not excel in the classroom. He was a good athlete, however, as he was offered several scholarships to attend college. But lacking the money to go to college, Hickock got a job as a railway trackman and married his 16-year-old girlfriend after graduating from high school. In 1950, Hickock was involved in a serious car accident in which he suffered extensive head injuries. Later, during the trial, his attorney argued that these injuries resulted in organic brain damage, which significantly altered Hickock's personality. It is debatable, however, whether the head injuries he suffered gave rise to criminal tendencies, considering that he was arrested for breaking into a drug store in 1949, one year prior to the accident.

Over the next several years, Hickock bounced around from job to job, working as an ambulance driver, a car painter, and a garage mechanic. It was during this time that he began to act on his previously latent pedophiliac impulses. In early 1957, when he was working as a garage mechanic, he started dating a 16-year-old girl, which prompted Hickock's wife to file for divorce. Although Hickock married the girl, he began to drink heavily, neglect his business, and write bad checks. Toward the end of 1957, he was arrested for burglarizing a home in Johnson County, Kansas. Hickock was convicted, and given a 5-year sentence at the Kansas State Penitentiary in Lansing. There, he shared a cell with Perry Smith, his future partner-in-crime, and Floyd Wells, the man who gave him the idea for the Clutter murders.

After serving 17 months of his sentence, Hickock was released from prison on August 13, 1959. In October, Hickock sent Perry Smith, who was released earlier on July 6, 1959, a couple of letters in which he urged Smith to join him in pulling off the "perfect score." Taking a Greyhound bus from Idaho, Smith arrived in Kansas City on November 12, 1959. A few days later, on the afternoon of November 14, the pair began the 400-mile drive from Olathe to the Clutter house in Holcomb. They arrived at midnight, and Smith initially wanted to back out when he saw the lights come on at a house about a hundred yards from the Clutters'. They both had a drink and then entered the house through an unlocked door. They first went to the bedroom where Herbert Clutter was sleeping, awoke him, walked to his office, and asked him where his safe was. Clutter replied that he didn't have a safe. Hickock and Smith proceeded to tie up all four members of the family and took Mr. Clutter and his 15-year-old son, Kenyon, down to the basement, while they looked for the safe.

Unsuccessful in their search, Hickock and Smith talked it over, deciding that they would not leave any witnesses. Smith then cut the throat of Herbert Clutter and shot him in the head. He then shot the other three members of the Clutter family. Sixteen-year-old Nancy, the only one whose mouth wasn't taped, pleaded with them, "Oh no! Oh, please. No! No! No! No! Don't! Oh, please don't! Please!" After killing all four members of the Clutter family, the two men ran out to the car and drove away, arriving in Olathe at about noon the next day. Although Hickock was led to believe that Clutter had at least $10,000 in his home, the pair netted only $40.

Using money obtained from bad checks, Hickock and Smith were on the run until January 2, 1960, when they were arrested in Las Vegas. While awaiting trial, Smith remarked, "Am I sorry? If that's what you mean — I'm not. I don't feel anything about it. I wish I did. But nothing about it bothers me a bit. Half an hour after it happened, Dick was making jokes and I was laughing at them. Maybe we're not human. I'm human enough to feel sorry for myself. Sorry I can't walk out of here when you walk out. But that's all." That spring, Hickock and Smith were convicted of the four murders and sentenced to death. They were hanged on April 14, 1965.

Familicides: I Love You to Death

The discussion of familicide has, to this point, focused on cases where parents kill their spouse and children. During the 1940s, we see several instances of progeny familicide. Less common than parental familicide, these incidents involve offenders, usually adolescent males, who kill their parents and siblings (see Table 10). Moreover, compared to those who commit parental familicide, these offenders are more likely to use guns and are much less likely to commit suicide.

On December 19, 1941, Richard Dehler, 16 years old, used a shotgun to kill his parents, younger sister, and younger brother at their farmhouse in Little Falls, Minnesota (*New York Times*, December 21, 1941; p. 34:5).

"Tired of being bossed around," Dehler made preparations to kill his family that afternoon. He siphoned gas from a tank and spread it around the premises. After the evening meal, he completed his chores, took a shotgun from the house, and told his father he was going to shoot rabbits.

Instead, Dehler used the shotgun to kill his family. He then set the house on fire and drove to the nearby town of Buckman, where he was told that his family's house was on fire. Dehler drove back to the house to help extinguish the blaze. Dehler left to phone relatives to tell them of the "terrible accident" and was arrested when he returned.

The familicide in Butte, Montana, in 1949 was notable in that it was committed by the daughter of the family — one of the few times this happened in twentieth-century America. On December 31, Lorraine Knapp, a 21-year-old miner's daughter, used a .22-caliber rifle to kill her mother,

Table 10.
Patterns of Familicides, 1900–1999

Variables	Parental	Progeny	Other	All Familicides
Average Death Toll	4.67	4.56	4.84	4.68
Average Wounded Count	0.45	0.12	0.54	0.40
Weapon Type				
Gun	62%	72%	73%	64%
Other	29%	26%	23%	29%
Fire	9%	2%	4%	7%
Public Location	8%	0%	12%	7%
City > 250,000	29%	15%	31%	26%
Assault Weapon	1%	0%	4%	1%
Interracial	2%	4%	5%	2%
White Offenders	78%	94%	80%	81%
Average Offender Age	35.24	23.67	30.04	32.63
Percent Offenders 30–49	62%	21%	27%	52%
Percent Offenders ≥ 50	6%	3%	7%	6%
Male Offenders	87%	92%	94%	88%
Suicidal Offenders	64%	16%	22%	53%
Average Offender Count	1.04	1.06	1.15	1.05
White Victims	80%	95%	84%	83%
Average Victim Age	17.42	31.91	26.25	20.81
Victims Age <16 or > 40	68%	69%	49%	68%
Male Victims	41%	52%	42%	43%
Region				
Midwest	30%	37%	34%	32%
East	29%	24%	30%	28%
South	21%	25%	22%	22%
West	20%	14%	14%	18%
N	271	63	27	361

two brothers, sister, and herself (*New York Times*, January 1, 1950; p. 42:1). Knapp had been doing office work in a garage in Dillon, Montana, until six weeks before the shootings. Unemployed in Butte, her brothers said she had been brooding and acting strangely. Her two brothers, 16-year-old George and 18-year-old Jack, discovered the killings. The familicide in Butte was noteworthy in another respect: it was the first time the *Times* used the term "mass killing" to describe a multiple murder.

Six years earlier, however, the *Times* first used the phrase "mass slayings" to describe the murders committed by Austin Cox in Ogden, Utah, on July 23, 1943 (*New York Times*, July 25, 1943; p. 27:4). Six months before the killings, District Judge Lewis Trueman granted a divorce to Wanda Mae Carter Cox, who alleged that her husband, Austin Cox, was mean, jealous, and had threatened to tear her tongue out. They had been married only a couple of months, but she had already recently given birth to a child. Cox was enraged about the divorce and said that he got "a bum deal in court." After he was arrested, he told police that, "I'm afraid I'm losing my mind." He claimed to have recently suffered a severe blow to the head while working in a war plant. And the trouble with his wife, he added, had upset his "mental equilibrium."

On the day of the shootings, he learned from a friend where his ex-wife was currently staying. Cox grabbed a shotgun and headed over to the home of Jane Stauffer. Even though his wife was not there — she was miles away when the shootings occurred — Cox killed Stauffer and her three friends after they asked him to leave. Cox then drove to the home of Judge Trueman, whom Cox blamed for the divorce. As Trueman was turning on a light, Cox shot him from outside the house. With police officers in pursuit, Cox drove to the police station, where he pointed his gun at a group of officers, one of whom wounded Cox by shooting him. Cox was arrested, but only after putting up a fight in which officers beat him into submission.

During the 1950s, familicides accounted for 62 percent of the mass killings, the second-highest percentage for the twentieth century. One of these incidents was committed by Ernest Ingenito on November 17, 1950, in Vineland, New Jersey. Ingenito, a 26-year-old television repairman and dishonorably discharged World War II veteran, shot nine relatives of his estranged wife, five fatally, before he was arrested by police (*New York Times*, November 18, 1950; p. 1:2). As a child, Ingenito was constantly picked on due to his small size. He was often beaten by his father and was later sent to reform school as a chronic runaway. Ingenito served in the

Army in World War II, but was dishonorably discharged in 1946 for hitting an officer. After his discharge, Ingenito got married and had two children. In July of 1950, however, his wife, Theresa, left him and took their two kids to live with her parents. Theresa and her family refused to let Ingenito see their children.

Depressed about not being able to see his children, Ingenito got into his car, armed with three pistols and a rifle, and drove to his wife's house. Arriving there at 9 P.M., Ingenito asked to see his children, but his wife replied that a court order prohibited him from visiting with them. Ingenito then opened fire, wounding his wife and killing her parents. He crossed the street where he saw his wife's grandmother, whom he killed by shooting her in the head. Next, Ingenito fatally shot his wife's aunt and uncle and wounded her 9-year-old cousin. Ingenito then drove to the home of Frank and Hilda Mazzoli, uncle and aunt of his wife, and wounded both of them. When Ingenito was arrested several hours later, he told police, "I'm the one you're looking for." Sentenced to life in prison, Ingenito was full of remorse — not for what he had done, but for the fact that his victims died so quickly and did not suffer a slow death (*New York Times*, January 20, 1951; p. 8:2).

In contrast to the massacre committed by Ingenito, which was clearly motivated by revenge, there were several familicides during the '50s where the motive was more "altruistic." On May 3, 1953, Carol Tiedeman MacDonald, a 29-year-old graduate of Barnard College and psychology student at Columbia University, killed her four children by carbon monoxide poisoning in Mahwah, New Jersey (*New York Times*, May 4, 1953; p. 1:1). She was married to 31-year-old Kenneth MacDonald, a real estate and insurance broker who was a football star at Rutgers and a lieutenant in the Pacific theater in World War II. Having left his wife three months before, MacDonald decided that he wanted a divorce. To "protect the children from the disgrace" of the impending divorce, Carol MacDonald planned to kill herself and her four children, who ranged in age from 2 to 7.

At around midnight, she awoke the children, put warm jackets and coats over their pajamas, and took them to the station wagon, which was parked in the garage. Discovering that the car had little gas, she drove to a service station, bought gasoline, and returned to the garage. She parked the car, left the motor running, and closed the garage doors. Leaving the children in the car, she went inside and wrote six suicide notes. MacDonald returned to the garage an hour or two later, for she later claimed to have changed her mind about killing her children. It was too late, however, because her children were dead. At 6 A.M., she called her brother, who hurried to the home and then notified police. MacDonald was later transferred to the Bergen Pines County Hospital because she had attempted to commit suicide in prison (*New York Times*, May 5, 1953; p. 20:2).

In another "altruistic" familicide, Dr. Ben T. Galbraith, a 36-year-old cardiologist, killed his wife and three children on March 17, 1955, in McAlester, Oklahoma (*New York Times* "Doctor slays family," March 23, 1955; p. 22:4). Galbraith grew up as the youngest of five children in a socially prominent home. At about age nine, he began to experience pseudo-epileptic attacks where he was not unconscious but was immobile in a grotesque way. He graduated from college and went to medical school. After completing his internship, he got married to his wife, Kitty, and they soon had their first child. It was around this time that he suffered his first breakdown in which he experienced paranoia and hallucinations (Karpman, 1955). Galbraith was diagnosed as paranoid schizophrenic but, when it was learned that he could not continue his residency because of it, his diagnosis was changed to manic-depressive psychosis.

Galbraith and his wife had two more children, but their home life was persistently stormy. For at least a couple of years before the killings, he had been encouraging his wife to get a divorce and, at one point, had even held a gun to her head. He also drank a lot and had an affair with a laboratory technician. About six months before the murders, he began thinking that his wife and children would starve to death. He was worried that he was suffering a permanent mental breakdown, and wanted to get away so that he could work out his mental troubles without anyone around him.

On March 17, 1955, he got a motel room in Norman (about 100 miles away), where he continued to worry about the fate of himself and his family. He began to believe that his family would be better off dead, that they would have a better life in Heaven. He drove back to his home, where he injected his wife with morphine. She awoke, so he hit her over the head with a liquor bottle and then injected her with more morphine. After killing his wife, Galbraith injected his sleeping children with morphine. When this did not kill them, he injected them with poison. Galbraith set the home on fire and drove to Norman. He returned the next morning to make his medical rounds, and feigned surprise when presented with the news that his family was dead. Faced with overwhelming evidence, however, he later confessed. After a battle between prosecution and defense psychiatrists, a jury decided that Galbraith was competent to stand trial. He was convicted and given two life sentences. While waiting to stand trial, Galbraith attempted to commit suicide on four separate occasions; once by jumping from a moving car, twice by taking sedatives, and another time by cutting his wrists (Karpman, 1955). On December 7, 1959, Galbraith finally succeeded in killing himself by using a razor blade to sever the main artery in his right thigh (*New York Times*, December 8, 1959; p. 60:1).

Racial Terrorism: The Birmingham Bombing

The 1964 Civil Rights Act was a milestone in the struggle for racial equality, for it essentially ended Jim Crow by prohibiting the segregation of blacks in public places, creating the Equal Employment Opportunity Commission, and protecting the voting rights of blacks (Reeves, 2000). Progress was costly, however. After the Supreme Court handed down the Brown v. Board of Education decision in 1954, efforts to desegregate in the South were often met with hatred and hostility.

Few places were as violently opposed to the Civil Rights movement and as deeply divided along racial lines as Birmingham, Alabama. From the end of World War II to the early 1960s, there were approximately 50 unsolved bombings that occurred on "Dynamite Hill," a white residential section where blacks had been trying to buy homes (*New York Times*, July 24, 1983; Section 6, p. 12:1). When the Congress of Racial Equality (CORE) launched its desegregation campaign in 1961, freedom riders encountered violence in Birmingham and a number of other Southern cities. After nonviolent protests failed in Albany, Georgia and elsewhere in the South, Martin Luther King and the Southern Christian Leadership Conference (SCLC) selected Birmingham as a site for boycotts and demonstrations in the spring of 1963 because its police chief— Eugene T. "Bull" Connor, a hard-core segregationist — might react harshly, thereby arousing sympathy and support for the Civil Rights movement.

Connor responded as King hoped he would, arresting hundreds of blacks, including King himself, after they marched on City Hall in April. And on May 3, demonstrators congregating at the 16th Street Baptist Church were beaten, attacked by police dogs, and hit with high-pressure hoses. The brutality of the police force was broadcast on the nightly news, ultimately leading the Birmingham Senior Citizens' Committee to reach an agreement with the SCLC a week later to desegregate lunch counters, rest rooms, and drinking fountains. That night, however, bombs damaged the home of Martin Luther King's brother and the hotel where the SCLC had been staying, which led to rioting (Blum, 1990). Four months later, the racial terrorism in Birmingham got worse as a bomb exploded in the basement of the 16th Street Baptist Church, killing four black girls between the ages of 11 and 14. Once again, the bombing incited rioting, this time claiming the lives of two more black children and prompting Alabama governor George Wallace to call in state troopers and National Guardsmen.

Investigators quickly focused on four suspects: 59-year-old Robert "Dynamite Bob" Chambliss, 27-year-old Troy Ingram, 25-year-old Thomas E. Blanton Jr., and 35-year-old Bobby Frank Cherry. The four men were members of the Cahaba River group, a splinter group of the Eastview 13 Klavern — one of the more violent Klan units in the South. On September 29, two weeks after the bombing, Alabama authorities arrested Chambliss and another Klansman. The arrests were premature, however, because Chambliss was charged only with possession of dynamite, a charge that later fell apart in court. The federal investigation did not fare much better. In 1965, FBI agents in Birmingham requested permission to present evidence, which implicated Chambliss, Ingram, Blanton, and Cherry in the bombing, to state and federal prosecutors. But J. Edgar Hoover, who despised Martin Luther King and the Civil Rights movement, turned down the request, stating that the chances for conviction were "remote" (*New York Times*, July 24, 1983; Section 6, p. 12:1).

The investigation stalled until 1977, when the state of Alabama charged Chambliss with murder. Convicted, he was sentenced to life in prison, where he later died. Another suspect, Troy Ingram, died in a motorcycle accident and was never charged for the massacre. Thomas Blanton Jr. was convicted of the murders in 2001 and given a life sentence, whereas Cherry was convicted in 2002 for the bombing and sentenced to life in prison.

4

The Second
Mass Murder Wave,
1966–1999

As the 1950s drew to a close, the dominance the United States enjoyed during the postwar era was slowly beginning to fade as the economies of Japan and Western Europe started making significant strides on the road to recovery. Although the 1940s and '50s were some of the most prosperous years in U.S. history, poverty was still a major concern. America's inner cities were beginning to feel the full effects of "white flight" to the suburbs and the end of the Industrial Age, as low-wage manufacturing jobs were becoming obsolete. Racism, too, was a source of major concern. The civil rights movement, which formed in the mid–1950s to eliminate the oppressive, debilitating effects of racial discrimination, won significant victories with the 1964 Civil Rights Act and the 1965 Voting Rights Act.

The increased concern over poverty and racism was part of the larger effort to build the Great Society. During the mid–1960s, the Johnson administration created a number of policies and legislative acts that aimed to address not only poverty and racism, but also air and water pollution, education for the young, and medical care for the elderly. But the Great Society programs soon faced withering attacks from the right for going too far and from the left for not going far enough. The efficacy of these programs was further hampered by the race riots during the summers of 1965–1967 and by increased military spending for the escalating war in Vietnam, which was beginning to attract serious opposition, especially on college campuses.

The 1960s were, nevertheless, a time of heightened social activism. The U.S. Supreme Court, headed by Chief Justice Earl Warren, was, therefore, very much a product of its time. Beginning with *Brown v. Board of Education* in 1954, the Warren Court handed down a series of decisions, many of them controversial at the time, that reflected an egalitarian emphasis on the rights of individuals. Some of these decisions had a significant impact on the criminal justice system. For example, the *Mapp v. Ohio* decision in 1961 required police to obtain warrants, when possible, before conducting searches; the 1965 *Pointer v. Texas* decision affirmed the right of an individual to confront his accusers; and the *Gideon v. Wainwright* decision in 1965 provided a guarantee of legal counsel in criminal cases. On June 13, 1966, the Supreme Court ruled in *Miranda v. Arizona* that a defendant must be informed of his rights. And this law applied to any defendant who had not yet been tried.

On April 23, nearly two months before the Miranda decision, 24-year-old Maria Torres and her five children, all under the age of 5, were stabbed to death in their Brooklyn apartment (*New York Times*, April 28, 1966: p. 34:2). Police immediately began to question Torres' estranged husband, Jose Suarez, a 22-year-old factory worker who had spent 6 weeks in King's Park Hospital in 1965 after he attempted to kill himself with a bread knife. Suarez admitted to police that he had stabbed Torres and the five children, four of whom were his, more than 100 times. He claimed that the killings followed an argument in which his wife had used a knife to cut his leg. Suarez then seized control of the knife and began his killing spree (*New York Times*, April 29, 1966; p. 17:1).

Ordinarily, Suarez's confession would have been enough to result in a conviction and at least a life sentence. But Suarez had not been advised of his rights before he confessed to the murders, because New York State law did not require it at the time. For seven months, the Office of the District Attorney attempted to obtain evidence on Suarez other than the confession, but to no avail. Nevertheless, a grand jury indicted Suarez on November 4, 1966, and, appearing in court a week later, he retracted the confession and pleaded not guilty.

On February 20, 1967, Assistant District Attorney Nathan R. Schor moved to dismiss the charges, stating, "I daresay that if his questioning had conformed with the requirements of Miranda, this defendant would be in Sing Sing Prison serving several life sentences." State Supreme Court Justice Micahel Kern responded by saying, "Unfortunately the general public doesn't understand the law. Even an animal such as this one, and I believe this is insulting the animal kingdom, must be protected with all the legal safeguards. This is a very sad thing. It is so repulsive it makes one's blood run cold and any decent human being's stomach turn to let a thing like this out on the street." An hour later, Suarez was a free man (*New York Times*, February 21, 1967; p. 41:2). It is important to note, however, that Suarez is one of the few mass killers, and probably the only one, to be freed on account of this technicality.

Drug-Related Massacres: A New Strain in Mass Murder

Just as social activism increased during the 1960s, so, too, did the use of illegal drugs. Prior to the 1960s, illicit drug use was widely considered to be more of an ethnic problem. During the late nineteenth century, for example, Chinese immigrants were blamed for the spread of opium dens across the country, eventually leading to the 1909 Opium Exclusion Act, which made it unlawful to import opium for "medicinal purposes." Five years later, Congress passed the Harrison Act, which criminalized cocaine in addition to opium and its derivatives. During the 1930s, Mexican immigrants were linked to the growing use of marijuana, which had, for some, become an alternative to alcohol during Prohibition. Harry Anslinger, head of the newly created Federal Bureau of Narcotics, led a successful campaign to criminalize marijuana, resulting in the Marijuana Tax Act of 1937.

Although illegal drug use persisted throughout the 1940s and '50s, it did not begin to grow dramatically until the 1960s when it became part of the lifestyle of the burgeoning youth counterculture. The proliferation of illicit drug use, especially among white middle-class youth, engendered much interest and concern, prompting the creation of the Drug Enforcement Administration in 1973 and increasingly tougher drug laws, which has led to the recent explosion in the U.S. prison population. The increased demand for marijuana and harder drugs also spawned a lucrative black market for drug traffickers. As with Prohibition, violence has been part and parcel of the illicit drug trade, helping drive up homicide rates since the 1960s. The dramatic expansion of the illegal drug market also led to the appearance of the drug-related massacre.

The first drug-related mass killing reported by the *New York Times* occurred in Detroit on June 14, 1971. At 4:30 A.M., four men and four women, all of whom were black, were killed "execution-style" in a "dope house" near the area where the 1967 Detroit riot began (*New York Times*,

June 21, 1971; p. 59:4). Police found five handguns, five long guns, and drug paraphernalia in the home. Four of the victims had records involving narcotics and prostitution. Police suspected that it was either a drug rip-off or a "turf war," as the narcotics trade in Detroit, worth hundreds of millions of dollars at the time, was fragmented, with various factions vying for control (*New York Times*, June 15, 1971; p. 1:6).

The drug-related massacre in Detroit was merely a harbinger of things to come. The following year, three young women and a heroin dealer were killed in a shootout at the Club Harlem, a nightclub in Atlantic City (*New York Times*, April 4, 1972; p. 1:7). The shootings were the result of a drug war that began the previous October. Tyrone Palmer, the slain heroin dealer, was 24 years old and a major narcotics dealer in Philadelphia. He was born in South Carolina, but had grown up in Philadelphia, and started dealing narcotics at 18. Palmer quickly established himself as a major dealer by developing purchasing contracts in New York and Philadelphia for high-quality heroin (*New York Times*, April 4, 1972; p. 47:1).

In October of 1971, a rival gang stole a $243,000 heroin shipment that was supposed to go to Palmer. In retaliation, Palmer put out a contract for 36-year-old James Smith, a lower-level drug dealer in Philadelphia whom Palmer thought responsible for the stolen shipment. On March 2, Smith was murdered "gangland style" in Philadelphia. As a reprisal for the Smith slaying, a $15,000 contract was put out for the murder of Palmer. Palmer had just returned from a trip to Bermuda, where he had gone for the sake of an alibi for the Smith murder, when he was approached in the Atlantic City nightclub at 2 A.M. and murdered. In the melee that followed, three other people were fatally shot, five were wounded by gunfire, and six suffered injuries in the stampede for the doors.

In his research on the connection between drugs and violence, Paul Goldstein (1985) has noted that they are related in three ways: psychopharmacological, economic compulsive, and systemic. The psychopharmacological model holds that some individuals may become violent after ingesting specific substances such as alcohol, stimulants, barbituates, and PCP. The economic compulsive model, on the other hand, suggests that some drug users may commit economically-oriented violent crimes to support their habit. And the systemic model posits that violence is intrinsic to the buying and selling of drugs. Examples of systemic violence include disputes over territory between rival dealers, retaliation for robberies of drug dealers, the enforcement of normative codes within dealing hierarchies, and punishment for failure to pay drug debts. Later research has revealed that most drug-related violence falls into the systemic category (Goldstein, 1998). As suggested by the two examples presented above, the same is true with mass murder. Of the 55 drug-related massacres examined in this study, 40 (73 percent) were instances of systemic violence.

Table 11 illustrates the characteristics of the 55 drug-related massacres. As noted earlier, all 55 incidents occurred between 1971 and 1999. These massacres are more likely to take place in a residential setting in a large urban area in the South or on the East Coast. Like other felony-related massacres, they are usually committed by a small group of young black males who use guns to kill acquaintances or strangers. Moreover,

Table 11.
Characteristics of Drug-Related Massacres

Variables	Avg/Percent
Average Death Toll	4.45
Average Wounded Count	0.53
Weapon Type	
Gun	92%
Other	4%
Fire	4%
Victim-Offender Relationship	
Stranger	32%
Family	0%
Acquaintance	68%
Public Location	16%
City > 250,000	58%
Assault Weapon	0%
Interracial	8%
White Offenders	26%
Average Offender Age	25.08
Percent Offender 30–49	15%
Percent Offender ≥ 50	0%
Male Offenders	99%
Suicidal Offenders	2%
Average Offender Count	2.07
White Victims	42%
Average Victim Age	25.59
Victims Age <16 or >40	25%
Male Victims	69%
Region	
Midwest	14%
East	35%
South	31%
West	20%
N	55

the prevalence of suicidal behavior is again similar to that seen for ordinary homicide. Whereas the victims in other mass murders tend to be white, the victims in drug-related massacres are more likely to be black.

By the early 1980s, South Florida had firmly established its reputation as a hotbed for drug trafficking. Instability produced violence, however, as smugglers vied for control of the profitable drug trade. Inciardi (1990) reports that the increase in violence in South Florida during the early 1980s was due primarily to the city's cocaine wars. Prior to the 1980s, cocaine trafficking was relatively stable and well organized; Colombians shipped cocaine north to Miami, where Cuban middlemen distributed it locally or shipped it elsewhere. In the late 1970s, however, the Colombians decided to cut out the middleman and take over cocaine distribution in South Florida.

In the Miami area alone, seven of the ten mass killings that took place between 1980 and 1984 were drug-related. One of these cases occurred on January 8, 1980. The bodies of John Merino, Scott Bennett, Rodolfo Ayan, and Nicomedes Hernandez were found in a burning car on an Interstate 95 entrance ramp. Earlier that night, the four men went to the apartment of Joseph Macker to negotiate a narcotics transaction. Macker and his accomplices, Bernard Bolender and Paul Thompson, robbed, tortured, and killed the four men when they failed to produce the drugs they had promised.

Macker and Bolender were arrested almost a week later, and Macker confessed to the crime in exchange for a plea bargain (AP Wire, January 14, 1980; PM Cycle). In doing so, however, he identified Bolender as the one who took the leading role in the killings. Bolender was convicted of the four murders and sentenced to death; on July 18, 1995, he was executed in Florida's electric chair (UPI Wire, July 17, 1995; BC Cycle). Macker, on the other hand, received a seven-year sentence and was released from prison in 1987. And Paul Thompson, the other drug dealer involved in the killings, was released from prison in 1997 after serving 15 years (UPI Wire, July 18, 1995; BC Cycle).

Drug-related massacres were occurring at an increased pace elsewhere in the United States. At 4 A.M. on July 1, 1981, four people were brutally beaten to death and another was severely injured inside a home in the Laurel Canyon area of Los Angeles. The victims of this mass murder, which "came to symbolize fast California lifestyle gone awry," were 44-year-old William Deverell, 37-year-old Ronald Launius, 22-year-old Barbara Lee Richardson, and 44-year-old Joy Miller, in whose home they were killed. All four were pummeled with iron pipes and at least one base-ball bat. Susan Launius, 25-year-old estranged wife of Ronald Launius, managed to survive, but she was beaten so badly that she was left with brain damage and partial paralysis. Several days before the killings, three of the victims — Deverell, Launius, and Miller — had robbed Eddie Nash, an owner of striptease joints and Hollywood nightclubs, of $10,000, a large amount of cocaine, and other property. Police surmised that they were killed in retal-iation for the robbery, while the other two victims happened to be in the wrong place at the wrong time. And the man at the center of the police inves-tigation was 37-year-old John Holmes, the "nation's premier pornographic film star" (*Los Angeles Times*, April 14, 1988; Part 2, p. 1:2).

The police investigation was led by Tom Lange, who would later gain fame from the O.J. Simpson case. Police believed that in the weeks lead-ing up to the killings, Holmes had taken property stolen by Deverell, Lau-nius, and Miller to Nash's heavily secured home in Studio City, where he exchanged it for drugs. Desperate for more money, Holmes told Deverell, Launius, and Miller about the large amounts of cash and drugs at Nash's home. During an earlier visit to Nash's house, Holmes left the sliding glass door ajar, which enabled Deverell and the others to enter the home and rob Nash and his 300-pound bodyguard, Gregory Diles. The day after the robbery, an associate of Nash spotted Holmes wearing a piece of jewelry that had been stolen from Nash's home. Nash found out about Holmes' involvement in the robbery and threatened to kill him and members of his family if he did not reveal who the robbers were and where they lived. Holmes then led several armed men to the home in Laurel Canyon where Deverell and the others were staying.

He buzzed an outside intercom box, asked to be let in, and entered the home, which was described as a "drug den," with the other men behind him. Police linked Holmes to the crime after finding his bloody palm print on the rail of the bed where Ronald Launius had died. Holmes was brought in for questioning, but disappeared after being released on his own recog-nizance. In December of 1981, police arrested Holmes and charged him with the four murders after tracking him down in North Miami Beach, Florida. Because Susan Launius, the lone survivor, could not identify the killers, remembering only three "shadowy figures" in the night, the case against Holmes rested largely on the palm print and his admission to detec-tive Frank Tomlinson that he was there when the murders happened.

But Holmes maintained that he did not kill anyone. The jury believed him, because on June 25, 1982, he was found not guilty (*New York Times*,

June 26, 1982; p. 19:1). Even though Holmes was acquitted, he spent an additional 111 days in jail because he refused to testify to a grand jury about the killings. He never did name the other men who were there that night. On March 13, 1988, Holmes died of complications resulting from his infection with the AIDS virus. That same year, prosecutors charged Eddie Nash (Adel Nasrallah was his birth name) and Gregory Diles with the murders, claiming they had discovered new evidence linking the two to the crime. The prosecution argued that Nash, who served two years in jail in the mid–1980s on narcotics charges, had ordered the killings and Diles had helped carry out the order.

In 1990, a mistrial was declared after jurors voted 11 to 1 for convicting Nash and 10 to 2 for acquitting Diles. Later that same year, the district attorney's office tried the pair again. This time, Nash and Diles were both acquitted. The prosecution's case against the two was hampered by the fact that it had no physical evidence tying Nash and Diles to the massacre and that it relied upon testimony from heavy drug users and convicted drug dealers. The defense, on the other hand, argued that a man named "Fat Howard" Cook sent Paul Kelly and a few other men to the house to avenge a drug debt. Although the prosecution conceded that Kelly, who was in state prison at the time for a narcotics conviction, may have been one of the killers that night, they contended that it was still Nash who ordered the murders (*Los Angeles Times*, January 8, 1991; Part B, p. 1:2). In 2001, following a four-year investigation, Nash pled guilty to jury tampering and running a drug dealing and money laundering operation, but denied ever ordering the murders.

James Ashford and Gary Jones were convicted of the drug-related massacre they committed in Springfield, Illinois, on June 12, 1985. Ashford, a chronic drug abuser, and Jones went to the home of 27-year-old drug dealer Lonnie Davis to steal his money and drugs. But as Ashford would later say, "With all that dope and money, you don't leave any witnesses" (*Chicago Tribune*, June 25, 1985; p. 3C). Thus, Ashford and Jones already planned to kill Davis that night, but he was not alone. Also in the home that night were Michelle Lawson, Bernard Bowen, Johnetta Eady, and Helen Singleton. Lawson had gone there to buy marijuana from Davis, and she was in the rear bedroom when she heard the voice of Gary Jones, followed by gunfire (*Chicago Tribune*, June 14, 1985; p. 3C). Afraid, she ran to the basement to find a hiding place. She soon heard one of the women upstairs pleading with Ashford and Jones, "Not me, not me, I'll never tell" (UPI Wire, January 25, 1986; BC Cycle).

Following their pledge to not "leave any witnesses," Ashford and Jones silenced the pleas for mercy. Michelle Lawson then heard James Ashford descend the stairs to the basement. Satisfied that no one was down there, Ashford went back upstairs, where he and Jones stole the money and cocaine that were in the house. Ashford and Jones were picked up by the police a little more than a week later and were charged with the four murders.

In prosecuting what was called the "largest mass murder in the city's history," Sangamon County state attorney Bill Roberts argued that Ashford and Jones went to the house "to steal drugs and money. In so doing, they took the life of four human beings." He added, "This is probably the most terrible crime I've ever seen. To just go in and know when you're going that you're going to end the lives of four people is just unspeakable." Convicted of the murders, Ashford and Jones both received the death penalty (UPI Wire, August 19, 1986; BC Cycle).

Like Ashford and Jones, 23-year-old Lawrence "Pumpkin" Jackson and 24-year-old Robert Driskell were ex-convicts who abused drugs. And on the night of September 24, 1986, they needed money to feed their habit. Jackson and Driskell, who were both high at the time, decided to rob the home of Mark "Tiny" Brown, who was Driskell's cousin. However, because they knew their victims, they did not want to leave any witnesses who could later identify them (*Chicago Tribune*, June 24, 1988; p. 2C).

Entering Brown's apartment at the Henry Horner Homes, a housing project in Chicago, Jackson and Driskell stabbed Brown as he slept on the couch in the living room. They then stabbed Brown's fiancée, Vernita Winder; her daughter, 4-year-old Dana; and a friend, 23-year-old Shirley Martin. All four victims were killed after getting stabbed at least 10 times each. Driskell also tried to kill Vernita Winder's 6-year-old daughter, Urica, by stabbing her 48 times. Miraculously, she survived the attack and later telephoned for help (*Chicago Tribune*, June 29, 1988; p. 6C).

When police arrived on the scene, they saw Vernita Winder's 18-month-old daughter, Shanita, who was unharmed, playing in a pool of blood. In describing the scene, Detective James Maurer said, "It was really gruesome. There was blood splattered all over the place, from wall to wall" (*Chicago Tribune*, September 26, 1986; p. 7C). After committing the brutal murders, Jackson and Driskell stole a television set and a videocassette recorder, which they sold for $120 to buy cocaine. Urica Winder later testified against the two, and both were convicted of the murders. Jackson was given the death penalty, while Driskell received a life sentence (*Chicago Tribune*, February 10, 1995; p. 5S).

Felony-Related Massacres: "Tie 'em up and get the money"

As noted in Chapter 1, the emergence of the drug-related massacre was part of a larger trend in mass murder — an increase in felony-related mass killings. Except for the 1930s, felony-related massacres were very rare during the twentieth century until the 1970s. Since that time, however, these incidents have comprised roughly a quarter of all mass killings (see Table 12).

While the smaller percentage of felony-related massacres prior to the 1970s is partly attributable to the fact that the *Times* generally considers these incidents to be less newsworthy than other mass killings, it also likely reflects a genuine increase over the last three decades.

The worst robbery-mass murder in U.S. history occurred on February 18, 1983, when thirteen people were gunned down at the Wah Mee Club, a high-stakes gambling parlor in Seattle's International District. A fourteenth victim, 61-year-old Wai Chin, was shot in the head and neck, but he managed to survive and give police the names of the three men who committed the murders: 20-year-old Benjamin Ng, 22-year-old Kwan Fai "Willie" Mak, and 26-year-old Wai-Chiu "Tony" Ng (no relation to Benjamin Ng). Police quickly arrested Benjamin Ng and Willie Mak, but Tony Ng fled the country to Calgary, Alberta, where he lived for over a year and a half before he was arrested and returned to the United States in October of 1984 (UPI Wire, August 23, 1983; AM Cycle).

All three were immigrants from Hong Kong. Mak and Benjamin Ng had been involved in criminal activity at least two years before the massacre. In 1981, Mak, Ng, and another man had stolen a safe and were dumping it into Lake Washington when 71-year-old Franklin Leach came upon them as he was jogging. Afraid to leave an eyewitness, Benjamin Ng ran after Leach and fatally shot him. Ng pled guilty to the murder after he was sentenced for the Wah Mee massacre. Mak and Benjamin Ng had also talked for several years about robbing a gambling club in Seattle's Chinatown. They told a friend, Yen Lau, that they would "Tie 'em up and get the money and shoot them." The killing was necessary, according to Mak, "because they (Ng and Mak) knew a lot of people in Chinatown" (UPI Wire, August 18, 1983; AM Cycle).

Table 12.
Characteristics of Mass Murders, 1966–1999

Variables	Avg/Percent
Average Death Toll	5.23
Average Wounded Count	4.18
Weapon Type	
Gun	70%
Other	17%
Fire	13%
Victim-Offender Relationship	
Stranger	25%
Family	41%
Acquaintance	34%
Public Location	27%
Workplace	5%
Felony-Related	24%
Interracial	9%
White Offenders	62%
Average Offender Age	30.37
Percent Offenders 30–49	35%
Percent Offenders ≥ 50	4%
Male Offenders	94%
Suicidal Offenders	25%
Average Offender Count	1.31
White Victims	73%
Average Victim Age	27.76
Victims Age <16 or >40	55%
Male Victims	54%
Region	
Midwest	24%
East	26%
South	28%
West	22%
N	735

Shortly before the massacre, Mak and Benjamin Ng had joined the Hop Sing, a Chinese tong. Earlier, a Hop Sing leader had been roughed up by George Mar, a leader of a rival tong. Mak came up with a plan to rob the Wah Mee Club. In doing so, he could not only exact revenge on Mar, but also make some money while doing it. To carry out his plan, Mak enlisted the help of Benjamin and Tony Ng. Mak and Tony Ng had been "casual friends" for several years, but in the weeks leading up to the massacre they had frequently gambled together.

On the night before the murders, Ng ran up a $1,000 gambling debt to Mak. Yet Mak offered to forgive the debt if Ng helped him "get even with someone and make some money" (UPI Wire, September 28, 1983; AM Cycle). So it was that on the night of February 18, 1983, the three men entered the Wah Mee Club just before midnight. They herded the patrons into a section of the club, where they hog-tied them and took their money and wallets. After robbing the Wah Mee patrons and employees, Benjamin Ng and Mak began shooting, with Ng firing 26 shots and Mak 6. The three men then fled the club with approximately $10,000. (UPI Wire, April 8, 1985; BC Cycle).

Juries found Mak and Benjamin Ng guilty of the murders; Tony Ng, on the other hand, was acquitted of the killings, but he was convicted on thirteen counts of robbery. As the mastermind of the massacre, Mak was given the death penalty, whereas Benjamin and Tony Ng were both given life sentences. Several years after the robbery-mass murder, a California company began filming *The Border of Tong*, a low-budget, sensational film based loosely on the Wah Mee massacre (*Seattle Times*, February 18, 1993; p. A1).

While the Wah Mee murders represent one of the worst felony-related massacres, the 1994 mass murder in Kilgore, Texas, provides what is perhaps a more representative example. On July 21, 1994, 68-year-old Luva Congleton, 54-year-old Buddy Waller, 54-year-old Patricia Colter, and 44-year-old Duane Colter were murdered during a robbery at Katie's, a beer tavern in Kilgore. The lone survivor was 32-year-old Sandra Cash, who managed to call the police, despite getting shot five times (*The Dallas Morning News*, July 23, 1994; p. 1A). Less than 24 hours later, police arrested 16-year-old Marcus Smith, 31-year-old Ray Don Mosley, and his 19-year-old nephew, DaRoyce Mosley (*The Dallas Morning News*, July 24, 1994; p. 41A). Smith told police he had turned and fled before the shooting started, whereas DaRoyce Mosely said that he had spent the evening at a friend's house.

But Ray Don Mosley told police a different story. He said that after he shot Sandra Cash, he threw down his gun and watched his nephew shoot the four remaining people in the bar. When police confronted DaRoyce Mosley with his uncle's version of events and informed him that he was being arrested for murder, he exclaimed, "Oh, what have I done. I've ruined my life. I'm going to spend the rest of my life in jail." After changing his story several times, DaRoyce Mosley signed a confession in which he admitted to having shot the four dead victims. He claimed, however, that his uncle forced him to do the shootings by holding a gun to his head (*Texas Monthly*, February 1996; p. 82).

The arrest of DaRoyce Mosley came as shock to many residents of Kilgore, a town of 11,000 about 115 miles east of Dallas. His mother, Charline Mosley Jackson, was 14 years old, unmarried, and strung out on drugs when she gave birth to DaRoyce. She went on to have four more children, and DaRoyce often took care of his siblings, because his mother spent much of her time on the streets, abusing drugs and chasing men. When DaRoyce was in elementary school, he moved in with his mother's uncle and aunt, Joe Rogers and Johnnie Mae Johnson. He responded remarkably well to the change in environment, earning A's and B's in school, getting elected to the student council, attending church, and participating in athletics.

Although he aspired to attend the University of Texas at Austin after he graduated from high school in 1993, he decided to spend a year at Kilgore College so he could save money and get some basic coursework out of the way. By the spring semester of his freshman year, however, he was placed on academic probation after his grade point average dropped to 1.5. Instead of studying, DaRoyce spent his days playing pool and table tennis at the student union, and his evenings hanging out at a friend's house (*Texas Monthly*, February 1996; p. 82). To make matters worse for DaRoyce, his uncle, Ray Don, returned to Kilgore in June of 1994 after getting released from prison.

Growing up in the Goat Hill neighborhood — a poor, mostly black section of Kilgore — Ray Don Mosley developed a reputation as a violent, angry youth. As one Goat Hill resident said, "When we were growing up, we all ran the other way if we saw him. He'd rather hit you than talk to you" (*Texas Monthly*, February 1996; p. 82). He started his criminal career at an early age, committing mostly minor offenses as a teenager (*The Houston Post*, July 25, 1994; p. A13). It was also around this time that he assaulted DaRoyce's mother, Charline. After the two got into an argument one evening, Ray Don pulled out a knife and slashed Charline across her chest. But by the time he was in his mid–20s, he had been arrested for aggravated assault, sexual assault, drug–possession, attempted burglary, and fraud. Smith, though only 16, had a long juvenile record, and he and Ray Don would often swap stories about various crimes they had committed.

DaRoyce Mosley claimed that his uncle, shortly after his return to Kilgore, began pressuring him to rob Katie's, a place well known for its hostility towards blacks. According to DaRoyce, he decided to commit the robbery to get his uncle off his back. So it was that on the night of

July 21, DaRoyce Mosley, his uncle Ray Don, and 16-year-old Marcus Smith robbed Katie's. After putting on gloves, bandannas, and ski masks, the three walked to the beer tavern, shot all five people inside, and stole $308. For confessing that he shot the four dead victims, DaRoyce Mosley was convicted and sentenced to death. His uncle, Ray Don, was also convicted and given three life terms (*The Houston Chronicle*, February 27, 1996; p. 20). Marcus Smith, on the other hand, was given only a two-year sentence at a juvenile facility because a judge concluded that he left the bar before the murders were committed (*Texas Monthly*, February 1996; p. 82).

Gang-Related Massacres: "It was just something that happened"

In the years following the 1929 St. Valentine's Day Massacre there were few gang-related mass murders. In 1984, however, two occurred within six weeks of each other in Los Angeles, a city frequently depicted as the epicenter for the alleged rising tide of gang violence during the 1980s. On August 31, two gunmen burst into a South-Central Los Angeles home and killed four relatives of Kermit Alexander, a former All-American football star at UCLA who later played in the NFL with the Los Angeles Rams and San Francisco 49ers. The victims were his mother, 58-year-old Ebora Alexander; his sister, 24-year-old Dietra Alexander; and his two nephews, 13-year-old Damani Garner and 8-year-old Damon Bonner.

For nearly four weeks, police were baffled as to who committed these seemingly "motiveless murders," until they raided a drug operation run by the Rolling 60s Crips, one of the most violent gangs in Los Angeles. There, police found James Kennedy, 17, with a .30-caliber M-1 carbine, similar to the weapon used in the mass murder. When Kennedy was asked about the gun, he said it belonged to Tiequon Cox, another member of the Rolling 60s who was in jail after police picked him up three weeks earlier for suspicion of cocaine activity and carrying a loaded weapon. Detectives soon discovered that Cox's fingerprints matched a palm print found on a red metal locker in Dietra Alexander's bedroom. And by February of 1985, police received tips that helped them apprehend the other two gang members involved in the shootings — Horace Burns and Darren Charles Williams (*Los Angeles Times*, August 2, 1987; p. 9).

At the ensuing trials, prosecutors argued that the three men were paid $50,000 to $60,000 to commit the crime. A club owner wanted to get rid of a girl who was suing him after getting shot in his club, and he offered the three men money to kill her. So it was that on August 31, 1984, Cox, Burns, and Williams showed up at the house of Ida Moore at 5:30 A.M., asking to use her 1975 Chevy van to see a woman that owed Williams money. She refused to let them borrow her van, so she and a friend, Delisa Brown, offered to drive.

At around 7:30 A.M., Williams spotted the home and instructed Moore to park four or five houses down the street and keep the engine running. With Burns and the two women waiting in the van, Cox and Williams approached the home where Ebora Alexander lived with her daughter, Dietra. Cox and Williams entered the house through an open door and started firing. They killed everyone there except for two: Neal Alexander, Ebora's son, escaped out the back door after fighting with Cox and Williams, while Ivan, a 13-year-old grandson of Ebora, hid in a closet. After the shootings, Cox and Williams returned to the van, whereupon Cox said, "Get out of here. I just blew the bitch's head off." Although Cox, Burns, and Williams were able to collect the hit money, they later found out they went to the wrong house. Thus, Ebora Alexander, her daughter, and her two grandchildren were murdered in a case of mistaken identity. Apparently, this did not bother Burns in the least, who later remarked, "It was just something that happened."

The prosecution's case against Burns was the weakest, as he was in the van during the murders and, thus, did not do any of the shootings. Plus, he claimed he knew nothing about the murder plot. Yet, during the trial, he tried to slip Cox a note in which he encouraged Cox to take full responsibility for the shootings, since the evidence against him was the strongest. In return, Burns promised to sue the city for the "lies" they told about him and give half the money to Cox's younger brother and sister. The incriminating note was seized by a sheriff's deputy, however, who thought it was contraband. After the note was introduced as evidence in court, Burns was convicted of the murders, and sentenced to life in prison. Cox and Williams were also convicted; however, because they were the triggermen in the shootings, they received the death penalty. Cox, described as "defiant and insolent" during his trial, was called a "menace to society" by the judge who sentenced him to death (*Los Angeles Times*, May 3, 1991; Part B, p. 3:4).

On October 12, 1984, less than six weeks after the Alexander tragedy, another gang-related mass murder occurred in Los Angeles. This time, five youths — ranging in age from 14 to 18 — were killed and five others were wounded outside a birthday party in South Los Angeles (*San Diego Union-Tribune*, November 16, 1984; p. A13). About four weeks later, police arrested the "prime triggerman" in the shootings, 18-year-old Keith "Ace Capone" Fudge. Although Fudge's mother said he was "very religious" and "too timid to be involved in any sort of violence," he was an 11th-grade dropout who had a criminal record dating back to the age of 16. Moreover, he was a leader of the Van Ness Gangsters set of the Bloods street gang (*Los Angeles Times*, August 11, 1987; Part 2, p. 6:1).

On the afternoon of the shootings, Fudge's car was stolen, and he believed that Percy "Buddha" Brewer, a rival gang member of the Crips, was responsible. According to police, Fudge and two fellow gang members, Fred Knight and Harold Hall, drove to a birthday party where they thought Brewer would be. Fudge and Knight stepped out of the car, and approached the partygoers, who were waiting outside. Spotting Brewer, Fudge and Knight opened fire, killing Brewer and four others. Witnesses reported that Fudge and his two accomplices were "just cracking up and laughing" as they drove off (*Los Angeles Times*, December 12, 1987; Part 2, p. 3:2).

In early 1987, Fudge was tried for the murders, but a mistrial was declared after jurors deadlocked 11 to 1 in favor of convicting him (*Los Angeles Times*, April 10, 1987). In the summer of 1987, a second trial was held, and this time Fudge was convicted of the killings. On December 11, 1987, he was sentenced to death for the shootings the judge called "reminiscent of the gangland violence and massacres of the '30s." Knight was more fortunate, however. After a six-month trial in 1989, a jury acquitted him of the five murders due to conflicting eyewitness testimony (*Los Angeles Times*, December 21, 1989; Part B, p. 1:5).

Mass Public Shootings: "This is War!"

As discussed earlier, the Speck and Whitman massacres in the summer of 1966 ushered in the second mass murder wave in the twentieth century. Both were heavily-publicized incidents that were regarded as the "crime of the century." In fact, these massacres captured so much media attention that they later inspired 18-year-old Robert Benjamin Smith to commit a mass murder in the fall of 1966. Smith killed five and wounded two at the Rose-Mar College of Beauty in Mesa, Arizona, on November 12 (*New York Times*, November 13, 1966; p. 1:2). He claimed he got the idea for the murders, which he committed to "make a reputation" for himself, from the mass killings four months earlier in Chicago and Austin.

Smith moved to Mesa, which was a predominantly Mormon community, a year before with his parents and 5-year-old sister after his father had retired from the Army. Before that, the family moved from Army post to Army post. He was regarded as a loner by other students. A neighbor from Glen Burnie, Maryland, where the family lived before they moved to Mesa, recalled that, "the most outstanding thing about Benny was how close he stuck to home all day and every day. He didn't associate with other kids. The whole family was shy, they kept to themselves, but all of them were bright." In school, Smith received adequate grades, doing very well in the subjects that interested him (e.g., English and literature), but poorly in those that did not (e.g., math and science). As an accelerated student, he participated in teacher-guided seminar sessions in which students discussed philosophy and human motivation. One student recalled that Smith "didn't value human life very much" and "ridiculed love and compassion." Another student remembered that Smith felt that the United States should use germ warfare "to wipe out the people of Southeast Asia — they're all animals and they're not important" (*New York Times*, November 15, 1966; p. 60:3).

Shortly after the Speck and Whitman massacres, Smith began planning his own when his parents gave him a .22-caliber pistol for target practice. In planning the killings, he initially intended to return to his hometown, Houston, Missouri, where he was born. After discarding that idea, he settled on three sites: a school, where he intended to kill the teachers, Rose-Mar College, and another beauty shop. He selected Rose-Mar because he decided that there were not enough people at the other beauty salon. Smith bought some plastic sandwich bags, nylon rope, and a hunting knife, because he planned to bind and suffocate his victims. He rejected this plan, however, because he discovered the sandwich bags were too small for a victim's head. On Friday night, November 11, he made the necessary preparations for the next day, putting 200 feet of nylon cord, 25 plastic food sacks, a hunting knife, a .22-caliber pistol, and a box of ammunition in a brown paper sack.

Smith arose at 6:30 the next morning; dressed in a blue and white pinstriped shirt, blue trousers, and blue canvas shoes; and walked the mile and a half to the salon, with the brown paper sack in hand. He waited outside until he saw an employee enter the shop, and then followed her inside. He fired a shot into a mirror and ordered the five women and two girls to the back room. The women asked Smith if he was kidding. He put the gun against the head of Bonita Sue Harris, an 18-year-old employee, and said, "No, I'm not kidding." He then ordered everyone to lie with their heads in a circle, so that their bodies extended out like spokes on a wheel (*New York Times*, November 14, 1966; p. 46:4).

One of the girls told Smith there would be 40 people in the shop in a few minutes. Smith responded by telling her that he was sorry, but he didn't have enough ammunition for them. One of the women asked Smith which ones were going to die or if everyone was going to die. He replied that everyone was going to die and even though he had not planned on killing any children, he would because they grow up, too. One of the employees, 18-year-old Mary Margaret Olsen, asked Smith if he was serious. When he said that he was, she started praying. Smith asked what she was doing, and 19-year-old patron Carol Farmer said that she was praying "if you don't mind." Smith replied, "I do mind," and opened fire, shooting each victim twice. Only Bonita Sue Harris and 3-month-old Tamara Lyn Sellers survived. The manager of the beauty college, Eveline Cummings, called police after she heard "a popping noise" and saw Smith with the gun. When police arrived, Smith told them, "I shot some people. They're back there. The gun is in that sack." On October 24, 1967, Smith was convicted and sentenced to death.

The mass murder committed by Robert Smith provides one of the clearest examples of the copycat or contagion effect. However, of the 909 mass killings examined in this study, it was one of only five that exhibited clear-cut evidence that the offender was influenced by a previous mass murder. For example, before postal carriers Thomas McIlvane and Joseph Harris each committed a mass murder at post offices in the fall of 1991, they both mentioned the massacre carried out by another postal carrier, Patrick Sherrill, five years earlier at the post office in Edmond, Oklahoma. McIlvane, in particular, told co-workers that he was going to make "Edmond look like Disneyland." More recently, Seung-Hui Cho, who committed the nation's worst gun-related mass murder at Virginia Tech University on April 16, 2007, invoked the names of Eric Harris and Dylan Klebold — the two killers responsible for the Columbine massacre in 1999. In the package of photos and videos Cho mailed to NBC News between the two shooting incidents, he referred to Harris and Klebold as "martyrs."

Some scholars have adduced clusters of high-profile mass killings as proof that the media encourage some individuals predisposed to aggression to commit similar acts of violence. However, the occurrence of several well-publicized massacres within a relatively short period of time does not, in and of itself, constitute sufficient evidence of the copycat effect. The findings presented here suggest that a very small number of mass murderers are directly affected by prior mass killings. It is important to point out, however, that there may be some offenders who were encouraged by a previous mass murder but simply did not express it to others.

As dramatically illustrated by the mass murders committed by Charles Whitman and Robert Smith, the 1960s marked the beginning of the rise in mass public shootings. These mass killings are typically committed by white males in their 30s (see Table 13). These offenders usually target either acquaintances or strangers and, compared to other mass murderers, are more likely to use assault weapons. Moreover, mass public shooters are highly suicidal, as almost half exhibited suicidal behavior.

In 1967, Leo Held, a 39-year-old laboratory technician, fatally shot six and wounded six in Lock Haven, Pennsylvania (*New York Times*, October 24, 1967; p. 1:8). Held was described as a quiet, devoted father and husband who was a member of the Sugar Valley school board, a director of a local Boy Scout troop, and an avid hunter and woodsman. Yet Leo Held felt that people were out to get him. Held believed that his neighbor, Floyd Quiggle, burned leaves just to spite him, knowing that he was bothered by the smoke. Held also feuded with other neighbors, complaining that they were encroaching on his property line. He believed that his phones were tapped. He held a grudge against those in his car pool who had "blackballed" him three months before the killings "because of his reckless driving." Held was also resentful towards those who had passed him over at work, and was fearful that he was going to lose his job (*New York Times*, October 25, 1967; p. 26:3).

At 8 A.M. on October 23, Held attempted to even the score with those whom he felt had persecuted him. Armed with a .38-caliber Magnum revolver and a .45-automatic pistol, he walked into the Hammermill Paper Company plant, where he was a laboratory technician, and opened fire, killing five fellow employees and wounding four others. Next, Held drove to the Lock Haven Airport, where Geraldine Ramm worked. Ramm had carpooled with Held, and was one of those who had "blackballed" him. Held wounded Ramm by shooting her twice. He then drove to his home, and proceeded to break into the house of Floyd Quiggle, who was

Table 13.
Characteristics of Mass Public Shootings, 1900–1999

Variables	Avg/Percent
Average Death Toll	6.10
Average Wounded Count	4.73
Weapon Type	
Gun	100%
Other	0%
Fire	0%
Victim-Offender Relationship	
Stranger	42%
Family	8%
Acquaintance	50%
Public Location	100%
City > 250,000	26%
Assault Weapon	9%
Interracial	17%
White Offenders	73%
Average Offender Age	33.08
Percent Offender 30–49	41%
Percent Offender ≥ 50	8%
Male Offenders	99%
Suicidal Offenders	47%
Average Offender Count	1.15
White Victims	89%
Average Victim Age	36.04
Victims Age <16 or >40	49%
Male Victims	65%
Region	
Midwest	17%
East	22%
South	31%
West	30%
N	116

asleep in bed with his wife. After killing Quiggle and wounding his wife, Held entered his home, which soon became surrounded by police. Held left through the back door of his house and fired at police as he ran across the lawn. He dropped to the ground after getting hit by a police bullet in the right thigh. But Held would not surrender; he continued to fire at police as he lay on the ground. Police were able to apprehend Held after they shot him four times. Two days later, however, he died at the Lock Haven Hospital (*New York Times*, October 26, 1967; p. 63:3).

During the 1970s, there were a number of well-publicized mass public shootings. In 1972, Edwin Grace, an unemployed security guard, shot

12 people, six fatally, in Cherry Hill, New Jersey; the following year, Mark Essex went on a shooting spree in New Orleans, killing six and wounding ten; and Nazi sympathizer Fred Cowan fatally shot five people in New Rochelle, New York, in 1977.

There were several mass public shootings, however, that were not as well publicized. On July 23, 1977, Dewitt Henry, a 26-year-old unemployed truck driver, gunned down six people and wounded two police officers in Klamath Falls, Oregon (AP Wire, July 23, 1977; AM Cycle). Described as a "misfit and a loner," Henry was despondent in the weeks leading up to the shootings. His wife had recently left him, and he attempted to commit suicide three weeks before the shootings. Henry was also upset about not being able to find a job, and in the five days prior to the shootings, he took drugs, drank, and did not sleep. On the night of July 23, Henry went to Uncle Albert's Lounge, where he used to work as a bouncer, for he stood 6-foot-3 and weighed 230 pounds. Henry was asked to leave the bar after getting into an argument. He then went to a bar called Poor Ol' Dan's, where he told a waitress that he planned on seeking revenge at Uncle Albert's (AP Wire, July 25, 1977; AM Cycle).

At 2 A.M., Henry, who was armed with a .223-caliber semi-automatic civilian version of an M-16 rifle, began shooting at people waiting outside Uncle Albert's Lounge after it had closed. He then exchanged gunfire with state troopers as they arrived on the scene. After wounding two of the officers, Henry was wounded by a shotgun blast and taken into custody. At his trial, Henry's attorneys sought a verdict of innocent by reason of mental disease or defect, but the jury convicted him and he was sentenced to life in prison. After the verdict, Klamath County district attorney Ulys Stapleton said, "He wants you to believe he's crazy. He was angry. He was vengeful and he vented that anger. Guns were his equalizer. Guns made him equal to others and made up for a deficiency in his personality" (AP Wire, November 10, 1979; PM Cycle).

Although Henry was unsuccessful in his insanity plea, Edward Allaway was not. On July 12, 1976, Allaway, a 37-year-old janitor, gunned down seven and wounded two at the Cal State Fullerton campus. After graduating from high school, Allaway joined the Marine Corps, but was dishonorably discharged in 1958 after he contracted venereal disease three times. Allaway first began showing signs of mental illness in 1971, when he was married to his first wife, Carol. He believed that the Black Panthers wanted to kidnap her for sex, castrate him, and then kill them both. On one occasion, according to his wife, he was surprised to see her because he thought she had been kidnapped, drugged, and molested by a group of men. In response, Allaway put a bolt lock on their bedroom door and stashed two loaded guns underneath their bed. After his wife convinced him he needed help, Allaway admitted himself to Oakwood Hospital, a mental facility in Dearborn, Michigan (*Orange County Register*, July 1, 1995; p. B1).

Following the release from the hospital and divorce from his wife, Allaway moved to California, where he found a job as a janitor on the campus of Cal State Fullerton. He also married his second wife, Bonnie, who was described as a pretty, vivacious, 22-year-old blonde (*Orange County Register*, May 14, 1991; p. A1). But the paranoid delusions that troubled him before began to reappear. At Fullerton, co-workers in the campus media center joked that pornographic movies were made there. They teased Allaway that his wife may have even starred in the movies. In the investigation following the murders, police found about 20 commercially produced pornographic films in the media center. But no evidence was presented to prove that any pornographic movies were ever made there. And in his duties as janitor, Allaway was offended by the obscene graffiti and homosexual activity he regularly found in a men's restroom.

Like other mass murderers, such as Seung-Hui Cho, Allaway was paranoid and depressed. For example, he feared that his wife would be forced to perform in pornographic movies and that he would be forced to commit homosexual acts. In May, two months before the shootings, Allaway's wife left him. He grew increasingly troubled at work, and asked his supervisor to be transferred to another building, but nothing ever came of it. On the Friday before the killings, Allaway bought a .22-caliber semi-automatic rifle and shells. Although Allaway had formerly been a mental patient, which would have barred him from purchasing the gun, he failed to disclose this information on the gun purchase form (*Orange County Register*, October 9, 1987; p. B1).

At 8:30 A.M. on Monday, July 12, Allaway went to work armed with his semiautomatic rifle. Years later, Allaway described his thought process on the day of the shootings: "I went to work. I was so afraid, so scared. I can remember the morning. My thought was to quit the job, don't go to work, go on a vacation, go to work. I couldn't make a decision. I had a rifle. I said nobody would hurt me. Nobody's going to mess with me, so I could work all day long. When I make this statement, it tells you just how illogical I was — just how sick I had become" (*Los Angeles Times*, July 6, 1996; Part 2, p. 1:2). Allaway entered the library where he worked, and descended the two flights of stairs to the basement, where the media center was located. Moving quickly from office to office, Allaway shot nine people, killing seven. He then drove to a nearby Hilton Hotel, where his estranged wife was staying, and called the police. In the ensuing trial, Allaway was found not guilty by reason of insanity and sent to Atascadero State Hospital (*Orange County Register*, April 22, 1987; p. B1).

Although Levin and Fox (1985) have claimed that most people think mass killers are crazy, Edward Allaway represents a tiny percentage of mass murderers who were found not guilty by reason of insanity. Of the 909 cases studied here, I was able to obtain offender disposition data on 705 of the 1,186 mass killers. Despite the relatively large percentage (40 percent) of missing data, the remaining cases still provide a glimpse, however imperfect, of how frequently mass killers are found insane. As shown in Table 14, 22 percent of the offenders never went to trial because they were killed after the attack, either by their own hand or by police gunfire. For those who did, however, only 2 percent were found not guilty by reason of insanity. Of those who were found guilty, 3 percent received less than a life sentence, 21 percent a life sentence, and 12 percent the death penalty.

These findings challenge the notion, if it exists, that most mass killers are found insane. But insanity is a legal, not a medical, concept. Moreover, nearly a quarter of all mass murderers are killed before they are adjudicated. There may be many mass killers who can differentiate between right and wrong, but are nevertheless mentally ill. In their study of thirty mass murderers, Hempel and colleagues (1999) found that fifteen had a documented psychiatric history. Of these, six were diagnosed with schizophrenia, seven with depression, and two with other disorders.

The offender mental health data are, like the data for offender disposition, plagued by missing cases. That is, there were many cases in which

Table 14.
Disposition of Mass Murderers, 1900–1999

Disposition	Percent
Adjudged Insane	2
Death Penalty	12
Life Sentence	21
Less than a Life Sentence	3
Killed at the Crime Scene	22
Missing Data	40
N	1,186

there was no mention as to whether the offender had a psychiatric history or a diagnosed mental illness. This, of course, does not necessarily mean that these offenders did not suffer from mental illness, but simply that they were never diagnosed or, if so, it was not mentioned in the data. It is still possible, though, to at least generate a very conservative estimate of the prevalence of mental illness among mass murderers. Of the 1,186 mass killers in this study, at least 154 (13 percent) were diagnosed with some form of mental illness. Moreover the evidence suggests that at least 176 more (15 percent), although never formally diagnosed, exhibited symptoms of mental illness such as depression, paranoia, or sociopathy. Therefore, it is reasonable to estimate that between 13 percent and 28 percent of mass killers were plagued by a mental disorder. It is important to reiterate, however, that this is a conservative estimate of the prevalence of mental illness among mass murderers.

Gan Fong Chin provides another example of a mentally disturbed offender who used a gun to kill publicly. In 1978, the 48-year-old Chin gunned down four co-workers at the Cathay Terrace Restaurant in War-wick, Rhode Island, on June 17 (AP Wire, June 18, 1978; AM Cycle). Born in the Canton section of China, Chin immigrated to the United States in 1950. Described as quiet and introverted, he was married, had four children, and was a long-time employee of the Cathay Terrace Restaurant, where he was a cook. But in the mid–1970s, Chin began to have paranoid delusions in which he thought his family was trying to poison him. In an attempt to "ward off evil spirits," Chin covered the windows in his house with newspapers, strung fish hooks across them, and boarded his doors with panels bearing hand-painted pictures of Chinese warriors. He also carried a .32 mm pistol and would wear sunglasses when his family would eat meals together. By 1978, he believed that not only was his family trying to poison him, but his co-workers as well (UPI Wire, August 19, 1987; AM Cycle).

On June 6, Chin bought a 30–30 carbine, which he brought to work eleven days later in a gift-wrapped box. On June 17, after working at the Cathay Terrace Restaurant for approximately four hours, Chin removed the rifle from the box, loaded it, and began firing. Ignoring the 50 or so customers who were in the restaurant, Chin killed the co-owner, bartender, maitre d', and waitress. One of the patrons, a 66-year-old woman, suffered a fatal heart attack when Chin began shooting. After misfiring at one of the busboys, Chin fled the restaurant, but surrendered peacefully to police a short distance away. When police questioned Chin, he reportedly said, "They tried to poison me" (UPI Wire, August 31, 1987; AM Cycle). For the next nine years, Chin was held at the Institute of Mental Health, where he was diagnosed as a paranoid schizophrenic. In 1987, however, he was found competent to stand trial. Despite defense arguments that Chin was not criminally responsible because he was mentally ill, he was convicted and sentenced to life in prison (UPI Wire, September 1, 1987; AM Cycle). Chin died in 1988 at the age of 57 (UPI Wire, May 16, 1988; BC Cycle).

Although the mid–1960s marked the beginning of the rise in mass public shootings, the incidence of these cases began to accelerate dramatically in the 1980s and 1990s. Of the 116 mass public shootings from 1900 through 1999, 52 percent took place in the last two decades of the twentieth century. What might have accounted for the sharp increase in mass public shootings since the mid–1960s?

Beginning in the 1960s, the United States was profoundly affected by a number of significant social and cultural developments. The children born during the postwar boom were growing into adolescence and were, thus, starting to enter the peak crime years between the ages of 14 and 24. During the 1960s, for example, the percentage of the population aged 15–24 increased by 30 percent. Due to declining economic opportunities, booming college enrollment, and a rejection of the bourgeois, suburban lifestyle in which they had grown up, many young Americans were delaying or avoiding marriage altogether as the marriage rate plummeted by 14 percent during the 1960s. And more Americans started terminating marriages, too, as the divorce rate increased by more than 200 percent from 1960 to 1979. Yet, due to the sexual revolution, many Americans were still having sex, which helped bring about a dramatic increase in the number of illegitimate children and single-parent families. From 1960 through 1990, the illegitimate birth rate doubled while the number of single-parent households increased by more than 250 percent. Consistent with the decline of marriage and family, more Americans were becoming socially isolated as the percentage of adults living alone grew by 71 percent from 1960 through 1980. And America was also becoming a more mobile and transient society.

The growth of alienated, unattached, and under- or unemployed young men probably played some role in the dramatic increase in homicide rates and crime overall beginning in the 1960s. It also may have contributed to the rise in mass murder in general and mass public shooting in particular during the last third of the twentieth century. But this is merely speculation, which is a poor substitute for empirical analysis.

In 2002, Tomislav Kovandzic, Carlisle Moody and I published a study in which we examined the impact of right-to-carry concealed firearms laws (hereafter referred to as RTC laws) on the incidence of mass public shootings. Although we did not specifically address the issue of what has caused the prevalence of mass public shootings to increase since the 1960s, we included in our analyses a number of control variables we hypothesized might have an impact on the occurrence of mass public shootings. As a result, the findings from our study may shed a little bit of light on what may have caused mass public shootings to increase since the 1960s.

The question of whether RTC laws deter mass public shootings was first examined by John Lott and William Landes, who hypothesized that gun carrying by prospective victims may exert a deterrent effect on multiple-victim public shootings by increasing shooters' perception of risk. Further, because RTC laws presumably increase gun carrying and defensive use of guns in public places, they posited that these laws might increase the rate at which armed victims disrupt shootings and, thus, the severity of attacks. Using Poisson regression, Lott and Landes found that RTC laws significantly reduced the number of multiple-victim public shootings and the number of people killed and wounded.

Using a more refined measure of mass public shootings, we re-examined whether RTC laws have a deterrent effect on these incidents. Whereas Lott and Landes used Poisson regression, we selected a negative binomial model since the mean and variances for our variables were very different. In addition to our variable of interest, RTC laws, we included a number of control variables we thought might have an impact on the incidence of mass public shootings. For example, we analyzed several demographic variables along with measures pertaining to unemployment, social isolation, and social mobility. We also included a few controls generally associated with homicide in general: prison population and legal executions.

Our results showed that RTC laws did not have a significant effect on the incidence of mass public shootings or on the number of people killed and wounded. We did find, however, that prison population, income, and the percentage of 45–54-year-olds had a significant positive effect on the occurrence of mass public shootings, while legal executions were significantly associated but in the negative direction. These findings do not lend much support to the notion that employment troubles increase the incidence of mass public shootings. Nor do they lend credence to the view that mass public shootings have increased because America has become a more mobile, anonymous, and anomic society. It is important to note, however, that we did not include a number of controls that might have an impact on the prevalence of mass public shootings — marriage rates, divorce rates, and religiosity.

Whatever the reasons for the increase since the 1960s, it is, nevertheless, clear that the incidence of mass public shootings continued to accelerate during the 1980s, producing some of the most notorious mass murders in recent memory. In 1984, James Huberty gunned down 21 at a McDonald's in San Ysidro, California, and Patrick Sherrill fatally shot 14 at an Edmond, Oklahoma, post office two years later. In 1989, Patrick Purdy shot 30, killing five, at a Stockton, California, schoolyard, while Joseph Wesbecker murdered eight in Louisville later that year. In all four incidents, the killers chose specific sites at which to commit their attacks, but their selection of victims was relatively indiscriminate. The mass public shooting carried out by Alvin Lee King on June 22, 1980, in Daingerfield, Texas, provides another example, though perhaps not as well known, in which the offender randomly gunned down his victims in a public location.

Born in Wichita Falls, Texas, in 1934, King was raised in Corpus Christi, where his parents owned a liquor store, pawnshop, and jukebox leasing company. He became a teacher in 1957 and started teaching mathematics at Daingerfield High School in 1966. This was also the same year in which King accidentally killed his father. While visiting his parents in Corpus Christi, King was examining a 12-gauge shotgun when it slipped from his grasp and discharged. The blast hit his father in the face and neck, wounding him fatally. King eventually returned to Daingerfield and resumed his teaching duties (*Time* July 7, 1980; p. 18).

King was regarded as a brilliant teacher who was impatient with slow learners and indifferent with colleagues. As Sam Johnson, former principal of the high school, would later say, "He was highly intelligent in science and math, a big slide-rule man, but as far as old common sense, he didn't have a whole lot" (*New York Times*, June 24, 1980). King was considered an outsider in the small town of Daingerfield, which had a population of 2,800. Unlike most of his neighbors, who attended church on a regular basis, King was an atheist. Although all teachers at the high school were required at the time to sign an oath acknowledging the existence of God, he refused.

In 1972, King quit his job after being asked to teach mentally disabled students. He began working as a truck driver and then went back to school to earn his doctorate in psychology from East Texas State University. Several years later, King moved his family to a 100-acre farm outside Daingerfield, where he raised peas and cucumbers, collected guns and practiced judo. Always a loner, King kept a low profile until October 1979, when his 21-year-old daughter, Cynthia, who had recently moved away from home, filed charges of incest against her father. She claimed that King had forced her to have sex with him for over 10 years, beginning in 1967. The trial was scheduled to begin on June 23, the day before the shootings. King had asked several members of the First Baptist Church to serve as character witnesses, but they all refused.

At 11:20 A.M. on June 22, King burst into the First Baptist Church, armed with an AR-15 rifle, an M-1 rifle, a .22-caliber pistol, a .38-caliber revolver, and about 250 rounds of ammunition. He fired several shots into the crowd of 350 worshipers, shouted, "This is war!" and continued shooting, killing three and wounding ten. Three members of the congregation were able to wrest the M-1 away from King, but he then drew the .22-caliber pistol and killed two of the men (*Washington Post*, June 23, 1980; p. A8). King fled to a nearby fire station, where he attempted to commit suicide by shooting himself in the head. The investigation afterwards revealed that shortly before the killings, King had applied for Soviet citizenship but was turned down (*New York Times*, June 23, 1980; p. 14:1). Police also found that King had deposited $300 into a Swiss bank account and had passports for himself and his wife. After King recovered from his wounds, he was held for 17 months at the Rusk State Hospital for the Criminally Insane, where he underwent psychiatric testing. In December of 1981, he was found competent to stand trial. But on January 19, 1982, he committed suicide by hanging himself in his jail cell (AP Wire, January 19, 1982).

Seven months after King committed suicide, Carl Brown went on a shooting spree in Miami, killing eight and wounding three (*New York Times*, August 21, 1982; p. 7:1). A schoolteacher for 20 years, Brown was ordered to receive psychiatric treatment after he had been placed on medical leave in December of 1981. But his troubles began at least as early as the mid–1970s, when he was a teacher at Hialeah Junior High School. There, students had refused to sit in his class, complaining that he was often incoherent, that he spent teaching time to talk about his personal problems, and that he had no control over his classes. In 1981, Brown was transferred to Drew Junior High, where colleagues immediately noticed that he was disturbed. Donald Fussell, assistant principal at the school, noted, "It was apparent that he had some severe problems right from the beginning. As far as the classes themselves, there was no teaching, no learning going on. He would begin a meaningful conversation with you and would maintain it for 15 seconds. But if he talked longer than that, it would become fragmented" (UPI Wire, August 22, 1982; PM Cycle).

On December 3, 1981, a classroom incident occurred that led to Brown's dismissal. Brown got into an argument with two boys after he accused them of throwing books. During the argument, Brown described his sexual behavior with a girlfriend, and then threatened to use a stapler on the penis of one of the boys. In a memo filed after the incident, Principal Octavio Visideo reported that he "found Mr. Brown to be incoherent and unable to grasp the severity of the situation at hand" (UPI Wire, August 24, 1982; AM Cycle). He sought counseling for Brown, who began seeing a psychiatrist in January. Brown was later placed on medical leave in March.

Just as Brown's professional life started a downward spiral, so, too, did his personal life. His second wife, Sylvia Loynaz Brown, divorced him because of his earlier refusal to get help for his mental health problems. She said that he had once threatened "to plant bombs all over Miami and to get up on the roof and shoot everybody that comes by." Despite the apparent severity of Brown's mental illness, the psychiatrist whom he had been seeing, Dr. Robert A. Wainger, thought that Brown did not pose a "danger to anyone." Dr. Wainger saw Brown two days before the shootings and noted, "He did not indicate ... that he had any interest in harming anyone or himself" (UPI Wire, August 24, 1982; AM Cycle).

The next day, Brown visited Bob Moore's Welding and Machine Service, Inc., to complain about a $20 bill for work done on a small lawn-mower engine. After making a few "threatening remarks," Brown left the shop and went home. That night, while swimming in the pool behind his house, Brown told his 10-year-old son that he was "going to kill a lot of people" the next day. True to his word, Brown went out that morning and bought two shotguns, an automatic rifle, and ammunition from a Dade County gun shop. Brown returned home, tossed one of the new guns to his son, and asked him to join him. Frightened, the boy called his mother, who tried to call police but gave up after she was repeatedly transferred.

At around 11 A.M., Brown burst into the shop and began shooting. He killed eight and wounded three before he fled on his bicycle. When Mark Kram, who was at a nearby metal recycling shop, heard of the shootings, he grabbed two guns and jumped in his car to pursue Brown. After spotting him, Kram fired a shot that struck Brown in the back. Kram then drove his car into Brown, knocking him into a light pole. Brown was later pronounced dead, and Kram was not charged with killing Brown because he used "justifiable force." Police later noted that Kram might have saved lives because Brown might have been headed to the junior high school where he once worked (*New York Times*, August 24, 1982; p. 14:3).

Politicians responded to the shooting spree that was called "Miami's biggest mass murder" by introducing legislation requiring a 72-hour cooling off period before the purchase of rifles and handguns in the state of Florida. Brown's ex-wife claimed that such a waiting period might have prevented the mass shooting. She also blamed the gun shop that sold him the guns, saying, "He had been there many times. They must have known he was strange. It is amazing they let him buy those guns" (UPI Wire, July 2, 1983; AM Cycle).

Alvin Lee King and Carl Brown were generally indiscriminate in their selection of victims. John Parish, on the other hand, had specific targets in mind when he carried out his attack. Parish was a 46-year-old truck driver who moved to Dallas in 1980 to start working for Western Transfer Corporation. Before moving to Dallas, he had worked as a trucker for 18 years in places such as Indiana, Kentucky, Illinois, and Missouri (UPI Wire, August 10, 1982; PM Cycle).

Although co-workers at Western considered him to be an easy-going person, Parish had been banned from making deliveries to the warehouse of Jewel-T, a discount grocery store, where he was thought to be a troublemaker. And Parish, recently estranged from his wife, had also become involved in a pay dispute with his employers at Western. He alleged that the company had shorted him $1,600 in pay (*New York Times*, August 10, 1982; p. 16:1). When company officials showed him photocopies of records indicating he had been paid everything due him, he remained unconvinced. His brother, Murphy Parish, said, "He was getting tired of being shoved around and was going to go in and see them about it Monday. He said if they'd talk to him like a man, and not treat him like a fool, they could work it out." But Parish had no intentions of resolving the dispute, at least not in a peaceful manner. He was "tired of being messed around," and was going to make his employers pay for mistreating him (AP Wire, August 10, 1982; AM Cycle).

At 8 A.M. Monday, Parish arrived at the offices of Western, armed with a .25-caliber semiautomatic pistol, a .38-caliber pistol, and an M-1 carbine. Without saying a word, Parish killed his supervisor and two other truck drivers. He then stole a truck and drove the half block to another Western Transfer office, where he killed an executive secretary and wounded two others. Parish grabbed an office worker and ordered her to find him an executive's office, telling her she would die if the executive was not there. Parish decided not to kill her when she told him that she was the wife of a mechanic with the company. He told her, "That's the only reason I'm not going to kill you — the only reason." He then walked over to the Jewel-T warehouse, where he killed two workers and wounded another.

After leaving the warehouse, Parish stole an 18-wheel tractor-trailer and began exchanging gunfire with police, who had arrived on the scene. He proceeded to ram the truck into a police barricade, which seriously injured an officer and sent the truck sliding on its side into a nearby building. Parish emerged from the tractor-trailer cab, still firing at police. He was eventually killed after suffering seven or eight gunshot wounds.

The mass murder committed by Mansel "Sonny" Hammett in South Connellsville, Pennsylvania, provides another example of a disgruntled employee with specific targets in mind. Hammett, 39, earned $9 an hour loading cartons of bottles on wooden pallets at Anchor Glass, where he had been an employee for 18 years. His wife, Judith, also worked at Anchor Glass. Hammett was described by co-workers as quiet, competent, and reclusive, but overprotective of his wife. Co-workers also noticed that he had become increasingly disturbed over layoffs at the plant (*New York Times*, March 17, 1985; p. 26:6).

Anchor Glass had been operating in South Connellsville for nearly 70 years. But in recent years, the growing prevalence of foreign imports and plastics had hurt the glass-making industry, resulting in the closing of 15 of the 100 plants in the U.S. The difficulties in the glass-making industry were also felt at Anchor Glass, which had recently reduced its workforce from 1,200 to 600. The cutbacks created stress among the workers, not least for Hammett, as both workloads and pressure to meet production quotas increased. When quotas were not met, employees were suspended or dismissed. The mounting tension at the plant led some to speculate that violence was imminent. As one co-worker of Hammett said, "It's a pressure cooker in there. When we took breaks, people sometimes talked about how somebody someday was gonna go over the edge and start shooting. We actually talked about somebody coming in there with a gun someday. We just didn't know who or when" (*Washington Post*, April 5, 1985; p. A3).

On March 16, 1985, Hammett was that somebody. He was working the Saturday shift when Judith, who was also working that shift, came to speak to him. Hammett's supervisor, Donald Abbott, admonished Judith for interrupting her husband and told her to get back to work. Hammett replied, "She's my wife, she's allowed to talk to me." An argument ensued and Abbott called other supervisors, who suspended Hammett and threatened him with dismissal.

Furious, Hammett left the plant, bought 100 rounds of ammunition, and returned an hour later, armed with a .38-caliber revolver. He pistol-whipped a security guard who tried to stop him, and entered the quality control office, where he shot Donald Abbott and another supervisor. Hammett's wife struggled for the gun and pleaded with him to stop, screaming, "No, Sonny, don't do it. No, no, don't do it." But Hammett continued his shooting spree as he hunted down another supervisor, whom he wounded with a shot to the chest. Hammett had specific targets in mind, for when other coworkers tried to stop him, he fired shots over their heads (AP Wire, March 18, 1985; PM Cycle). With employees shouting at him and diving for cover, he located department manager Ralph Tomaro and quality control manager John Coligan in Tomaro's office, where he killed them both. After Hammett was unable to find plant manager Russell Watson, he returned to the center of the shop floor, and committed suicide by shooting himself in the chest.

In the early 1990s, the media focused the public's attention on problems like serial murder, stalking, and hate crimes. The growing emphasis on random violence led to a heightened fear of crime, which was evident during the 1992 presidential race. The steady increase in mass public shootings during the first half of the 1990s may have contributed to the rise in the fear of crime. For example, George Hennard committed what was, until the April 16, 2007, shooting at Virginia Tech, the worst gun-related mass murder in U.S. history when he murdered 22 and wounded 23 more at a Luby's Cafeteria in Killeen, Texas, in 1991. Later that year, James Johnson gunned down four people in a sniper attack in Missouri, and in 1992 Lynwood Drake killed six people in Morro Bay, California. In 1993, Kenneth Junior French fatally shot four and wounded eight at a restaurant in North Carolina, James Buquet killed four at a health club in California, and Colin Ferguson gunned down six and wounded seventeen on the Long Island Railroad.

On June 20, 1994, 20-year-old Dean Mellberg went on a shooting spree at Fairchild Air Force Base in Spokane, Washington. Shortly after graduating from high school in Lansing, Michigan, in 1992, he joined the Air Force (*Seattle Times*, June 21, 1994; p. A1). But within one month of joining, a staff psychiatrist at Lackland Air Force Base in Texas recommended Mellberg's discharge for "having some problems adjusting and getting along in basic training" (*Los Angeles Times*, June 22, 1994; p. 9:1). He was allowed to continue basic training, however, and was eventually assigned to Fairchild in April 1993 as an aircraft maintenance worker (*The Spokane-Review*, November 17, 1997; p. A1).

Mellberg's problems continued at Fairchild, where, according to his mother, his roommate began spreading rumors he was homosexual (*New York Times*, June 22, 1994; p. 14:1). His difficulties led to meetings with the staff psychiatrist and psychologist, who diagnosed him as mentally ill and imminently dangerous. Their diagnosis ultimately led to Mellberg's discharge on May 23, 1994, despite his efforts to fight it (*Los Angeles Times*, June 22, 1994; p. 9:1). On June 20, Mellberg arrived at Fairchild armed with a MAK-90 semiautomatic rifle. Bent on revenge, he went directly to the offices of the staff psychiatrist and psychologist, where he fatally shot both men (*Chicago Tribune*, June 22, 1994; p. 18N). Mellberg then walked through the base hospital and annex, firing as he went. He killed two more victims and wounded 22 others before he was shot by a military policeman.

As discussed later in Chapter 6, gun control proponents used a number of mass public shootings during the late 1980s and early 1990s — including the one committed by Dean Mellberg — to bring about a ban on assault weapons. Contrary to the claims noted earlier, assault weapons are used very rarely in mass killings; in fact, there were only 16 incidents that involved assault weapon use, and all took place since 1977. Despite the infrequent use of assault weapons among mass murderers, these guns may inflict greater fatalities due to their semiautomatic capability and ability to accept large ammunition clips.

Compared to other mass murders, incidents involving assault weapons have, on average, about one more fatality (see Table 15). The biggest difference, though, is not the number of victims killed, but the number of victims wounded. Table 15 indicates, for example, that assault weapon-related massacres produce twice as many wounded victims as other mass killings, or roughly four more wounded victims per incident. It is important to point out, however, that 11 of the 16 cases (69 percent) involved offenders who were armed with other, non-assault weapon guns. Moreover, it was unclear in eight of these cases whether the offender used only

Table 15.
Characteristics of Assault Weapons-Related Massacres

Variables	Avg/Percent
Average Death Toll	6.56
Average Wounded Count	8.19
Victim-Offender Relationship	
Stranger	47%
Family	20%
Acquaintance	33%
Public Location	81%
City > 250,000	53%
Interracial	21%
White Offenders	55%
Average Offender Age	32.82
Percent Offender 30–49	38%
Percent Offender ≥ 50	19%
Male Offenders	100%
Suicidal Offenders	45%
Average Offender Count	1.37
White Victims	72%
Average Victim Age	32.36
Victims Age <16 or >40	57%
Male Victims	64%
Region	
Midwest	13%
East	31%
South	31%
West	25%
N	16

an assault weapon. Therefore, of the eight unambiguous instances of assault weapon use, the average number of victims killed and wounded was 5.87 and 8.13, respectively, compared to 5.39 deaths and 3.97 wounded for all mass murders (see Table 1). These findings suggest that although assault weapons do not significantly increase the number of fatalities, they might increase the number of victims wounded.

The accelerated tempo of mass public shootings during the 1990s was dramatized by a number of high-profile workplace massacres. In 1991, postal carriers Joseph Harris and Thomas McIlvane both committed mass murders, sealing the reputation of the U.S. Postal Service as ground zero for the alleged explosion of violence that rocked the American workforce. In the same year, physics student Gang Lu killed five at the University of Iowa. John T. Miller murdered four in New York in 1992, and Gian Luigi Ferri killed eight and wounded six at a San Francisco law office in 1993.

Two years later, James Simpson and Willie Woods gunned down former co-workers in massacres they committed, while Arturo Reyes and Matthew Beck each fatally shot four victims in 1997. Finally, in 1999 Mark Barton killed twelve in Atlanta and Bryan Uyesugi gunned down seven in Honolulu.

The 1993 shooting carried out by Alan Winterbourne in Oxnard, California, provides an illustrative example of the long-term frustration often experienced by those who commit workplace massacres. After receiving a bachelor's degree in computer science from Cal Poly San Luis Obispo in 1985, Winterbourne began working at the Northrop Corporation in September of that year. In February of 1986, however, just five months after he started, Winterbourne quit his position as computer systems engineer. Six months later, he applied for state unemployment benefits, but his request was denied on the grounds that he had left his job voluntarily (*Los Angeles Times*, December 4, 1993; p. 1:4). In December of 1986, when Winterbourne appealed the state's decision, he told the administrative law judge that he quit his job out of fear for his personal safety. He explained that he could not elaborate, however, due to government secrecy (*San Diego Union-Tribune*, December 4, 1993; p. A3). Years later, Winterbourne told family members he was convinced that Northrop had conspired to prevent him from ever obtaining employment again (*Los Angeles Times*, December 11, 1993; p. 1:2).

To a certain extent, Winterbourne's paranoia may have been somewhat justified. After all, from 1986 to 1993 he had been rejected from every one of the 288 jobs to which he had applied. But it was not negative references from Northrop that prevented him from finding a job; rather, it was his appearance and demeanor. Winterbourne wore long hair and sported a scraggly beard. A potential employer later recalled that Winterbourne "wasn't rude or mean, there was something about him that wasn't quite right. He struck me as a bit strange, but I couldn't pinpoint quite what it was." Another remembered that Winterbourne "just seemed eccentric" (*Los Angeles Times*, December 4, 1993; p. 1:2)

In his struggle to find work, Winterbourne ran for Congress in 1990 because he thought "it would be a good job." In challenging incumbent Robert Lagomarsino in the Republican primary, Winterbourne's two main issues were cutting the federal deficit and repealing the 55 m.p.h. speed limit. He lost the election, although he did receive 11.4 percent of the vote (*Los Angeles Times*, December 3, 1993; p. 1:6).

At around the same time, Winterbourne began waging a campaign to remove stop signs from the neighborhood in which he shared a home with his mother. An avid bicyclist, he argued that the stop signs forced him to stop and get off his bike, instead of just rolling through the intersection. He also complained that because he was unemployed, he could not pay the traffic fines he had received for running the stop signs. Many who knew Winterbourne considered him to be gentle and mild-mannered. But the Ventura city transportation engineer, who received most of Winterbourne's complaints, told his boss he was afraid Winterbourne might come in and shoot him someday (*Los Angeles Times*, December 3, 1993; p. 1:6).

Frustrated by chronic unemployment and feeling that others were to blame for it, Winterbourne ultimately directed his rage toward the Oxnard unemployment office, the same office that had denied his claim for jobless benefits in 1986. On December 2, 1993, nearly seven years to the day after his appeal for unemployment benefits was rejected, he began a shooting spree at the Oxnard Employment Development Department (EDD) office. Twenty minutes before Winterbourne launched his attack, he dropped off documents showing his seven-year battle with unemployment at the *Ventura County Free Press*, the local newspaper.

At 11:41 A.M., he arrived at the Oxnard EDD office armed with a .44-caliber revolver, a 12-gauge shotgun, a .300-magnum rifle, and a .223-caliber "Mini 14" rifle. Ignoring the customers inside the building, Winterbourne started firing at employees, killing three and wounding four. After leaving the Oxnard EDD office, he gunned down a fourth victim, a police officer, while he was en route to the Ventura unemployment office. Upon his arrival there, Winterbourne was killed by police officers (*Los Angeles Times*, December 3, 1993; p. 1:5).

As illustrated by the case involving Clifton McCree, mass murderers who exact revenge at the workplace frequently threaten their victims prior to the attack. McCree, who had served in the Marines, began working in Fort Lauderdale's parks department in 1977, cleaning the city's beaches (*The Washington Post*, February 10, 1996; p. A2). Although he was given an "above satisfactory" rating in all of his annual evaluations and was promoted three times during his 18-year career, he had also been suspended four times for absenteeism, rude behavior toward tourists, and fighting with another worker. In 1981, he was asked to work on controlling his temper (Associated Press, February 11, 1996; AM Cycle).

But McCree's anger and hostility only became worse over time, leading several co-workers to file complaints against him in October 1994.

One of the complaints noted that McCree had threatened co-workers by telling them, "If you mess with my job, I will take you out." And employees reported that McCree had let everyone know that he kept a gun in his car (Associated Press, February 11, 1996; AM Cycle).

In response to the escalation of McCree's threatening behavior, the Fort Lauderdale parks department asked him to take a drug test, which he failed. As parks department officials prepared McCree's dismissal notice, they were aware of his potential for violence. One official, for example, noted that "one step and he may go off the deep end," while another stated that "there is evidence of a paranoid behavior and that Clifton may need medication in order to gain control.... We may want to escort him with a cop" (Associated Press, February 11, 1996; AM Cycle).

After he was fired in December of 1994, McCree eventually found work as a security guard. Yet he brooded about his firing from the parks department because he thought it was the result of racial discrimination. McCree, who was black, felt that his co-workers, who were white, should have been asked to take the drug tests, too. He wrote the NAACP a number of times, complaining that his employment prospects were ruined due to his firing by the city. On a number of occasions following his termination, McCree threatened his former co-workers that he would come back and kill them (*The Tampa Tribune*, February 10, 1996; p. 1). The sister of one of McCree's victims recalled that her brother told her, "If I don't come out of this, you sue the city, because I've been telling them for a year and a half that this man was going to do this."

In early February of 1996, McCree was fired for the second time from his job as a security guard (*New York Times*, February 11, 1996; p. 37). A few days later, he sent his wife, who was also out of work, and kids to the homes of relatives because he was unable to afford the repairs to his water heater after it broke. Hopeless and distraught, McCree made good on his lethal threats. On February 9, 1996, at 5 A.M., he burst into the city office trailer where park employees gathered to be assigned daily duties, and shouted, "Everybody is going to die!" before he opened fire. Armed with a Glock 9 mm handgun, McCree shot six former co-workers, killing five, before he committed suicide by turning the gun on himself. McCree left behind a suicide note in which he blamed his co-workers at the parks department for his inability to hold on to a job and, thus, to support his family. He wrote, "Since I couldn't continue to support my family, Life became nothing. I no longer wanted to live in this kind of world. I also wanted to punish some of the cowardly, racist devils that help bring this about, Along with the system" (Associated Press, February 10, 1996; AM Cycle).

Although the mass murder committed by Seung-Hui Cho at Virginia Tech occurred outside the timeframe covered by this research (1900–1999), it merits discussion here as the worst mass public shooting in U.S. history. On the morning of April 16, 2007, Cho shot and killed two students in the West Ambler Johnston residence hall. Approximately two hours later, he entered Norris Hall and shot 45 people over a nine-minute period, killing 30.

The incident was, aside from the inordinately high body count, largely typical of mass public shootings in general. Frequently characterized as loners, mass public shooters are often depressed, paranoid individuals who externalize the blame for their problems. From a very young age, Cho seldom communicated with others, including members of his own family. Growing up, he preferred solitude, often spending his time playing video games or shooting baskets by himself. Cho's reticence and intense introversion continued at Virginia Tech, where his depression first became evident during his junior year in December 2005. Similar to Richard Farley, who stalked a fellow employee before killing seven former co-workers in Sunnyvale, California, in 1988, Cho came to the attention of police after stalking two female college students. Following his meeting with the police, Cho sent a message to one of his roommates in which he indicated he was thinking about killing himself. Later evaluated at several mental health facilities, where he was ultimately declared mentally ill but not an imminent threat, Cho was allowed to undergo outpatient treatment rather than being involuntarily committed (*New York Times*, April 22, 2007; p. A1).

Residing just below Cho's withdrawn demeanor was a seething contempt for humanity that found expression in his writing. Many mass public shooters such as Charles Layman, Thomas McIlvane, and Clifton McCree — to name but a few — conveyed their intentions prior to their attacks by making threats or filing grievances. Cho was uncomfortable with oral communication and was in fact mocked when he was younger for his poor English and deep voice, and he did not verbalize his violent thoughts to others. There were signs, however, that he was preoccupied with violence. As an English major, his work was notorious among both his professors and fellow students for its crass brutality. In fact, several professors considered Cho's work to be so disturbing that he was removed from one class and later had to be tutored by the head of the English department. Moreover, after reading one of Cho's plays, a fellow classmate told a friend that "this is the kind of guy who is going to walk into a classroom and start shooting people" (*New York Times*, April 22, 2007; p. A1). That Cho's actions did not come as a complete surprise to those who knew him is consistent with other mass public shooters such as Clifton McCree or Joseph Wesbecker. For example, in 1989 when Wesbecker began his attack at the Standard Gravure plant in Louisville, Kentucky, where he killed eight and wounded 12, one employee heard the gunfire and knew that "crazy Joe Wesbecker" had come to the plant to make good on the threats he had been making for months (Holmes and Holmes, 1992).

The unbridled misanthropy that Cho expressed in his student writing was on full display in the multimedia "manifesto" he mailed to NBC News between the shootings. In his manifesto, he railed against hedonism, trust funds, cognac, gold necklaces, and rich brats with Mercedes. Speaking to the camera in one of his video clips, Cho asked, "Are you happy now that you have destroyed my life?" Much like George Hennard, who repeatedly asked, "Tell me, was it worth it?" when he carried out his attack at Luby's cafeteria in Killeen, Texas, in 1991, Cho felt justified in exacting vengeance against the society he held responsible for his shortcomings. It did not matter that Cho did not have a personal grudge against most, if not all, of the victims he shot. Rather, as members of society and, more narrowly, the Virginia Tech community, they represented what was, to Cho, the bane of his existence.

Like most mass public shooters, Cho planned the assault well in advance. Available evidence indicates he had been planning the shootings since the purchase of his first gun in February 2007, two months before the massacre, although it seems likely that he had been fantasizing about the attack longer than that. In the two months leading up to the mass murder, Cho spent several thousand dollars buying two firearms, ammunition, a hunting knife, and a chain, which he used to seal the doors of Norris Hall so that it would be difficult for law enforcement to disrupt the second, more deadly set of shootings (*New York Times*, April 22, 2007; p. A1). Cho was methodical and calculating not only in how he carried out the assault, but also in the steps he took to maximize the publicity for his actions. In addition to mailing the multimedia packet to NBC News, Cho committed the mass murder on a Monday morning, thus ensuring that the incident would dominate news coverage for an entire week. As shown earlier, 54 of the 116 mass public shooters (47 percent) from 1900 through 1999 committed suicide afterwards. Like these 54 mass murderers, Cho ended the attack by turning the gun on himself, believing that his life had already been destroyed.

"The Youth Movement": Juvenile Mass Murderers

Mass public shootings are seldom committed by offenders under the age of 18. In fact, there were only three that occurred in the twentieth century, and all took place during the late 1990s. Kip Kinkel killed his parents and then went on a shooting spree at his high school in Oregon in 1997; Mitchell Johnson and Andrew Golden fatally shot five victims and wounded ten others at their school in Jonesboro, Arkansas, in 1998; and Eric Harris and Dylan Klebold killed thirteen and wounded twenty-five at Columbine High School in 1999. Garnering enormous media coverage, these and other incidents incited a moral panic over school shootings.

Although these cases dramatically illustrate the youth movement in mass murder during the 1990s, they are atypical in that youthful offenders are usually involved in either progeny familicides or felony-related massacres (see Table 16). Compared to other mass murderers, offenders under the age of 18 are less likely to use guns and more likely to use personal, hands-on type weapons. Moreover, young mass murderers are much less suicidal; in fact, Table 16 shows a steady progression in suicidal behavior as mass murderers get older.

The mass murder committed by Bruce Brenizer provides a fairly typical example of a progeny familicide during the 1990s. On April 22, 1991, the 15-year-old Brenizer killed his father, his father's girlfriend, and her three daughters in Cushing, Wisconsin (Associated Press, June 9, 1993; AM Cycle). When he was very young, Brenizer began living with his father, Rick, after his parents divorced. Soon after the divorce, Rick began dating Ruth Berentson, who eventually moved in with her two daughters, Heidi and Mindy. The couple added to their family when Ruth gave birth to a daughter, Crystal, in 1986.

Over time, however, Bruce Brenizer developed a deep-seated hatred for his family and the conditions under which he was forced to live. He claimed that his father was physically and emotionally abusive towards him (*Star Tribune (Minneapolis)* "Brenizer pleads guilty," April 23, 1993; p. 1A). He alleged, for example, that his father taunted him about being fat and told him he looked like a girl. Weeks before the murders, Brenizer wrote in his diary, "My dad pisses me off so damn much, I sometimes feel mad enough to kill all the damn [people in this] ... house."

As Brenizer's anger intensified, he began planning how he would kill his family. On April 21, the day before the murders, he shared his plan

Table 6.
Patterns of Mass Murder by Offender Age, 1900–1999

Variable	Under 18	Ages 18–23	Ages 24–29	30 and Over
Average Death Toll	4.77	5.17	6.08	5.75
Average Wounded Count	1.40	8.77	10.70	5.75
Weapon Type				
Gun	55%	64%	71%	68%
Other	27%	17%	18%	20%
Fire	18%	19%	11%	12%
Victim-Offender Relationship				
Stranger	16%	35%	33%	18%
Family	44%	24%	34%	51%
Acquaintance	40%	41%	33%	31%
Public Location	12%	30%	34%	27%
City > 250,000	40%	43%	41%	32%
Assault Weapon	2%	3%	2%	3%
Workplace	0%	6%	2%	9%
Felony-Related	23%	34%	29%	15%
Interracial	7%	12%	10%	9%
White Offenders	63%	53%	59%	73%
Male Offenders	95%	95%	93%	93%
Suicidal Offenders	5%	10%	20%	47%
Average Offender Count	1.53	1.75	1.58	1.24
White Victims	75%	70%	70%	81%
Average Victim Age	24.05	29.78	28.57	27.49
Victims Age <16 or >40	63%	50%	56%	62%
Male Victims	52%	59%	54%	52%
Region				
Midwest	35%	24%	26%	28%
East	26%	27%	23%	28%
South	21%	28%	30%	25%
West	18%	21%	21%	19%
N	61	176	188	393

with his stepbrother, Jesse Anderson, who lived with Brenizer's biological mother. He told Anderson he would "kill Ruth and the kids and then wait for his dad to get home." The following day, Brenizer came home from school and then used baling twine to tie up Heidi and Mindy Berentson. He claimed he overheard the two girls talking about escaping and killing him; as a result, he dragged them outside and shot them in the head with a .30–30 rifle. When the other three family members arrived, Brenizer greeted his father by shooting him in the chest and head (Associated Press, May 19, 1992; AM Cycle). As Ruth Berentson was trying to call 911, Brenizer cut the phone line and then fatally shot her as she tried to run away. He then killed five-year-old Crystal by shooting her in the head (*Star Tribune [Minneapolis]*), April 15, 1992; p. 1B).

Afterwards, Brenizer called Jesse Anderson and begged him to help get rid of the bodies. When Anderson asked Brenizer whether he understood that he had just killed five people, Brenizer responded that Anderson was trying to make it sound like he was a "mass murderer." The two boys then disposed of the bodies by placing them in the family's station wagon and setting it on fire at a wooded site two miles away. Brenizer was arrested about a month later after a fisherman discovered the station wagon on May 11. Convicted of the five murders, Brenizer was sentenced to life in prison in 1993. He was first sent to a mental institution, however, because a judge ruled he was insane when he killed the three girls (*Star Tribune (Minneapolis)*, June 13, 1993; p. 1B).

Another mass killing committed by juveniles occurred two years later in Yakima, Washington. In 1991, Michael and Lynn Skelton, and their two sons, 12-year-old Jason and 6-year-old Bryan, moved from California to Washington to escape the rise in violent crime. But on March 24, 1993, the Skeltons were bludgeoned and stabbed to death inside their mobile home. The killers were two 14-year-old boys, Miguel Gaitan and Joel Ramos, who were classmates of Bryan Skelton (Associated Press, December 21, 1993; PM Cycle). Police arrested the pair after they had bragged to friends about the killings; in fact, Gaitan told one friend he had enjoyed it. Although a motive was never clearly established, police suspected that Gaitan and Ramos committed the murders to impress members of a street gang (Associated Press, December 22, 1993; Part B, p. 2:3).

Gaitan grew up in an abusive home in which his father would beat him on a regular basis. But when Gaitan was nine years old, his father was murdered in Oxnard, California. This filled Gaitan with rage; he easily became angry and on one occasion had threatened to harm one of his teachers. A few months before the murders, he wrote a paper for an English class in which he said he wanted to grow up to be a "cop killer," so that he would be famous among youth gang members (*The Seattle Times*, January 2, 1994; p. B1).

The 1990s produced several of the worst mass murders in twentieth-century America. In the first attack on the World Trade Center in 1993, terrorists detonated a car bomb in the basement garage of the building, killing six and wounding more than a thousand. The bombing was the first terrorist mass murder on American soil since 1975, when a bomb at LaGuardia Airport in New York killed eleven and wounded seventy-five.

Earlier that year, four people were murdered and twelve more were wounded when a bomb exploded at the Fraunces Tavern in New York. No one was charged for either bombing, although the Puerto Rican terrorist group, FALN, was believed to have been responsible for the one at LaGuardia.

The largest mass murder in twentieth-century America occurred on April 19, 1995, when Timothy McVeigh parked an explosives-laden Ryder truck outside the Federal Building in Oklahoma City. The explosion killed 168 people and wounded 500. McVeigh was convicted of the massacre and executed in 2001, while his accomplice, Terry Nichols, was sentenced to life in prison after he was found guilty for his role in the bombing.

Before the Oklahoma City bombing, the record for the worst mass murder in twentieth-century America belonged to Julio Gonzalez, who killed eighty-seven in 1990 when he set fire to the Happy Land Social Club in New York City. Gonzalez set the fire because he was angry that his ex-girlfriend, who worked at the club, rebuffed his attempt to reconcile. It is ironic, perhaps, that she was one of only five survivors to escape the blaze. Gonzalez was later convicted and sentenced to 25 years to life.

Due largely to the inordinately high body count, the mass murder committed by Gonzalez captured a great deal of publicity. However, aside from the number of victims and the amount of media coverage, the Happy Land massacre is a fairly typical example of a mass murder involving the use of fire as a weapon. Like most mass murders, including fire-related cases, it was committed for the sake of revenge. But unlike most mass murders, which are committed after much planning and deliberation, it was an impulsive act of violence. This is consistent with most fire-related cases, however, where the violence is generally episodic. Having taken place in New York City, the Gonzalez case was like other fire-related massacres, which are more likely to occur in an urban area in the East (see Table 17). At 36, Gonzalez was older, though, than the average age of the offender who uses fire to commit mass murder.

The case involving Jose Tapia and Jose Garcia provides an instance of a fire-related massacre perpetrated by younger offenders. In the early morning hours of February 27, 1993, Garcia, 18, and Tapia, 16, set fire to an apartment building in Providence, Rhode Island (*The Providence Journal-Bulletin*, July 7, 1995; p. 1B). The fire killed Carlos Chang, his wife, and four children, who ranged in age from seven to eighteen. Chang and his family had emigrated to the U.S. from Guatemala two years earlier in 1991. Chang's brother-in-law, Ivan Ponce, was the only one who survived the blaze (*The Providence Journal-Bulletin*, July 12, 1995; p. 1B).

Table 17.
Patterns of Mass Murder by Weapon Type, 1900–1999

Variable	Guns	Hands-On	Fire	Bombs/Explosives
Average Death Toll	4.92	4.52	6.82	20.32
Average Wounded Count	1.30	0.53	4.86	113.25
Victim-Offender Relationship				
Stranger	24%	15%	28%	70%
Family	42%	63%	26%	15%
Acquaintance	34%	22%	46%	15%
Public Location	32%	16%	12%	89%
City > 250,000	37%	40%	45%	38%
Workplace	7%	1%	0%	6%
Felony-Related	27%	14%	8%	0%
Interracial	8%	7%	9%	13%
White Offenders	67%	72%	55%	87%
Average Offender Age	30.26	29.83	28.39	34.21
Offender Age 30–49	36%	38%	39%	28%
Offender Age ≥ 50	6%	4%	3%	13%
Male Offenders	96%	89%	82%	100%
Suicidal Offenders	34%	27%	9%	25%
Average Offender Count	1.32	1.12	1.32	1.75
White Victims	79%	77%	66%	88%
Average Victim Age	28.59	21.63	26.92	34.38
Victims Age <16 or >40	50%	65%	72%	44%
Male Victims	58%	45%	51%	59%
Region				
Midwest	24%	34%	33%	20%
East	23%	27%	38%	50%
South	29%	20%	20%	15%
West	24%	19%	9%	15%
N	600	187	102	20

Earlier that night, Garcia and Tapia were involved in a fight in which Tapia's cousin, William Cifredo, suffered serious injuries after he was dragged for nearly 450 feet under a car (*The Providence Journal-Bulletin*, November 17, 1995; p. 1B). Vowing to exact revenge against the driver of the car, Jorge Giep, Garcia and Tapia set fire to the apartment building where they thought Giep lived. It turned out to be the wrong building, however. Convicted of the mass murder, both Garcia and Tapia were sentenced to life in prison. However, because Tapia expressed remorse for his role in the mass killing, he was granted eligibility for parole in 21 years (*The Providence Journal-Bulletin*, July 7, 1995; p. 1B).

Mass murderers who use fire as a weapon usually kill acquaintances or strangers (see Table 17). Some, however, target family members, as evidenced by the case involving Tracey Shaw. While growing up in Philadelphia, Shaw was raped at the age of 13 and again at the age of 16. She received psychiatric treatment when she was hospitalized after both rapes. Shaw never quite recovered, however, as she began abusing drugs and alcohol. Moreover, she became involved with physically abusive men and, from 1986 to 1994, had five children by three different fathers (*The Dallas Morning News*, February 26, 1995; p. 41A).

In 1994, Shaw started dating 30-year-old Andre Broggins, who later moved in with her and her five children. They frequently fought with each other, however, and on several occasions Shaw threatened to kill herself and her five children if Broggins moved out. Shortly before Christmas, Broggins packed up his belongings and left, much to the chagrin of Shaw, who pleaded with him to stay. Shaw also received a notice that she was going to be evicted on December 24 for failure to pay rent (*Pittsburgh Post-Gazette*, July 20, 1996; p. C5).

In the early morning hours of December 23, Shaw followed through on part of her earlier threats to kill herself and her five children when she set fire to their home. The fire killed six people — four of Shaw's children and two others who were spending the night (*The Houston Chronicle*, December 24, 1994; p. 24A). Shaw escaped the blaze with her 6-month-old son, Nathaniel. She was later convicted of the murders and sentenced to life in prison (*The Houston Chronicle*, July 25, 1996; p. A22).

Familicides: "Your husband is coming to kill you"

In 1975, James Ruppert committed what was, at the time, the largest familicide in U.S. history when he killed eleven family members. His record was short-lived, however, because George Banks murdered thirteen in Wilkes-Barre, Pennsylvania, in 1982. But Banks' record was also short-lived because Ronald Gene Simmons committed what is currently the largest familicide in the nation's history when he killed fourteen family members and two others during December of 1987. Due mainly to the large body counts, each of these incidents received extensive publicity. In discussing family massacres during the second mass murder wave in the twentieth century, I focus on several cases that were not as well publicized but are perhaps more representative of familicides during this time.

Loxley Sexton met his wife, Linda, in the early 1960s when they were in the Army. Despite the fact that he was married with four children at the time, he began having an affair with Linda, who soon became pregnant. He decided to leave his family and marry Linda. In between the births of their second and third children, the couple moved to Snohomish, Washington, in 1968. For the fourteen years the family lived there, Sexton had difficulty holding on to a job. Linda tried to shoulder some of the burden by working as a registered nurse at Providence Hospital in Everett, Washington, but this did little to alleviate the family's constant financial strain. Their troubles did not end there, however, as Sexton argued frequently with his wife because he thought that her mother was interfering in their marriage (AP Wire, July 3, 1982; AM Cycle).

The couple's marital strife also took its toll on the children. The oldest child, Deborah, had previously seen a doctor for stress-related problems, while the second child, Bobby, had been treated for an ulcer. The mounting tension within the home proved to be too much for Linda, who took the three children and moved into her mother's house in Thompson Falls, Montana, on June 24, 1982. During the next week, Sexton called his wife to reconcile, but she had no desire to return. Sexton, who had once told a neighbor, "I gave up four children for her [Linda] and I will never give up these children," figured that if he could not have his wife and children, he would kill them (UPI Wire, July 4, 1982; BC Cycle).

On July 2, 1982, Sexton drove to his mother-in-law's house in Thompson Falls. Arriving at 10:30 P.M., Sexton barged into the house, armed with a .22-caliber rifle and .22-caliber magnum revolver. After tearing the telephone cord from the wall, Sexton ordered 14-year-old Curt McGowan, a friend of Bobby's, to leave. As McGowan watched from outside the house, he heard Sexton's youngest son, eight-year-old Michael, yell, "Don't daddy — don't." Sexton then gunned down his wife, three children, and mother-in-law. As Sexton left the house, he encountered McGowan, telling him, "I don't have no quarrel with you." While McGowan went to a neighbor's house to call the police, Sexton went back inside the home and committed suicide by shooting himself in the head (AP Wire, July 4, 1982; AM Cycle).

On January 7, 1988, Malcolm T. Gray, a 40-year-old unemployed Vietnam veteran, killed his wife and three sons in Laclede, Idaho, before he committed suicide. Originally from Tennessee, Gray and his wife moved to Laclede in 1979. He soon encountered racial harassment in Laclede, which is north of the Aryan Nation headquarters in Hayden Lake, because he was black and his wife was white. After marital problems led to a divorce, Gray married Minnie "Serena" Brooks, who was 20 years his junior. Over the next several years, Brooks gave birth to three sons: Nathan in 1982, Jonathan in 1985, and Justin in 1986 (UPI Wire, January 10, 1988; AM Cycle).

But Gray had trouble finding work, and the financial hardship caused the family, which had neither a telephone nor electricity, to become more and more isolated. The inability to find employment also took a mental and emotional toll on Gray (UPI Wire "Man who killed family was despondant [sic], says suicide note," January 9, 1988; BC Cycle). Several months before the killings, he barged into the home of a couple who lived nearby, threatening the husband with a gun. After the couple was able to calm Gray down, he told them he had tried to commit suicide earlier in the day, but was unsuccessful. He reasoned that if he could kill them, he could also kill himself. They urged him to seek counseling at the Veterans Hospital in Spokane, Washington (UPI Wire, January 12, 1988; BC Cycle).

But Gray felt that his situation was hopeless. On January 7, he used a .44-caliber pistol to kill his wife and three sons. He then set the house on fire, and walked down to the end of the driveway, where he killed himself. Gray left a note in the mailbox in which he referred to himself as the "personification of evil, weakness and evil of the most sophisticated type." He added, "This I will say — those persons who masquerade as my family are not. With all my heart, I begged others to help me but no one would help me. The evil was overpowering" (AP Wire, January 12, 1988; PM Cycle).

The 1989 mass murder committed by Raymond Navarro in Los Angeles provides a vivid illustration of the physical abuse that sometimes precedes familicides. Navarro and his wife, Maria, were high school sweethearts. Although they had frequent arguments, which were considered minor at the time, they eventually got married and had three children — Claudia, Denise, and Raymond Jr. — over the next several years. By early 1987, however, Raymond Navarro, who drank heavily and was known to have a "very bad temper," had started to become verbally and physically abusive towards his wife and children. For example, he beat the face of Raymond Jr., who was two years old at the time, for wetting his pants. Two months after this incident, Maria Navarro moved into a women's shelter.

Raymond and Maria soon reconciled, however, after he received psychological counseling. But when she returned, she found that nothing had changed. In August of 1987, the couple were having an argument when he started pushing her and breaking furniture. She tried to escape and seek refuge in the apartment manager's office, but he caught her at the door and began punching her in the face, leaving a cut on her forehead. Although the police arrested Raymond Navarro, he forced her to drop the charges by threatening to kill her if he was put in jail. As she said later, "I never did nothing [about it] because I was scared of him because he also [was] threatening my family" (*Los Angeles Times*, August 29, 1989; Part 1, p. 3:1). In January of 1988, Raymond and Maria Navarro were having another argument when he threatened her by asking, "How would you like to wake up one day and have one kid instead of three? You're going to pay. I'm going to get you through the kids." The next month, Raymond Navarro was arrested again after he tried to physically force his wife to leave a public building. Afterwards, she said, "I was scared for me and the baby because I know what he would do."

In March of 1988, Maria Navarro filed for divorce and moved out of the apartment, taking the three children with her. Raymond Navarro, who was unemployed, moved into the apartment where his parents and two brothers were living. Though separated, Navarro kept an "obsessive vigil" on his wife by tracking her every movement. This prompted Maria Navarro to obtain a temporary restraining order against her estranged husband, which prohibited him from having any contact with her. During their separation, Navarro began to drink more and was arrested in June of 1989 on a cocaine possession charge. He also brooded over the impending divorce, blaming not only his wife, but her aunts, too, for what he regarded as "meddling" in their marital affairs (*Los Angeles Times*, August 29, 1989; Part B, p. 1:4).

On August 27, 1989, Navarro decided to exact revenge against his wife and her "meddling" aunts. Maria Navarro was having a small party to celebrate her 27th birthday when she received a phone call at about 10:45 P.M. from one of Raymond Navarro's brothers, who warned her, "Your husband is coming to kill you." Maria Navarro called 911 to report the threat. After determining that Raymond Navarro had not yet arrived at the house, the dispatcher told her, "OK, well, the only thing to do is just call us if he comes over there ... I mean, what can we do? We can't have a unit sit there and wait and see if he comes over." Maria Navarro responded by saying, "Oh, my God." The dispatcher then told her, "So if he comes over don't let him in. Then call us." Maria Navarro thanked the dispatcher, and hung up (*Los Angeles Times*, August 30, 1989; Part B, p. 1:1).

A few minutes later at 11 P.M., Raymond Navarro burst into the house, uttered a profanity in Spanish, and started firing. Wearing a "serene" expression on his face, Navarro shot six people, killing his wife, two of her aunts, and a family friend. At one point, he chased a woman who was trying to hide in the bathroom, and said, "Do you want it, too?" before he shot her. Navarro was arrested five hours later at his parents' home, which was only two miles away. He was convicted of the murders, and sentenced to life in prison without the possibility of parole (*Los Angeles Times*, May 9, 1991; Part B, p. 3:1).

5

The News Media's
Presentation of Mass Murder

So far, this book has attempted to provide a historical perspective on mass murder in the United States by not only detailing its incident, victim, and offender characteristics during the twentieth century, but also by situating the patterns and prevalence of mass murder within a broader social, political, and economic context. But the material presented in the preceding chapters does not fully correspond with the historical claims made about mass murder. In particular, the mid–1960s did, indeed, mark the onset of a mass murder wave, but it was hardly unprecedented. When mass murder was identified as a new crime problem in the 1980s, why did claimsmakers think there were very few mass killings that occurred in the U.S. prior to the 1960s? Or, to put it another way, why did they fail to take into account the mass murder wave during the 1920s and '30s?

Part of the answer to these questions lies in the primacy of the news media as a source of information on mass killings. Previous research has shown that the public depends heavily on the news media for information on crime. Graber (1980, p. 50) found, for example, that the media are regarded as the primary source of information on crime by 95 percent of the public. While the influence of the press is pervasive, this influence declines when alternative sources of information are available such as knowing someone who has been accused of a crime, having been victimized personally, or knowing family members, close friends, or acquaintances who have been victimized (Graber, 1980, p. 51). But the extent to which the public relies on the media may be greater for mass murder than for other crimes considering that mass killings are a relatively rare occurrence, affecting a small number of people on the whole. With few if any interpersonal experiences available to most people, the media are the primary and perhaps the only information source on mass murder for an overwhelming majority of the public.

In light of this influence, several scholars have surmised that public perceptions have been heavily influenced by widely publicized massacres, resulting in a distorted popular stereotype. Fox and Levin (1998, p. 431) have stated, for example, that "the widely held view [is] that the victims of massacres are usually strangers to their killer who selects them on a random basis after he 'goes berserk.'" Similarly, Petee et al. (1997, pp. 318–9) have specified that "the public perception of these offenders is generally that of a disgruntled, White male, 30 to 40 years of age, who usually commits suicide at the conclusion of the homicidal episode."

Prior research has also suggested that the media's coverage of mass killings increases the public's fear of crime (Fox and Levin, 1994, p. 139–40; Levin and Fox, 1996, p. 55). The fear-of-crime literature indicates that news of distant, random crimes of violence does not increase the public's fear (Chiricos, Eschholz and Gertz, 1997, p. 349; Heath, 1984, p. 274; Liska and Baccaglini, 1990, p. 372). This suggests that while mass killings may increase the fear of crime locally, they are not likely to affect crime fear from afar. Massacres that attract widespread news coverage are therefore not significantly more likely to increase the public's fear of crime than those that obtain mostly local coverage. Previous studies have further speculated that the extensive publicity given to mass killings encourages individuals predisposed to violence to commit similar acts of bloodshed (Fox and Levin, 1994, pp. 140–42; Levin and Fox, 1985, pp. 22–26; Rappaport, 1988, p. 41). As discussed earlier, however, the copycat effect is evident in only a very small number of mass killings.

While news coverage has been the primary, if not the sole, source of information on mass murder for the general public, it has also been an important data source for those who have made claims about it, namely, academics. To be sure, the Supplementary Homicide Reports are an invaluable source of official data on mass murder; in fact, without these data, it would have been exceedingly difficult to do this research. Because the SHR provide a record of when and where most mass killings have occurred in the U.S. since 1976, these data illuminate the dark figure of mass murder. Moreover, because the SHR can be used to shed light on which mass killings are not reported by news organizations such as the *New York Times*, these data are valuable in terms of revealing the extent to which the *Times* underreports mass murders and, more generally, the biases of new coverage as a source of data. As shown earlier, this information was crucial for delineating the patterns and prevalence of mass murder not only for the 1976–1999 period, but also for the 1900–1975 period.

Despite the considerable value of the SHR, only a few scholars have used it to study mass murder (Duwe, 2000; Fox and Levin, 1998; Levin and Fox, 1985, 1996). Some have erroneously assumed that the SHR are ill-suited to examine mass murder (Petee et al. 1997), whereas others have made the interesting claim that no official data exist on mass killings (Holmes and Holmes, 2000). Researchers have, therefore, relied mainly on news coverage as a data source, which is understandable since it is easily accessible and, compared to the SHR, it tends to provide more detailed information.

But this is not, in and of itself, a problem. After all, news accounts have been an important data source on mass killings for this research, especially for the 1900–1975 period. What is a problem, however, is that researchers have not acknowledged or demonstrated an awareness of the limitations involved with using news coverage as a data source. Rather, most seem to assume, perhaps because of the infrequency with which mass killings occur, that high-profile cases are typical of mass murder in general. As we see in the next chapter, though, the uncritical use of celebrated cases as typifying examples has led to a number of inaccurate claims about the nature and incidence of mass murder.

Considering that news accounts have been the predominant source of information on mass killings for the general public and claimsmakers alike, the news media's presentation of mass murder warrants close scrutiny. Identifying what is newsworthy about mass murder is especially important, then, because the incidents that garner extensive news coverage are more likely to influence public perceptions and social policy decisions. Indeed, high-profile crimes have been the catalyst for the identification of social problems such as missing children (Best, 1990), serial murder (Jenkins, 1988, 1994), drug violence (Brownstein, 1995; Chermak, 1997), stalking (Lowney & Best, 1995), and money laundering (Nichols, 1997).

Routine crime stories seldom foster conditions that are favorable for the social construction of crime problems because they simply provide a primarily factual account of what happened. In contrast, celebrated crimes are reported in great detail and followed closely over time (Chermak, 1995, pp. 28–41). Moreover, high-profile cases generate a great deal of interest and concern, providing reporters and sources (e.g., law enforcement officials, prosecutors, politicians, academics, interest group activists, etc.) with an opportunity to make claims about new or recurring crime problems

(Chermak, 1997, p. 705; Daly, 1995, p. 15; Ericson et al. 1987, p. 70; Ericson, Baranek & Chan, 1989, p. 4; Ericson, Baranek & Chan, 1991, p. 74; Kappeler, Blumberg & Potter, 1996, p. 6). While claimsmakers use highly publicized crimes to raise public awareness of a social problem, they also utilize these cases to typify the nature of the problem (Chermak, 1997, p. 714; Nichols, 1997, p. 337). In doing so, claimsmakers shape the perception of the problem (Best, 1987, p. 106; 1990, p. 79). And perceptions, as Best (1995, p. 259), Loseke (1989, p. 202) and others have pointed out, help shape the policy recommendations to control a problem.

Research on the content of crime news has long shown that the news media misrepresent the social reality of crime. Although news organizations are obligated to inform the public, they are also compelled to generate revenue, for they are businesses whose primary purpose is to create a profit (Brownstein, 1995, p. 86; Chermak, 1994, p. 567; Lotz, p. 10). News organizations turn a profit by presenting news that attracts a large audience, which, in turn, attracts more advertising dollars (Chermak, 1995, p. 23; Ericson, Baranek and Chan, 1987, p. 50; Gamson, Croteau, Hoynes and Sasson, 1992, p. 377).

Since the inception of the penny press in the 1830s, the media have viewed the reporting of crime as a way to boost sales of their product, which explains why crime has long been a popular news item (Chermak, 1994, p. 567; Harris, 1932, pp. 1–2; Sherizen, 1978, p. 208). Limitations on time and space, however, preclude the press from reporting all or even most of the crimes that occur (Chermak, 1995, pp. 18–9; Krajicek, 1998, p. 13). In an effort to make crime news more entertaining and, thus, more appealing to consumers, the news media overrepresent violent, interpersonal crimes because they are dramatic, tragic, and rare in occurrence. Indeed, previous studies have consistently shown that the most serious and least frequently occurring offenses such as murder, assault, and robbery are most often reported, while the far more prevalent property and white-collar crimes are less likely to receive coverage (Antunes and Hurley, 1977, p. 759; Chermak, 1994, p. 569; 1995, p. 118; 1998, p. 67; Davis, 1952, p. 327; Garofalo, 1981, p. 323; Graber, 1980, p. 39; Harris, 1932; p. 78; Humphries, 1981, p. 195; Marsh, 1988, p. 509; Sheley and Ashkins, 1981, p. 499; Sherizen, 1978, p. 216; Smith, 1984, p. 290; Windhauser, Seiter and Winfree, 1990, p. 77).

Although murder is a staple of crime news, accounting for 12 percent to 45 percent of all crime stories (Antunes and Hurley, 1977, p. 759; Chermak, 1994, p. 569; 1995, p. 118; Graber, 1980, p. 39; Liska and Baccaglini,

1990, p. 365; Sherizen, 1978, p. 216; Sheley and Ashkins, 1981, p. 499), only a few studies have looked at the news media's coverage of homicide (Johnstone, Hawkins, and Michener, 1994; Wilbanks, 1984). Examining local newspaper coverage of homicides that occurred in Miami in 1981, Wilbanks (1984, pp. 111–112) found that multiple victims was the best predictor of story length and the number of stories presented. Similarly, in their study of local homicide coverage in Chicago's two daily newspapers, Johnstone, Hawkins, and Michener (1994, pp. 866–868) reported that multiple victims was the strongest predictor of whether a homicide was reported and how prominently it was covered. They also found that inter-racial murders stimulated more prominent coverage and that white victims, female victims, child victims, multiple offenders, and unusual killing method each significantly increased the odds that a homicide was selected for presentation in at least one of the newspapers. Finally, Pritchard and Hughes (1997) analyzed local newspaper coverage of 100 murders that occurred in Milwaukee during 1994, finding that white participants, female offenders, female victims, and youthful or elderly victims were significant predictors of story length and the number of stories presented.

The Wilbanks (1984) and Johnstone et al. (1994) studies suggest that although homicides are highly newsworthy, they are not always reported, especially in larger cities. For example, Wilbanks (1984, p. 108) discovered that 40 percent of 569 cases went unreported, whereas Johnstone et al. (1994, p. 863) found that 76 percent of Chicago's murders in 1987 were not reported by the *Tribune* and that 83 percent were not covered by the *Sun-Times*.

Because mass murder is a shocking, infrequently occurring crime involving a relatively large number of fatalities, it is an eminently newsworthy event. Still, there are some mass killings that attract more media attention than others. The ensuing sections in this chapter analyze how the news media covered mass killings during the twentieth century. The analysis begins by examining the amount of attention the *New York Times* gave to mass murder between 1900 and 1999. This chapter then analyzes which characteristics influenced the extent to which the *Times* covered mass killings. Finally, a broader perspective is provided by looking at newspaper, network television news, and weekly newsmagazine coverage of 495 mass murders that occurred between 1976 and 1996.

New York Times, *1900–1999*

Although the *New York Times* clearly does not encompass all of the news coverage devoted to mass murder during the twentieth century, there is reason to believe it might be fairly representative. As one of America's most prestigious newspapers, the *Times* has long been regarded as the standard bearer for print and broadcast media alike. Because the news media are highly self-referential (Ericson, Baranek, and Chan, 1987), it is reasonable to infer that other newspapers followed the *Times'* lead and employed similar reporting practices with respect to mass killings. But even if this is not a reasonable inference, the figures below show, at the very least, the extent to which one of America's most influential newspapers covered mass murder in the twentieth century.

As Figures 3 and 4 reveal, the mid–1960s marked the beginning of a dramatic increase in the amount of coverage given to mass killings. Of the 909 mass killings from 1900 through 1999, 540 (59 percent) were reported by the *Times*. Nearly one-third (N = 173) of the 540 cases took place between 1900 and 1965. The last one-third of the twentieth century, however, accounted for a little more than two-thirds (N = 367) of the 540 cases.

Figure 3. Average Number of Times Stories Per Mass Murder, 1900–1999

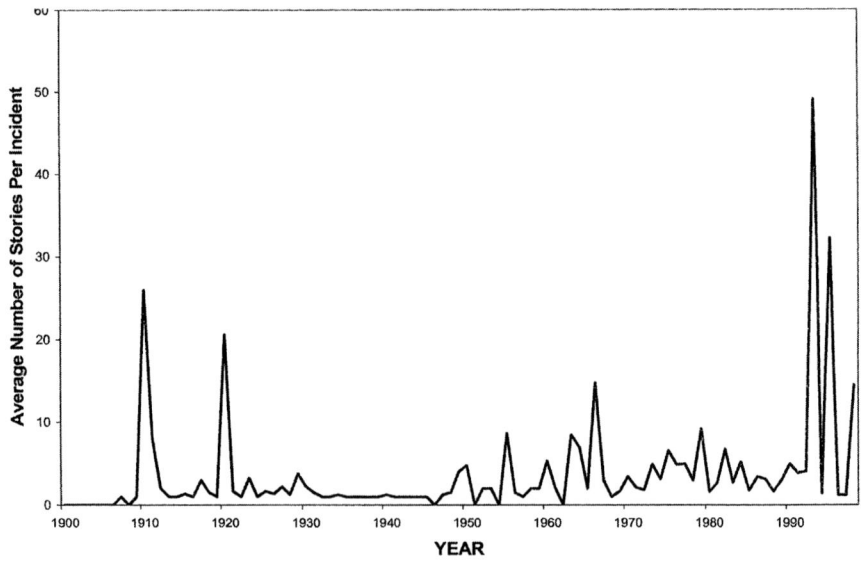

Figure 2. Total Number of Stories Reported by the New York Times, 1900–1999

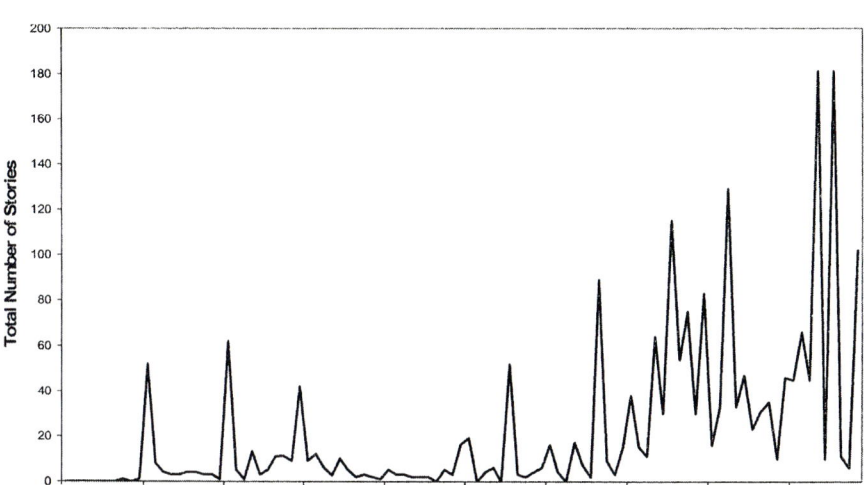

As the number of mass murders reported by the *Times* began to increase in the mid–1960s, so, too, did the amount of attention given to these incidents. Indeed, from 1900 through 1965, the average number of stories on the 173 mass killings was 2.42. During the first mass murder wave, however, this average was even lower. For example, during the 1926–1935 period, the average number of stories per mass killing was 1.67. But from 1966 through 1999, the average number of stories on the 367 mass murders was 6.36, nearly three times the average from 1900 through 1965 and roughly four times the average during the first wave.

Due to the growing number of mass killings reported by the *Times* from 1966 through 1999, combined with an increase in the number of stories per incident, the total number of stories per year rose substantially over the last one-third of the century (see Figure 4). The average number of stories per year was 7.35 in 1900–1965, and was slightly higher at 11.78 stories per year during the first mass murder wave (1926–1935). During the 1966–1999 period, however, the number of stories per year was 83.60. Thus, the total annual amount of coverage during the second mass murder wave was approximately seven times that of the first mass murder wave and about 11 times that of the whole 1900–1965 period.

What Makes a Mass Murder More Newsworthy?

Are there certain types of mass murders the *New York Times* is more likely to report? Of the cases that get reported, which ones are more likely to receive greater coverage? The first question was addressed by examining which of the 649 mass killings from 1976 through 1999 were reported by the *Times*. The second question, on the other hand, was addressed by analyzing which characteristics affected the number of stories the *Times* presented on the 540 mass murders it reported from 1900 through 1999 (please see the Appendix for a more detailed discussion of the methodology used).

During the 1976–1999 period, the *Times* was more likely to report mass killings involving larger body counts (wounded and fatal victims), public locations, strangers as victims, workplace violence, interracial victim-offender relationships, suicidal offenders, white victims, and incidents that took place in the East (see Table 18). Mass murders involving victims who were known to the offender (e.g., family member or acquaintance) and those committed in connection with criminal activity (i.e., felony-related massacres) were slightly less likely to be reported by the *Times*. To check for spuriousness among the bivariate relationships shown in Table 18, a multivariate logistic regression model was estimated to determine the effect that a given variable had on the probability that a massacre was reported by the *Times*, controlling for the effects of the other independent variables.

In Table 19, we see that death toll and wounded count were strong positive predictors of whether a mass killing was presented, increasing the odds 1.97 and 1.11 times for each additional fatal and wounded victim, respectively. The results also indicate that a mass murder was 3.38 times more likely to be reported if it involved gun use, 2.80 times more likely if it took place in a public location, 2.74 times more likely if it involved strangers as victims, 3.28 times more likely if it involved victims under 16 or over 40, and 5.33 times more likely if it took place in the East.

While the *Times* was much more likely to report mass public shootings (i.e., strangers as victims, gun use, and public locations) involving relatively large numbers of fatal and wounded victims, did these same characteristics also increase the number of stories presented? As shown below in Table 20, death toll, wounded count, strangers as victims, and interracial victim-offender relationships each significantly increased the number of stories the *Times* devoted to a mass killing during the 1900–1975 period (see Model 1). We see similar results for the 1976–1999 period

Table 18.
Mass Murders Reported by the New York Times, 1976–1999

Variable	New York Times: 1976–1999	Overall: 1976–1999
Average Death Toll	6.42	5.22
Average Wounded Count	8.48	4.31
Weapon Type		
Gun	68%	69%
Other	17%	17%
Fire	15%	14%
Victim-Offender Relationship		
Stranger	31%	24%
Family	37%	40%
Acquaintance	32%	36%
Public Location	40%	27%
Assault Weapon	4%	3%
Workplace	10%	5%
Felony-Related	19%	25%
Interracial	14%	9%
White Offenders	65%	61%
Average Offender Age	29.52	29.19
Percent Offenders Age 30–49	41%	36%
Percent Offender Age ≥ 50	5%	4%
Male Offenders	95%	94%
Suicidal Offenders	31%	24%
Average Offender Count	1.30	1.30
White Victims	78%	72%
Average Victim Age	29.90	28.02
Victims Age <16 or >40	61%	56%
Male Victims	54%	55%
Region		
Midwest	22%	26%
East	33%	23%
South	22%	29%
West	23%	22%
N	280	649

(Model 2), except for strangers as victims, which did not have a significant impact. In addition, mass murders in 1976–1999 were likely to receive significantly more coverage when they involved gun use, public settings, and offenders between the ages of 30 and 49. Proximity also had a significant positive impact, as massacres occurring in the East significantly increased the number of stories reported. This finding is hardly surprising, of course, given that the *Times* is apt to devote more attention to massacres that occur in or near New York. Over the entire 100-year period

Table 19.
Logistic Regression Analysis of *New York Times*
Coverage of Mass Murder, 1976–1999

Variable	B	S.E.	Exp (B)
Death Toll	0.68*	0.14	1.97
Wounded Count	0.11†	0.05	1.11
Weapon Type			
Gun Use	1.22*	0.38	3.38
Other Weapon Use	1.18*	0.41	3.25
Victim-Offender Relationship			
Percent Stranger Victims	1.01*	0.36	2.74
Percent Acquaintance Victims	0.37	0.28	1.44
Public Setting	1.03*	0.29	2.80
Assault Weapon Use	-0.86	0.91	0.42
Workplace Massacres	7.85	16.59	2560.66
Felony-Related	-0.67	0.31	0.51
Interracial	-0.05	0.47	0.95
White Victims/Offenders	0.22	0.25	1.24
Offender Age			
Percent Offenders 30–49	-0.03	0.25	0.97
Percent Offenders over 50	-0.20	0.58	0.82
Percent Offenders Male	0.51	0.31	1.66
Percent Suicidal Offenders	0.42	0.29	1.52
Offender Count	0.13	0.16	1.14
Victims' Age <16 or >40	1.19*	0.39	3.28
Percent Victims Male	-0.22	0.23	0.80
Region			
East	1.68*	0.30	5.33
South	-0.39	0.28	0.68
West	0.02	0.30	1.02
Constant	-6.47		
-2 Log Likelihood	570.59		
N	649		

*significant at the .01 level
†significant at the .05 level

(Model 3), mass murders received significantly more attention when they were locally-occurring incidents in which the offender gunned down a relatively large number of victims, especially those outside his own race, in a public location.

    Overall, the findings in this section suggest that the *Times* coverage of mass murder began to increase sharply in the mid–1960s. The increase in coverage, moreover, is likely due to the growing frequency with which mass public shootings began to occur over the last one-third of the twentieth century. As noted in Chapter 1, 95 (82 percent) of the 116 mass

Table 20.
OLS Regression Analyses on the Effect
of Mass Murder Characteristics
on the Number of Stories in the *New York Times*

Variable	Model 1 (1900–1975)			Model 2 (1976–1999)			Model 3 (1900–1999)		
	b	B	t-ratio	b	B	t-ratio	b	B	t-ratio
Death Toll	0.45*	0.31	5.27	0.26*	0.14	2.45	0.36*	0.22	5.17
Wounded Count	0.16*	0.31	5.11	0.13*	0.15	2.50	0.15*	0.21	5.04
Weapon									
Gun	1.67	0.11	1.15	6.62*	0.28	3.02	4.42*	0.22	3.41
Other Weapon	2.94	0.19	1.95	4.17	0.14	1.66	4.15*	0.19	2.94
Victim-Offender									
Relationship									
Stranger	3.56*	0.19	3.04	0.60	0.03	0.35	1.85	0.08	1.68
Family	-0.08	-0.01	-0.08	-0.91	-0.04	-0.46	-0.23	-0.01	-0.21
Public Setting	0.34	0.02	0.34	4.01*	0.18	2.37	2.11*	0.11	2.12
Workplace	-4.96*	-0.15	-2.68	-6.94*	-0.18	-2.53	-4.87*	-0.14	-2.86
Felony-Related	1.11	0.06	0.96	-1.62	-0.06	-0.80	-0.30	-0.01	-0.26
Percent Interracial	5.45*	0.18	2.58	7.74*	0.22	3.59	6.76*	0.19	4.51
Pct. White									
Victims/Offenders	2.18	0.10	1.84	0.33	0.01	0.20	0.59	0.02	0.56
Offender Age									
Pct. Offenders									
30–49	-0.40	-0.03	-0.47	3.05*	0.13	2.09	1.41	0.07	1.62
Pct. Offenders > 50	-0.78	-0.03	-0.54	0.80	0.01	0.25	-0.73	-0.02	-0.43
Percent Offenders Male	-0.07	-0.00	0.08	1.36	0.04	0.65	0.17	0.01	0.16
Pct. Suicidal Offenders	-0.87	-0.06	-0.98	-2.91*	-0.12	-1.82	-2.02*	-0.10	-2.18
Offender Count	-0.26	-0.03	-0.48	0.42	0.03	0.40	0.01	0.01	0.16
Pct. Victims Age <16									
or >40	-2.22	-0.11	-1.95	4.22	0.11	1.78	-0.31	-0.01	-0.25
Percent Victims Male	-1.23	-0.05	-0.93	-0.58	-0.02	-0.42	-1.02	-0.04	-1.06
Region									
East	1.01	0.07	1.22	5.72*	0.24	3.31	3.11*	0.15	3.51
South	-0.91	-0.05	-0.91	-0.93	-0.04	-0.48	-0.96	-0.04	-0.94
West	0.05	0.00	0.08	-0.32	-0.01	-0.17	-0.01	-0.00	-0.07
Year	0.04	0.10	1.85	0.01	0.05	0.89	0.02	0.05	1.18
Constant	-3.44			-17.70			-5.66		
Adjusted R²	.46			.16			.23		
N	260			280			540		

*Notes: *Significant at the .05 level*

public shootings occurred between 1966 and 1999. And mass public shootings, as the analyses in this section have demonstrated, were more likely to not only be presented by the *Times*, but also to receive significantly more coverage when they did get reported.

Although the findings presented here suggest that the *Times* has considered mass public shootings with relatively large body counts to be highly newsworthy, particularly in relation to other mass murders, to what extent can this be said about other newspapers? And how does the *Times* coverage of mass murder compare with other news media such as network television news and weekly newsmagazines such as *Time* and *Newsweek*? The following sections focus on these questions by examining newspaper, network television news, and weekly newsmagazine coverage of 495 mass murders that took place between 1976 and 1996 (please see the Appendix for a more detailed discussion of the methodology used).

Newspapers, 1976–1996

Of the mass killings that occurred between 1976 and 1996, nearly all were reported by at least one newspaper. Most of these incidents, however, were not widely publicized. Indeed, the distribution of newspaper scores revealed that a large majority of massacres garnered limited, mostly local coverage. Yet, much of the press coverage was non-local, as evidenced by the finding that 21,845 (73 percent) of the 30,027 newspaper articles were stories on non-locally occurring incidents. Given the infrequency with which mass murders occur, newspapers seldom reported locally occurring massacres because they rarely had the opportunity to do so. For example, of the 247 incidents from 1976 through 1996 reported by the *New York Times*, only 39 (16 percent) occurred locally. Instead, newspapers relied heavily upon the major wire services (e.g., Reuters, AP, or UPI) to provide accounts of non-locally occurring massacres. The bulk of the non-local coverage, however, was confined to a relatively small minority of mass killings. These were the most newsworthy mass murders, for they attracted a great deal of local and non-local attention.

In Table 21, which shows the characteristics that stimulated greater coverage, we see findings similar to those for the *New York Times*. For example, the number of fatal and wounded victims were two of the strongest positive predictors of the extent to which mass killings were reported. Incidents committed with guns and other weapons received significantly more coverage than those committed with fire, while strangers as victims, interracial victim-offender relationships, and public locations were found to have a significant positive effect on the amount of newspaper coverage. Although assault weapon use and workplace violence did not result in greater *Times* coverage, they significantly increased the extent to which mass murders were reported by newspapers in general.

Table 21.
OLS Regression Analysis of Newspaper Coverage, 1976–1996

Variable	b	B	t-ratio
Death Toll	29.37*	0.39	10.87
Wounded Count	3.93*	0.11	3.06
Weapon			
Gun	141.68*	0.19	3.56
Other Weapon	155.74*	0.17	3.48
Victim-Offender Relationship			
Stranger	89.74†	0.11	2.56
Family	-17.90	-0.03	-0.50
Public Setting	91.66*	0.12	2.77
Assault Weapon	576.70*	0.27	7.38
Workplace	166.58†	0.10	2.43
Felony-Related	-44.62	-0.06	-1.33
Percent Interracial	95.23†	0.08	2.06
Percent White Victims/Offenders	6.37	0.01	0.21
Offender Age			
Percent Offenders 30–49	34.57	0.05	1.21
Percent Offenders over 50	85.00	0.05	1.35
Percent Offenders Male	-1.41	-0.01	-0.04
Percent Suicidal Offenders	-18.55	-0.02	-0.56
Percent Victims Age	67.03	0.06	1.52
Percent Victims Male	-17.63	-0.03	-0.70
Population Group	-21.81	-0.03	-0.81
Region			
East	-1.37	-0.01	-0.04
South	-25.03	-0.03	-0.76
West	13.38	0.02	0.38
Year	6.45*	0.11	3.00
Constant	-803.77		
Adjusted R^2	.43		
N	493		

*significant at the .01 level
†significant at the .05 level

Network Television News, 1976–1996

Of the mass murders from 1976 through 1996, 104 were reported by ABC, NBC, or CBS in their evening newscasts. The network television news media reported roughly one-fifth the number of mass killings reported by newspapers (104 compared to 495). Much of this difference, however, is due to the large disparity in the number of sources examined (3 for network television newscasts compared to 117 for newspapers).

Network television news organizations presented fewer mass murders because they not only have less news space, but also because they provide strictly national coverage, whereas newspapers focus on stories of local and national interest. While the emphasis on national news coverage helped limit the number of incidents that were reported, it also figured prominently in determining which mass murders were selected for presentation. More specifically, the network television media focused on mass killings that had broad news appeal. As shown in Table 22, the amount of newspaper coverage given to these cases was nearly four times greater than the overall average, indicating that the massacres appearing on network evening newscasts were also well publicized by newspapers.

The figures in Table 22 also indicate that network evening newscasts overrepresented mass killings involving large numbers of fatal and wounded victims, strangers as victims, public locations, assault weapon use, workplace violence, interracial victim-offender relationships, suicidal

Table 22.
Descriptive Statistics of Mass Murder
Network Television News Coverage, 1976–1996

Variable	Report Mass Murders	Non-reported Mass Murders
Average Newspaper Score	438.76	45.64
Average Death Toll	7.62	4.47
Average Wounded Count	5.31	0.80
Percent Gun Use	69%	66%
Percent Other Weapon Use	16%	24%
Percent Strangers as Victims	45%	20%
Percent Family Victims	27%	39%
Public Setting	60%	19%
Assault Weapon Use	9%	1%
Workplace Massacres	18%	1%
Felony-Related	23%	26%
Interracial	23%	8%
White Victims/Offenders	81%	66%
Percent Offenders 30–49	41%	37%
Percent Offenders over 50	8%	3%
Percent Offenders Male	94%	94%
Percent Suicidal Offenders	36%	24%
Percent Victims Age	58%	57%
Percent Victims Male	55%	54%
Population Group	33%	26%
East	26%	24%
South	25%	29%
West	28%	20%
N	102	391

offenders, and white victims and offenders. On the other hand, the networks provided a representative depiction of the remaining characteristics.

As seen in Table 23, a multivariate logistic regression model was estimated to determine the effect that a given variable had on the probability that a mass murder appeared on a network television newscast, controlling for the effects of the other independent variables. Death toll was a strong positive predictor of whether a mass killing was reported, increasing the odds 1.88 times for each additional fatal victim. The results also indicate that a mass murder was 4.57 times more likely to be reported if it involved strangers as victims, 4.18 times more likely if it occurred in a public setting, and 23.80 times more likely if it was a workplace massacre.

Table 23.
Logistic Regression Analysis of Mass Murder
Network Television News Coverage, 1976–1996

Variable	B	S.E.	Exp(B)
Death Toll	0.63*	0.12	1.88
Wounded Count	0.06	0.03	1.06
Percent Gun Use	0.78	0.60	2.18
Percent Other Weapon Use	1.25	0.64	3.50
Percent Strangers as Victims	1.52*	0.42	4.57
Percent Family Victims	1.04	0.50	2.84
Public Setting	1.43*	0.38	4.18
Assault Weapon Use	0.49	1.02	1.63
Workplace Massacres	3.17*	0.85	23.80
Felony-Related	0.30	0.42	1.35
Percent Interracial	0.06	0.51	1.06
Percent White Victims/Offenders	0.30	0.42	1.35
Percent Offenders 30–49	-0.23	0.33	0.79
Percent Offenders over 50	0.75	0.72	2.12
Percent Offenders Male	0.15	0.48	1.16
Percent Suicidal Offenders	0.54	0.39	1.72
Percent Victims Age	0.27	0.56	1.31
Percent Victims Male	-0.07	0.31	0.93
Population Group	-0.17	0.34	0.84
East	0.04	0.40	1.04
South	-0.41	0.41	0.66
West	-0.42	0.43	0.66
Constant	-7.30		
-2 Log Likelihood	322.41		
N	493		

*significant at the .01 level

Weekly Newsmagazines, 1976–1996

There were 23 mass murders from 1976 through 1996 that were reported by weekly newsmagazines such as *Time, Newsweek,* or *U.S. News & World Report.* Due to greater space limitations, weekly newsmagazines reported the fewest number of mass killings (23). But these massacres were highly newsworthy because, like the network television media, weekly newsmagazines try to attract a national audience. The exceptional news appeal of the incidents reported by the newsweeklies is borne out by the finding that the amount of newspaper coverage given to these cases was 13 times greater than the overall average (see Table 24). Along with extensive newspaper coverage, all 23 incidents were reported on network television newscasts. The figures in Table 24 thus provide a good description of the most celebrated mass killings.

Table 24.
Descriptive Statistics of Mass Murder
Weekly Newsmagazine Coverage, 1976–1996

Variable	Reported Mass Murders	Non-reported Mass Murders
Average Newspaper Score	1,368.73	71.67
Average Death Toll	14.49	4.70
Average Wounded Count	8.85	1.41
Percent Gun Use	90%	66%
Percent Other Weapon Use	5%	18%
Percent Strangers as Victims	62%	20%
Percent Family Victims	14%	38%
Public Setting	90%	24%
Assault Weapon Use	38%	1%
Workplace Massacres	33%	3%
Felony-Related	5%	26%
Interracial	26%	10%
White Victims/Offenders	83%	69%
Percent Offenders 30–49	67%	36%
Percent Offenders over 50	10%	4%
Percent Offenders Male	100%	93%
Percent Suicidal Offenders	62%	25%
Percent Victims Age	59%	57%
Percent Victims Male	54%	54%
Population Group	33%	36%
East	14%	25%
South	29%	28%
West	43%	20%
N	21	472

These figures indicate that newsweekly magazine accounts heavily overrepresented mass murders involving large numbers of fatal and wounded victims, gun use, strangers as victims, public locations, assault weapon use, workplace violence, interracial victim-offender relationships, white victims and offenders, and older, suicidal offenders. By contrast, profit-motivated massacres were underrepresented in newsweekly coverage.

The results presented in Table 25 reveal that death toll was, once again, a strong positive predictor of whether a mass murder was reported, increasing the odds 2.19 times for each additional fatal victim. Also, a mass killing was 187.87 times more likely to be reported if it was carried out in a public setting, 20.24 times more likely if it involved the use of an assault weapon, 13.97 times more likely if it involved strangers as victims, and 11.75 times more likely if it involved offenders between the ages of 30 and 49.

Table 25.
Logistic Regression Analysis of Mass Murder
Weekly Newsmagazine Coverage, 1976–1996

Variable	B	S.E.	Exp (B)
Death Toll	0.78*	0.24	2.19
Wounded Count	0.01	0.02	1.01
Percent Gun Use	1.36	1.43	3.91
Percent Strangers as Victims	2.64[†]	1.14	13.97
Public Setting	5.24[†]	2.16	187.87
Assault Weapon Use	3.01[†]	1.31	20.24
Workplace Massacres	-0.12	1.18	0.89
Felony-Related	-2.43	1.66	0.09
Interracial	-0.98	1.26	0.37
White Victims/Offenders	-1.03	1.58	0.36
Percent Offenders 30–49	2.47[†]	1.24	11.75
Percent Offenders over 50	0.43	1.99	1.53
Percent Offenders Male	-0.74	1.50	0.48
Percent Suicidal Offenders	1.45	1.06	4.25
Percent Victims Age	1.34	1.56	3.81
Percent Victims Male	-0.71	0.88	0.49
Population Group	-2.32	1.36	0.10
East	-1.63	1.52	0.20
South	-1.65	1.35	0.19
West	-1.81	1.51	0.16
Constant	-12.73		
-2 Log Likelihood	50.50		
N	493		

*significant at the .01 level
[†]significant at the .05 level

Summary

Despite numerous differences in format, there was much agreement among the different types of news coverage in terms of which characteristics made a mass killing more newsworthy. The most newsworthy mass murders involve offenders who use guns, especially assault weapons, to kill a relatively large number of victims in a public location such as the workplace. These characteristics enhanced the news value of a mass murder because the news media are compelled to market a crime product that sells. In pursuit of this objective, news organizations engage the audience by appealing to their emotions, presenting informative yet entertaining crime news that depicts crisis and conflict, tragedy and melodrama (Ericson et al., 1987, p. 15; Kappeler et al., 1996, p. 6). The emphasis on news as theater is evidenced by the high priority given to violent, interpersonal crimes such as robbery, assault and, in particular, homicide. But the news media place an even greater premium on mass murders because, as one of the rarest and most extreme forms of violence, these incidents are more likely to seize the public's attention by stirring their emotions.

Although almost every mass killing is locally newsworthy, only a small minority are nationally newsworthy. The mass murders that garner greater media exposure are more newsworthy largely because they are riveting, emotionally evocative incidents that epitomize news as theater — a good and bad morality play involving pure, innocent victims and offenders who seemingly went berserk in a public setting. The strong effects that death toll and, to a lesser extent, wounded count had on all types of coverage suggest that tragedy figured prominently in determining the news value of a mass murder. More specifically, the higher the body count, the more newsworthy the mass killing because it was more serious, shocking, and tragic.

But massacres were even more tragic when strangers were killed. These incidents conjure up images of random violence because the slaughter of strangers connotes an indiscriminate selection of victims. As a result, a sharp distinction is drawn between victims and offenders: victims are depicted as blameless or virtuous while offenders are characterized as evil, crazy, and less than human. Moreover, the seemingly random selection of victims broadens the news interest by conveying the impression that anyone could be a victim of a mass killing. In contrast, massacres involving non-strangers as victims had a more limited news appeal because these incidents tend to be regarded as more of an intimate matter in which the victims are less likely to be portrayed as innocent or blameless. For example, although family massacres almost always received local newspaper coverage, they seldom captured the national spotlight.

Publicly occurring massacres generated a great deal of media attention because they were sensational, highly visible events that had widespread significance. These incidents usually involved a number of persons who witnessed and survived the attack, which gave the news media an invaluable means to deliver a fascinating first-hand account to the audience, allowing them to vicariously experience the horror of the event. In addition, the audience is generally more apt to identify with the victims of these incidents, for they were killed simply because they were in the wrong place at the wrong time. Conversely, mass murders in residential settings had less significance as news items because they were private incidents that rarely had any survivors.

The results also indicate that the high-profile mass murders were more newsworthy because they were more unusual. For example, with the exception of gun use, the characteristics that heightened the news value of a mass killing were among the least frequently occurring for mass murder. Furthermore, the findings regarding workplace massacres and assault weapon use suggest that novelty also enhanced the news value of a mass murder. While these massacres were unusual and often dramatic displays of violence, their importance as news items may have been augmented by the perception that emerged in the late 1980s that workplace violence and assault weapon use constituted new trends in crime and, more narrowly, mass murder. The extensive publicity given to these incidents may partly account for the exaggerated claims that have been made.

The majority of mass killings receive mostly local coverage. Although the locally-reported incidents are more representative of mass murder, these cases are insulated in that they are generally known only on a local basis. But the well-known incidents are the most extreme and atypical instances of mass murder, which is precisely why they are more newsworthy. To be sure, it is hardly surprising to find that the news media present a distorted image of mass murder, for research has consistently shown that news reporting misrepresents the social reality of crime. Yet, the overemphasis placed on the rarest and most sensational mass killings is significant because these cases are likely to have a greater impact on the social construction of mass murder, which is addressed in the next chapter.

6

The Social Construction
of Mass Murder

In contrast to the objectivist approach, which defines social problems in terms of their objective conditions, the constructionist tradition views social problems as the product of "the activities of individuals and groups making assertions of grievances and claims with respect to some putative conditions" (Spector and Kitsuse, 1977, p. 75). Constructionists criticize the objectivist perspective on the grounds that it neglects the subjective nature of social problems. Whereas objectivists link the emergence of problems to concrete changes in society, constructionists contend that shifting conditions do not, by themselves, produce social problems (Adler, 1996). Rather, they maintain that a condition becomes a social problem only when people bring it to the public's attention by making claims about it (Best, 1990). For example, in his study on the "discovery" of child abuse in the 1950s and 1960s, Pfohl (1977) concluded that although child abuse existed "throughout the ages" and had not become more prevalent of late, it gained recognition as a social problem when pediatric radiologists helped raise public awareness of it to enhance, Pfohl claimed, the marginal reputation of their specialty within the medical community. Similarly, Tierney (1982) found that wife beating arose as a social problem in the 1970s not because it had become more common, but because a burgeoning women's movement helped make the problem more visible by effectively mobilizing resources to provide aid to battered women.

Woolgar and Pawluch (1985) have argued, however, that the constructionist perspective is internally inconsistent because it is implicitly based upon objectivist assumptions. They contend that constructionist explanations depend upon finding a discrepancy between the claims that have been made about a condition (e.g. the incidence of child abuse grew to the extent that people began to take notice) and the objective reality of that condition (e.g. the incidence of child abuse did not increase or it just stayed the same). In doing so, however, researchers assume that they know the objective reality of social conditions, which is, in theory, contrary to the subjectivist approach. Constructionists attempt to manage this theoretical tension through "ontological gerrymandering," a term Woolgar and Pawluch (1985) use to describe the selective relativism found in the constructionist literature. That is, analysts question the truth status of claims made about social conditions, yet they conceal the objectivist assumptions upon which their analyses depend by failing to apply the same level of scrutiny to statements that are presented as factual. As Woolgar and Pawluch (1985) point out, however, such statements are merely another set of claims and, thus, should not be immune from ontological doubt.

The issues raised by Woolgar and Pawluch stimulated a great deal of debate, resulting in a split between strict and contextual constructionists. For strict constructionists, the solution to ontological gerrymandering is to avoid making any assumptions about the objective conditions of social problems. Contextual constructionists have pointed out, though, that this is an impossible standard to achieve. More important, they contend that making assumptions about social phenomena is perfectly reasonable, so long as the assumptions are defensible and do not damage the analysis (Best, 1989, p. 347). Because strict constructionists subscribe to a phenomenological perspective, they maintain that one set of claims cannot be used to judge another set of claims. But contextual constructionists argue that claims can be evaluated because they assume we can attain a sufficient knowledge of objective conditions (Best, 1989, p. 348).

In this chapter, I use a contextual constructionist approach because it holds greater promise in terms of explaining the emergence of mass murder as a crime problem. Some may argue, however, that this study falls outside the constructionist tradition because I focus on the objective conditions of mass murder by describing its patterns and prevalence from 1900 through 1999. But as Woolgar and Pawluch (1985) correctly point out, "perhaps all attempts at accounting (explaining) depend upon presenting at least some state of affairs as objective." I treat the descriptive findings in this study as more objective, or more credible, than the prior claims that have been made about mass murder, because they are based on stronger, more technically sound evidence. It is important to note, however, that this study is not merely an exercise in debunking, for a number of valid claims have been made about mass murder. Rather, I attempt to adhere to the constructionist perspective by focusing on the claims-making process, which involves examining the content of claims, identifying the values and interests of claimsmakers, and determining what policies have been implemented to control mass murder.

Constructionist studies have noted that when claimsmakers attempt to raise public awareness of a crime problem, they frequently use typifying examples to characterize the offender, the victim, and the crime itself (Lowney and Best, 1995, p. 33). Previous studies have shown that claimsmakers often depict offenders as monsters or less than human (Cohen, 1972; Hall, Critcher, Jefferson, Clarke, and Roberts, 1978; Jenkins, 1988; Kappeler, Blumberg, and Potter, 1996), victims as innocent or blameless (Adler, 1996; Best, 1987; Kappeler et al., 1996), and crimes as random (Adler, 1996; Best, 1991, 1999; Kappeler et al., 1996; Lowney and Best, 1995; Sacco, 1995, p. 150). Emphasizing these characteristics enables claimsmakers to highlight the problem's harmful dimensions, elicit sympathy or support for their cause, and convey the notion that the problem could affect anyone at any time. The typification process is central to the construction of a crime problem because, as Best (1987, p. 106) points out, it shapes the perception of the problem in general.

In addition to providing typifying examples, claimsmakers often present statistics to illustrate the scope and prevalence of the problem. Larger numbers suggest that a problem is serious and demands attention; as a result, claimsmakers commonly assert that a problem is an "epidemic" (Chiricos, 1996; Jacobs and Henry, 1995; Jenkins, 1988; Kappeler et al., 1996), or that it is increasing and getting worse (Best, 1987, 1991; Nichols, 1997). But the incidence and growth estimates provided by claimsmakers are often flawed or greatly exaggerated (Ben-Yehuda, 1986; Best, 1987; Fishman, 1978; Jacobs and Henry, 1995; Jenkins, 1988, 1994; Kappeler et al., 1996; McCorkle and Miethe, 1998).

A number of scholars have noted that such exaggerated or distorted claims can sometimes result in a moral panic. The moral panic concept, developed by Cohen (1972, p. 9) in his study of Mods and Rockers in 1960s England, refers to a "condition, episode, person or group of persons [that] emerges to become defined as a threat to societal values and interests." Cohen (1972, p. 204) adds that his point is "not that there's nothing there," but that the societal response is "fundamentally inappropriate" to the damage that the threat poses to society. Elaborating on Cohen's work, Goode and Ben-Yehuda (1994) posit that a moral panic is defined by five criteria: a heightened level of concern, hostility directed towards those considered responsible for the problem, consensus about the seriousness of the threat, disproportionate concern about the nature of the threat, and volatility, i.e., the threat may erupt as suddenly as it disappears.

When claimsmakers call attention to a problem, they usually prescribe solutions to control the problem. The solutions offered are often based not only on the way claimsmakers have typified a problem, but also on their values and interests (Loseke, 1989). For example, in his research on the social construction of serial murder, Jenkins (1988, 1994) notes that the FBI characterized serial murder as a crime committed by offenders who wandered from state to state, killing many victims in a number of different jurisdictions. A major reason why serial killers were so "successful," the FBI asserted, was because of the lack of networking and coordination across jurisdictions, i.e., linkage blindness. The FBI's proposal to combat linkage blindness and, by extension, serial murder involved the creation of the National Center for the Analysis of Violent Crime (NCAVC), a law enforcement clearinghouse and resource center headquartered at the FBI Academy in Quantico, Virginia. Jenkins (1988) points out that even though efforts to expand the role of federal law enforcement had been previously met by serious opposition, the FBI had by that time established "ownership" of the serial murder problem. Consequently, the FBI's claims were accepted, and the NCAVC became operational in 1984.

Previous research has noted that claimsmakers are successful when they establish ownership of a problem — their claims are accepted and viewed as authoritative (Gusfield, 1981, p. 10). Because claimsmakers compete in a social problems marketplace (Hilgartner and Bosk, 1988), they often experience failure before they taste success. But by concentrating almost exclusively on claimsmaking activity, most studies fail to adequately explain why claimsmakers suddenly succeed. In his study on the Boston garroting hysteria of 1865, Adler (1996, p. 261) argues that an external spark, or triggering event, is needed to transform a previously unsuccessful claimsmaking campaign into a successful one. Although theoretical discussions of social problems seldom mention triggering events, Adler points out that scholars have implicitly recognized their importance in creating concern over youth disturbances (Cohen, 1972), crimes against the elderly (Fishman, 1978), and adolescent drug abuse (Ben-Yehuda, 1986). A review of the constructionist literature reveals that triggering events have also led to the identification of social problems such as missing children (Best, 1987), serial murder (Jenkins, 1988, 1994), stalking (Lowney and Best, 1995), and money laundering (Nichols, 1997).

Closely related to the idea of a triggering event is the landmark narrative concept put forth by Nichols (1997) in his study on the social construction of money laundering. According to Nichols, the prosecution of the currency reporting violations at the First National Bank of Boston was a landmark narrative in that it led to the creation of a new crime category, money laundering, and was eventually regarded as the definitive example of this type of crime. The news media helped establish the Bank of Boston case as a landmark narrative, Nichols argues, by giving it considerably more coverage than other cases of money laundering and by presenting it as a distinctive, uniquely important case. Moreover, federal law enforcement agencies saw the case as an opportunity to call for new legislation that criminalized money laundering. These efforts were successful, for they resulted in passage of the Money Laundering Control Act of 1986. Nichols concludes that claimsmakers in the mass media and government exploited the Bank of Boston case in pursuit of organizational goals — namely, the sale of news products and the expansion of government power.

Unlike most constructionist studies, which emphasize the efforts of primary claimsmakers, I argue that the news media have had a decisive impact on the social construction of mass murder. Following Adler (1996) and Nichols (1997), I suggest that the occurrence of highly publicized massacres helps explain why, in the early 1980s, claimsmakers saw the mid–1960s as the onset of an unprecedented mass murder wave. And just as the Bank of Boston case was seen as the landmark narrative for money laundering, so, too, were these celebrated massacres cited as the definitive examples of mass murder. I further explore the landmark narrative concept by looking at the role that several high-profile massacres have played in the creation of three additional crime problems — assault weapon use, workplace violence and school shootings.

As shown later, claimsmakers have characterized mass murder as a crime involving angry, disturbed loners who indiscriminately gun down innocent victims in a public place. And recall that previous research has shown that when claimsmakers typify crime problems, they characterize them as random, the victims as innocent, and the offenders as monstrous deviants. Because most research has focused on the efforts of primary claimsmakers, scholars often imply that claimsmakers deliberately select unusual and dramatic typifying examples to galvanize the public and attract policymakers' attention. I suggest, however, that the way crime problems are usually typified is largely due to the news media's preference for presenting informative yet entertaining crime news that appeals to the emotions of the audience. The news media therefore give much more attention to crimes involving predatory offenders who randomly prey upon innocent victims. And claimsmakers succeed in calling attention to a crime problem by capitalizing on the massive publicity surrounding a celebrated crime. But claimsmakers' exploitation of high-profile crimes may also be due to the fact that these are cases with which they and their audience are already familiar.

"Discovering" Mass Murder

One of the central questions of this study is why, in the 1980s, claimsmakers saw the mid–1960s as the beginning of an unprecedented mass murder wave. As noted in Chapter 1, the first mass murder wave in the 1920s and '30s did not draw much attention because it was composed mainly of familicides and felony-related massacres, which, then as now, are not as newsworthy as other mass killings. During the 1940s and '50s, the terms "mass killing" and "mass slaying" entered the American lexicon, but mass murder rates, like those for crime in general, were low. Academic research on mass murder began to appear in the 1950s, but it consisted entirely of psychological and psychiatric case studies (Banay, 1956; Gavin and Macdonald, 1959; Karpman, 1955). The parochial scope of these studies may have therefore precluded a widespread recognition of mass murder.

As the incidence of mass murder accelerated in the mid- to late 1960s, there was a corresponding increase in the amount of media attention devoted to mass killings, evidenced most dramatically by the growing number of high-profile cases. Previous research has likewise suggested that the late 1960s marked the beginning of a dramatic rise in serial killings, or at least in the number publicized by the media (Hickey, 1991; Jenkins, 1994). The growing prevalence and publicity of serial killings caught the attention of several researchers during the mid–1970s, who coined the phrase "serial murder." The creation of this phrase brought about a more limited meaning for the term "mass murder," and the media eventually popularized the distinction between the two types of multiple murder in the early 1980s.

Since the introduction of the serial murder concept and the concomitant redefinition of mass murder, serial murder has clearly garnered the lion's share of attention — from journalists and scholars alike. Fox and

Levin (1994, p. 144) have attributed the imbalance to the fact that serial murder poses a greater threat to law enforcement, generates 'more fear and anxiety, and is more sensational. However, the media's initial interest in serial murder during the early 1980s was due largely to the FBI's promotion of the problem. Before the 1970s, the FBI's interest in serial murder and, more specifically, in psychological profiling was virtually nonexistent. This was largely due to the enormous influence of longtime Director J. Edgar Hoover, who eschewed the "soft sciences" and psychological approaches to crime (Douglas and Olshaker, 1995). Thus, it was not until after Hoover's death in 1973 that the FBI's Behavioral Science Unit (BSU) began devoting more attention to psychological profiling. Even though members of the BSU were given permission in 1978 by then–Director William Webster to provide profiling consultation to local and state law enforcement agencies, profiling was still regarded with some suspicion by many in the Bureau (Douglas and Olshaker, 1995).

But the emerging serial murder problem provided the BSU with an opportunity to establish profiling as a legitimate investigative technique. During the late 1970s, the serial murders committed by the likes of Edmund Kemper, John Wayne Gacy, and Ted Bundy captured a wealth of media coverage. The FBI capitalized on the increased publicity by supplying the media with grossly exaggerated figures on the scale and prevalence of serial killings. Moreover, the Bureau depicted serial murder as a crime without historical precedent. Although the FBI were later the first to correct their hyperbolic claims, they still helped create the enduring impression that the 1960s marked the beginning of an unprecedented and ever-growing serial murder wave (Jenkins 1988, 1994).

It is within this context that claims about mass murder first began to appear. Although it has, compared to serial murder, received far less attention, there has been a similar tendency to view mass murder as a crime endemic to late twentieth-century America. While the redefinition of mass murder may have helped convey this impression, the perception that the mid–1960s marked the onset of an unprecedented mass murder wave is largely due to the surge in high-profile cases since that time. Before the mid–1960s, there were few celebrated mass killings. Indeed, popular and academic discussions on mass murder prior to the mid–'60s have generally identified the same handful of cases (e.g. the St. Valentine's Day Massacre, the Howard Unruh mass murder, and the massacre of the Clutter family in Holcomb, Kansas) as if these were the only mass killings that occurred during that era. As illustrated later, claimsmakers have relied on high-profile cases not only as indicators of both short- and long-term trends in the prevalence of mass murder, but also as typifying examples.

Establishing Ownership

Once mass murder was redefined and identified as a new crime, it was soon clear that criminologists James Alan Fox and Jack Levin established ownership of the problem. In 1985, they published their pioneering book on multiple murder, becoming the first scholars to systematically study the subject. Six years later, the *New York Times* claimed that the book was still widely regarded as the most authoritative work on the topic (*New York Times*, October 19, 1991). Consequently, when the news media began devoting more attention to mass murder in the late 1980s and early 1990s, they turned to the experts on the subject — Fox and Levin.

In examining several types of media coverage for this study, I located 17 newspaper articles, two television news broadcasts, and one television program that explored the general topic of mass murder. Although this does not encompass all of the feature stories on mass murder since the early 1980s, it probably covers most that were presented by the media. The news media used a total of 47 sources for the 20 stories. Since some of the sources were quoted in more than one story, there were a total of 24 different "experts" cited by the media. Of the 24 experts, 17 were academics, three were law enforcement personnel, three were non-academic psychologists or psychiatrists, and one was a legal director of an advocacy group. Fox and Levin were, by far, the most quoted authorities on mass murder, as they were used as a source in 11 and 10 stories, respectively. The next most quoted expert was Park Dietz, author of a 1986 article on mass murder, who was used as a source in three stories. The remaining 21 authorities were quoted in either one or two stories.

Typification of Mass Murder

After mass murder was identified as a new crime, efforts were made to characterize what kind of problem it was. One of the earliest instances came in the 1984 article that appeared in the *New York Times*. In discussing the then-recent massacre committed by James Huberty at a McDonald's restaurant in San Ysidro, California, the article reported that "mass murderers like Mr. Huberty ... kill groups of people in a single outburst" (August 27, 1984; p. 1:1). In Levin and Fox's (1985) book published the following year, they claimed that mass killers were not "crazed, glassy-eyed lunatics" which was, according to them, the prevailing image of mass murder at the time. Rather, they emphasized how "extraordinarily ordinary" mass killers were. Levin and Fox later modified their views, however, when they began serving as sources for feature stories on mass murder. For example, they started making the important distinction between mass and serial murder, which they did not do in their book. In addition, they developed a profile of the typical mass murderer, which the news media began to disseminate.

Although the news media did a few feature stories on mass murder after the much-publicized massacres committed by James Huberty in 1984 and Patrick Sherrill in 1986, it was not until the late 1980s that the press began devoting serious attention to the "growing" mass murder problem. Indeed, of the 20 feature stories I located, 15 appeared between 1988 and 1993. These stories were usually presented in the wave of publicity following one or more high-profile massacres. To put the incident (or incidents) in perspective, the news media turned to the experts, who provided commentary on trends in the prevalence of mass killings and on what constitutes the typical mass murder. As noted in the introduction, claimsmakers unanimously asserted that mass murder was on the rise. To their credit, however, scholars like Fox and Levin rightly noted that it was still an infrequent occurrence. For example, in a 1991 newspaper article, Levin said, "The only positive thing I can tell you that might be comforting to some people is that ... it's still rare. And you're more likely to contract leprosy than you are to be killed by a mass murderer" (*Dallas Morning News*, October 17, 1991).

In the feature stories from 1988–1993, Fox and Levin introduced their profile of the typical mass killer. In a newspaper article presented after the 1991 massacre committed by George Hennard, Fox claimed, "Mass murderers fit a fairly rigid profile. They tend to be white males in their 30s or 40s who have a long history of frustration and failure. They tend to be loners, or people who feel isolated. And they either own guns or are very familiar with them" (*Washington Post*, October 19, 1991; p. A13). In another article, Levin estimated that in 95 percent of mass murders, there is a precipitating event such as a divorce or job termination (*Dallas Morning News*, October 17, 1991). A number of claimsmakers also depicted mass murderers as highly suicidal. After the heavily publicized 1989 massacre committed by Marc Lepine in Montreal, Elliott Leyton, author of *Hunting Humans*, claimed that "mass killers make their social statement and then die, either by their own hand or a hail of police bullets" (*Maclean's*, April 21, 1986). Similarly, Jack Levin asserted in a 1993 newspaper article that "in 95 percent of all mass murder cases, the killer dies on the spot, either by his own hand or by police" (*Chicago Sun-Times*, January 13, 1993; p. 4).

Claimsmakers also characterized the nature of mass murder through the use of typifying examples. For instance, in discussing the topic of mass murder after the shooting spree carried out by George Hennard, a *Washington Post* article reported that "Hennard ... fits what experts say is the classic profile of a mass killer" ("Hennard said to fit classic profile of mass killer," October 19, 1991; p. A13). Likewise, a 1993 newspaper article reported, "Gian Luigi Ferri was a textbook case of a mass murderer" after he killed 8 and wounded 6 at a law office in San Francisco (*The Ottawa Citizen*, "California gunman a 'textbook' murderer," July 5, 1993; p. A6). And in discussing the 1993 mass murder committed by Colin Ferguson, James Fox declared, "Ferguson is as classic and typical as you can get" (Arts & Entertainment network, *Massacres*, 1996).

In Table 26, I describe the characteristics of the cases used by claimsmakers as typifying examples of mass murder. Examining news coverage and the academic literature on mass murder, I identified the cases claimsmakers cited to illustrate the nature of mass murder. In addition, I noted the identity (news media-journalist or academic) of those who cited cases as typifying examples. Because Fox and Levin have played a prominent role in constructing mass murder, I also depict the characteristics of the mass killings they cited as typifying examples in their media interviews and academic work.

Table 26 shows that claimsmakers were more likely to use mass murders involving large body counts, strangers as victims, public locations, assault weapon use, workplace violence, interracial victim-offender relationships, and older, suicidal offenders, and slightly more likely to use incidents involving gun use and white offenders. Conversely, they were less likely to use felony-related massacres as typifying examples. Perhaps the most interesting finding, though, is the extent to which the typifying examples were publicized. Indeed, the average newspaper score of these cases was almost 20 times greater than the overall average. Moreover, the mass murders used as typifying examples received five times as much coverage from the *New York Times*, were four times more likely to appear on a network television newscast, and were 11 times more likely to be featured in a newsweekly magazine.

Table 26.
Descriptive Statistics of Mass Murders Used
as Typifying Examples, 1900–1999

Variables	Media Exemplars	Academic Exemplars	Fox and Levin Exemplars	Overall Exemplars	Mass Murder Overall, 1900–99
Avg. Newspaper Score[a]	1135.16	4350.73	2562.86	2402.52	126.95
Pct. Reported by TV Networks[a]	92%	95%	84%	86%	18%
Pct. Reported by Newsweeklies[a]	58%	62%	53%	45%	4%
Avg. # of NYT Stories	14.14	58.72	25.74	33.17	6.29
Average Death Toll	13.82	15.52	15.58	13.46	5.39
Average Wounded Count	8.37	64.44	18.64	34.19	3.97
Weapon Use					
Percent Gun Use	82%	74%	73%	75%	67%
Percent Other Weapon Use	15%	26%	22%	21%	21%
Percent Fire	3%	0%	5%	4%	12%
Victim/Offender Relationship					
Percent Strangers as Victims	55%	63%	53%	51%	24%
Percent Family Victims	18%	18%	22%	27%	44%
Pct. Acquaintance Victims	27%	19%	25%	22%	32%
Public Setting	77%	78%	75%	70%	28%
Assault Weapon Use	18%	22%	15%	12%	2%
Workplace Massacres	29%	26%	33%	27%	5%
Felony-Related	18%	4%	13%	13%	22%
Interracial	21%	30%	25%	24%	8%
Percent White Offenders	76%	70%	76%	74%	67%
Average Offender Age	34.78	33.89	34.34	33.63	30.12
Percent Offenders 30–49	59%	54%	49%	52%	37%
Percent Offenders over 50	6%	7%	10%	7%	5%
Percent Offenders Male	97%	100%	95%	96%	93%
Percent Suicidal Offenders	47%	56%	48%	48%	29%
Avg. Offender Count	1.18	1.22	1.10	1.23	1.28
Percent White Victims	86%	82%	81%	84%	78%
Average Victim Age	29.84	35.38	33.81	32.23	27.51
Pct. Victims Age <16 or >40	52%	50%	58%	58%	55%
Percent Victims Male	52%	53%	55%	56%	55%
Region					
Midwest	35%	30%	28%	35%	27%

Variables	Media Exemplars	Academic Exemplars	Fox and Levin Exemplars	Overall Exemplars	Mass Murder Overall, 1900–99
East	18%	22%	27%	25%	26%
South	12%	22%	15%	13%	26%
West	35%	26%	30%	27%	21%
N	34	27	40	56	909

ᵃ*Based on data from 1976–1996 (N=495)*

These findings indicate that claimsmakers clearly prefer to use high-profile mass murders as typifying examples. This is likely due to the fact that news coverage is by far the most accessible source of information on mass killings. Unlike hate crimes, for example, there is neither a government agency nor an interest group that has specifically collected data on mass killings. Although the SHR represent an invaluable source of information on mass murder, scholars have, with few exceptions, not utilized these data. As a result, claimsmakers tend to use high-profile cases as typifying examples because these are the cases with which they are the most familiar. But these are also the cases with which the general public is the most familiar. Using high-profile cases as typifying examples serves claimsmakers' interests in that they are trying to call attention to a new crime problem, and well-publicized, sensational cases are more likely to help them achieve that goal. In doing so, however, claimsmakers have presented a distorted image of mass murder because, as shown in the previous chapter, the high-profile cases constitute the least representative examples of mass murder. This is significant because, as the next section illustrates, the popular image of mass murder has shaped the policy proposals to control it.

The Solutions to Control Mass Murder

The policy proposals to control mass murder have consisted of stronger gun laws, especially a ban on assault weapons, and efforts to prevent workplace and school violence. But crime problems can be framed in a number of ways. That mass murder has been framed mainly as a gun problem and, to a lesser extent, as a workplace and school violence problem is a reflection not only of the most publicized mass killings, but also of the values and interests of claimsmakers themselves, particularly those who have established ownership. For instance, mass murder could easily be framed as a domestic violence problem given that familicides are the most common mass killing. Moreover, various interest groups relating to domestic violence were already in existence by the mid–1980s, when mass murder was being constructed as a new crime problem. However, mass murder has not been framed as a domestic violence problem largely because familicides seldom attract national media attention. The mostly local coverage not only insulates these cases in that they are generally known only on a local basis, but it also inhibits the opportunity for claimsmaking.

Mass murder could also be framed as a mental health problem. Indeed, in a 1988 newspaper article, forensic psychiatrist Park Dietz stated that he "never came across one who wasn't at least partially interested in suicide" (*New York Times*, January 3, 1988; p. 1:1). He said, "Depression is very common and easily treated. If we are sensitive to it we could prevent suffering, a few suicides and perhaps the occasional incident of mass murder." According to Fox and Levin, however, mass murder is not a mental health problem because it is unpredictable. Levin has claimed, for example, "There simply aren't many warning signs to recognize mass murder" (*Dallas Morning News*, October 17, 1991). Moreover, as Fox stated in a 1991 newspaper article, "You cannot spot them ... of the thousands who fit the profile, there are very few who will kill anyone, much less commit mass murder. It's a very large haystack and very few needles" (*Houston Chronicle*, October 20, 1991).

Harsher penalties are often advanced as a solution for crime problems, but not for mass murder. One obvious reason for this is that mass killers already tend to receive the maximum punishment allowed by law. But another reason that stiffer penalties are considered unnecessary may be due to the popular, albeit erroneous, belief that the vast majority of mass killers die at the scene of the crime.

Mass Murder as a Gun Problem

As the two most quoted authorities on mass murder, Fox and Levin have figured prominently in framing it as a gun problem. In their profile noted above, they identified access to, and familiarity with, firearms as a characteristic typical of mass murderers for several reasons. First, according to Fox and Levin (1998), firearms are the most effective means of mass destruction. As Levin stated in a 1991 newspaper article, "It's very difficult to kill a lot of people with a knife. They just won't hold still" (*Dallas Morning News*, October 17, 1991). Second, in their own research they found that the percentage of gun use is significantly greater among mass murders (79 percent) than among single-victim homicides (68 percent) (Fox and Levin, 1998). It is important to point out, however, that Fox and Levin obtained an inflated percentage of gun use for mass murder by excluding every fire-related case reported to the SHR. When I attempted to account for the fire-related cases in the SHR data, I found that the difference in levels of gun use between mass murder and ordinary homicide essentially washes out. Finally, Fox and Levin have alleged that mass murders have recently become more lethal. In their 1994 book, they contend that "the increased availability of high-powered, rapid-fire weapons ... is ... a large part of the reason why the death tolls in mass murders have climbed so dramatically in the recent past."

In discussing the ways to control mass murder, Fox and Levin (1994, pp. 270–271) have reasoned that conventional gun control measures, such as background checks and waiting periods, would not necessarily prevent massacres from occurring because few mass killers have criminal records and most carry out their attacks after much planning and deliberation. Instead, they argue that the most effective gun control policy for mass murder would be to ban rapid-fire weaponry and oversized ammunition clips. Fox and Levin point out that this may not prevent mass murders from occurring, but it might reduce the number of people harmed in such attacks.

Fox and Levin are not the only ones who have framed mass murder as a gun problem, for others have also made claims, including journalists, law enforcement officials, politicians, attorneys, academics, gun control activists, and friends and family members of mass murder victims. Beginning with the 1966 massacre committed by Charles Whitman, claimsmakers have frequently capitalized on the extensive publicity surrounding high-profile mass public shootings to call for stronger gun laws. For example, after James Huberty gunned down 21 at a McDonald's in 1984, gun control advocates used this incident to argue for handgun registration, waiting periods, and bans on machine guns and armor-piercing bullets (Andrews, 1984). In 1987, David Burke killed 42 and himself in 1987 by causing a Pacific Southwest Airlines (PSA) flight to crash after he shot the pilot. John Phillips, executive board member of Handgun Control, Inc., responded to the incident by declaring, "The PSA situation absolutely illustrates the need for tougher handgun control" (UPI Wire, December 24, 1987).

In the late 1980s and early 1990s, gun control advocates began calling for a ban on assault weapons, i.e., semiautomatic and automatic hand-guns and rifles with a military-style appearance. The event largely respon-sible for initiating the frenzy over assault weapons was the Stockton, California, mass murder committed by Patrick Purdy in January of 1989 in which he used an AK-47 rifle to kill 5 Asian-American children and wound 30 others. Indeed, a 1995 article in the *Chicago Tribune* (May 29, 1995; 5M) said, "The massacre of five children as they ran screaming that sunny January morning, and the wounding of 30 others, including a teacher, packed such emotional power it ignited the nascent anti-assault weapons movement." Bob Walker, legislative director of Handgun Con-trol, Inc., added that the Stockton schoolyard massacre "was clearly the single event that captured people's attention" (*Chicago Tribune*, May 29, 1995; 5M).

The massively publicized Purdy massacre sparked a flurry of claims-making activity on the part of gun control proponents and helped lead to changes in gun laws. In response to the massacre, California governor George Deukmejian and Attorney General John Van de Kamp both held press conferences, vowing to pass an assault weapon ban. Robert M. Ack-erman, Dickinson School of Law professor, responded to the tragedy by stating, "What the recent school tragedy in Stockton, Calif., bears out is that semiautomatic assault rifles like the AR-15 and AK-47 are the weapons of choice of mass murderers" (*New York Times*, March 2, 1989; A7). While this claim is patently false — as only 2 percent of mass murders are com-mitted with any kind of assault weapon, never mind assault rifles — it is important because it illustrates the notion often held by supporters of gun control in the years following the Stockton massacre that outlawing assault weapons such as the one used by Purdy will avert future outbreaks of mass murder. Indeed, in the wake of the Stockton massacre, the state of Cali-fornia passed the Roos-Roberti Weapon Control Act, which banned the sale and possession of assault weapons. Moreover, several months later the Bush administration banned the importation of foreign-made assault weapons, even though gun control proponents later contended that this piece of legislation was a largely symbolic gesture that did not target the real problem — domestic-made assault weapons.

In September of 1989, nearly eight months after the Stockton inci-dent, Joseph Wesbecker, like Purdy, used an AK-47 rifle to kill 8 and wound 12 at the Standard Gravure plant in Louisville, Kentucky, where he was formerly employed. The widely publicized Wesbecker incident was heralded by *Newsweek* (September 25, 1989) as an "unwelcome reminder of last January's schoolyard slaughter in Stockton, California." A *Chicago Tribune* editorial declared that the massacre was "a cause for hysteria on assault rifles" and mentioned that "the event must be noted for what it is: another reminder that it is past time to rid ourselves of vicious weapons of no legitimate purpose" (*Chicago Tribune*, September 18, 1989). L. Stanley Chauvin, then-president of the American Bar Association, declared, "This is a classic case. Assault weapons are used for no earthly purpose other than to kill people. As long as they are available, people will be killed" (*Los Angeles Times*, September 15, 1989).

An editorial in the *St. Louis Post-Dispatch* contended that "Joseph Wesbecker is a classic example" of why gun licenses, police background checks of gun buyers, and handgun registration and permits are needed. The editorial further proclaimed, "This slaughter shows again ... the need to restrict semi-automatic military-style assault weapons," because, "with the help of reasonable gun control measures, this tragedy might very well have been prevented" (*St. Louis Post-Dispatch*, September 17, 1989). And Rep. Pete Stark (D-Calif.) warned, "There will be more and more mindless mass murders until the President and Congress put controls on the sales of assault weapons" (*Los Angeles Times*, "Louisville mayhem seen spurring gun debate; activists on both sides expect new drive to widen curbs on assault weapons," September 15, 1989). Along with the Stockton massacre, the Wesbecker incident helped fuel the enactment of an assault weapon ban in New Jersey in 1990 as well as similar bans in at least 30 cities and counties.[1]

On October 16, 1991, George Hennard gunned down 23 people at Luby's cafeteria in Killeen, Texas. Having taken place just two days before the House of Representatives was to vote on an anticrime bill that included a ban on semiautomatic weapons and multiple-bullet gun clips, this incident provoked a loud chorus of demands for stronger gun laws. Ann Richards, then-governor of Texas, responded to the massacre by saying, "The dead lying on the floor of Luby's cafeteria should be evidence enough that we are not pursuing a rational ... posture" (*Houston Chronicle*, October 19, 1991). On the floor of the House of Representatives, Rep. Chet Edwards (D-Texas) implored, "Don't let the tragedy in my district yesterday be the tragedy in your neighborhoods tomorrow. We cannot bring back the lives of 22 citizens lost yesterday. But, with your vote, we can still save some lives" (*New York Times*, October 18, 1991). Despite the pleas of Edwards and other congressmen, the House of Representatives rejected the ban on the sale and ownership of semiautomatic weapons and multiple-bullet gun clips. Jeffrey Y. Muchnick, lobbyist for the Coalition to Stop Gun Violence, said, "This vote is disgraceful. It's hard to believe members are so callous when people are being killed" (*New York Times*, October 18, 1991).

The Killeen massacre also engendered the political activism of Suzanna Gratia Hupp, who lost both of her parents in the lethal rampage. Family members, friends, or colleagues of mass murder victims occasionally become advocates for issues such as gun control. Gratia Hupp, however, who was inside Luby's with her parents during the attack but left her gun in her car on account of the state's gun laws, launched a crusade to permit licensed gun owners to carry concealed handguns. She later won a seat in the Texas legislature and due in part to her persuasive arguments, a right-to-carry concealed firearms law was passed in Texas in 1996. And Gov. Ann Richards' opposition to the law contributed to her defeat in the next gubernatorial election, and the first political victory of her opponent, George W. Bush.

The movement to ban assault weapons picked up momentum in July of 1993 when Gian Luigi Ferri killed 8 and wounded 6 with a TEC-DC-9 semiautomatic pistol at the law offices of Pettit and Martin in San Francisco. In response to the massacre, Thomas A. Hagemann, former U.S. attorney, posed the question, "Isn't it obvious that better gun control will help — not solve, but help — our peculiarly American problems of widespread, violent crime, of instantaneous mass murders, gang warfare and a growing sense that no street is safe?" (*Houston Chronicle*, July 11, 1993). Dianne Feinstein, Democratic senator from California, asserted, "By depriving Ferri (and a series of demented killers before him) of easy access to weapons of war, a federal ban could have saved lives" (*Washington Post*, July 23, 1993). Shortly after the Ferri mass murder, the lawyers at Pettit and Martin formed a gun control advocacy group which they named the Legal Community Against Violence and later opened a joint office with Handgun Control, Inc., at the law firm's old office. In early 1994, California senator David Roberti proposed a bill banning ammunition clips holding more than 15 bullets, adding that such a change in the law would have prevented Ferri's mass murder. Referring to assault weapons, Roberti declared, "These are not weapons for hunting and self-defense. They are weapons for crime and mass murder" (*San Francisco Chronicle*, February 23, 1994; A20).

In December of 1993 — less than one month after the enactment of the Brady bill — Colin Ferguson opened fire on the Long Island railroad commuter train, killing 6 and wounding 17. This incident received an enormous amount of news coverage and predictably led to a number of claims by gun control proponents, chief among them President Bill Clinton. Clinton responded to the tragedy by saying, "The rapid fire of the gun was something that almost paralyzed all the people on the car. When the guy had to change clips and was wrestled to the ground, that seems to me to be a pretty good argument for the Feinstein amendment," which proposed to ban assault weapons and large ammunition clips (*Newsday*, December 9, 1993). An editorial in the *New York Times* declared, "The message of the mass murder in New York is clear: We need to get handguns off the streets." Similarly, an *LA Times* editorial asserted that the "gunman, like countless other killers, was able to commit his crime with great efficiency because of relatively easy access to a concealable handgun with a high-volume ammunition clip." The aftermath of the Long Island railroad shooting also brought with it the gun control activism and political rise of Carolyn McCarthy, whose husband was slain while her son was critically wounded in the attack. McCarthy later won a seat in the House of Representatives after she beat incumbent Dan Frisa in an election in which she campaigned solely on the issue of gun control.

In June of 1994, Dean Mellberg used a MAK-90 semiautomatic rifle to kill 4 and wound 22 at the Fairchild Air Force Base in Spokane, Washington. An editorial in the *News Tribune* claimed, "The shooting spree ... is doubly tragic because it could have been prevented. Dean Mellberg may have pulled the trigger on his MAK-90 semiautomatic rifle, but poor security and ridiculously easy access to assault weaponry surely played a role" (*News Tribune*, June 23, 1994). After using a number of high-profile mass murders involving assault weapons from the late 1980s through the 1990s, gun control activists scored a major victory in 1994 when Congress passed a federal assault weapon ban.

Mass Murder as a Workplace Violence Problem

In the late 1980s and early 1990s, a movement began that sought to heighten awareness regarding the alleged increase of workplace violence. By most accounts, 1986 marked the beginning of the rise in workplace violence for that was the year in which Patrick Sherrill, a postal worker, killed 14 and wounded 6 at the post office in Edmond, Oklahoma. The view that the Sherrill massacre was the vanguard for the increase in workplace violence is expressed by Kelleher (1997, p. 86) who wrote, "Patrick Sherrill's crime in 1986 inaugurated the modern era of the violent workplace and forever changed the traditional American view of a safe work environment."

The reverberations of Sherrill's lethal attack were widespread, for Kelleher (1997, p. 169) notes that "even though Patrick Sherrill was not the first employee to commit mass murder in the workplace, his crime garnered significant national attention in the media and among several government agencies, such as the National Institute of Occupational Safety and Health (NIOSH), the Centers for Disease Control (CDC), and the Occupational Safety and Health Administration (OSHA). His actions marked the first widespread, public recognition of the potential for massive and lethal violence in the workplace." Moreover, the Sherrill massacre prompted a congressional hearing on the issue of violence in the U.S. Postal Service (United States House of Representatives Committee on Post Office and Civil Service, 1987). Thus, in many ways, Patrick Sherrill did for workplace violence what Patrick Purdy did for the assault weapons movement. That the Sherrill and Purdy massacres were largely responsible for inciting the hysteria over workplace violence and assault weapons is consistent with Adler's (1996, p. 261) contention that a triggering mechanism is needed to stimulate the development of a moral panic. In both situations, the massacres provided an external spark that focused popular sentiment in such a way that the public was receptive to the claims made by both groups of claimsmakers.

In the years following the Sherrill massacre, the workplace mass murders committed by the likes of Richard Farley, Joseph Wesbecker, Gian Luigi Ferri, and Thomas McIlvane (to name a few) received a great deal of publicity and helped fuel the perception that workplace violence was a "growing menace" (DiLorenzo and Carroll, 1995). Suplee (*Washington Post*, October 1, 1989; p. D1), for example, proclaimed that "mass murder has seized the workplace with unprecedented fury." Meanwhile, Kelleher (1997, p. 169) asserted, "Since 1986, the American workplace has been besieged by a continuing series of mass murders carried out by employees or ex-employees who harbored a deep sense of revenge against their employers." The McIlvane massacre was especially noteworthy because he, like Sherrill, was a postal worker who exacted revenge at the workplace, this time the post office in Royal Oak, Michigan, in the fall of 1991. His deadly rampage also led to congressional hearings (United States House of Representatives Committee on Post Office and Civil Service, 1992) and, along with a handful of other violent acts by postal workers, crystallized the image of the U.S. Post Office as the center for the alleged rising tide of employee violence.

Due in part to the prominence that workplace violence achieved as a result of the high-profile mass murders, federal agencies such as the CDC, NIOSH, and the Bureau of Labor Statistics (BLS) began to conduct research on workplace violence and eventually announced their findings in 1993. As Larson (1994) mentions, though, the misinterpretation of these findings produced a heightened level of concern. The BLS, for example, found that homicide is the second-leading cause of workplace fatalities, a fact not lost on newspaper reporters who, according to Larson (1994), "often insert this finding when reporting the latest murder by a disgruntled employee, conveying the impression that workers are to blame for elevating homicide to the number two position." Along the same lines, since mass murders committed by disgruntled employees dominated the initial depiction of workplace violence, the findings that there were between 750–1,000 victims of workplace homicide annually imparted the faulty notion that current or former employees were responsible for most if not all of these incidents. Research later showed, however, that disgruntled employee violence constitutes a small portion of workplace violence, as evidenced by the findings that co-workers account for only 6 percent of violent acts in the workplace (Bureau of Labor Statistics, 1994a) and roughly the same percentage of workplace homicides (Bureau of Labor Statistics, 1994b, 1995; Windau and Toscano, 1994).

In the late 1980s and 1990s, workplace massacres were commonly used as typifying examples to show that the "epidemic" of workplace violence was a serious problem in need of greater attention (de Becker, 1988; DiLorenzo and Carroll, 1995; Mantell, 1994; Minor, 1995; *Newsweek*, 1993; Schneider Denenberg, Denenberg, Braverman, and Braverman, 1996; *Workers' Comp Executive*, 1993). For instance, Minor (1995, p. ix) detailed the exploits of David Burke, Richard Farley, and the three postal service mass murderers and cited these cases as "examples of the growing trend of workplace violence." In a *USA Today* article, Michael Mantell cited the post office mass killings as well as the massacres committed by Eric Houston and Courtney Matthews as examples of workplace violence and asserted that "the stories continue at hundreds of workplaces each year" (*USA Today*, April 5, 1994). In an article in the *New York State Bar Journal*, DiLorenzo and Carroll (1995) recounted the crimes of Richard Farley and two other disgruntled employees, conceding that though "these three incidents may shock the reader, they illustrate an increasingly serious problem facing both management and workers: violence in the workplace."

The solutions proposed to address workplace violence have generally included proactive strategies such as pre-employment screening, increasing security, and threat assessment; a crisis plan that deals with a violent incident when it occurs; and reactive measures like public relations damage control and employee re-entry programs (Anfuso, 1994; Cawood, 1991; Johnson, Kiehlbauch, and Kinney, 1994; Minor, 1995; Slora, Joy, and Terris, 1991). Despite the fact that co-worker violence is rare, much of the attention has focused on pre-employment screening and threat assessment, which are tailored to identify potentially violent workers. Larson (1994) points out, for example, that workplace violence consultants typically "concentrate on co-worker violence to the exclusion of far more common robbery-related murders. Antiviolence seminars for corporate executives have proliferated, and can convey the impression that massacres are almost commonplace." As reported earlier, however, workplace massacres are far from commonplace, for they occurred, on average, less than once every two years during the twentieth century. Yet, as Larson (1994) notes, workplace violence consultants have profited greatly from the corporate fear engendered by the panic that to some extent they helped create. Although the emergence of the workplace violence panic can be traced to other factors such as the alleged rise in lawsuits against businesses failing to anticipate employee violence, workplace massacres have undoubtedly fostered the recognition of workplace violence as a serious problem. In doing so, these incidents shaped the perception of the problem that, in turn, justified the implementation of violence prevention programs as well as increased involvement by government agencies such as the CDC, NIOSH, and OSHA.

Mass Murder as a School Violence Problem

Most recently, mass murder has been framed as a school violence problem. Beginning in 1997, a string of school shootings took place throughout the United States. Luke Woodham killed three and wounded seven in Pearl, Mississippi; Michael Carneal fatally shot three and wounded five more in Paducah, Kentucky; Kip Kinkel murdered four and wounded 22 in Oregon; and Mitchell Johnson and Andrew Golden shot fifteen victims, five fatally, in Jonesboro, Arkansas. But the incident that came to define the essence of the school violence problem was the now infamous Columbine massacre in Littleton, Colorado, in 1999. Garnering international media coverage and intense public interest, the Columbine massacre has served as the landmark narrative for the school violence problem and has led to adoption of zero tolerance policies at schools and fevered debate over how the nation's youth are affected by bullying and violent media, especially video games. The concern over school shootings has surged once again following the April 16, 2007, massacre at Virginia Tech, where disgruntled student Seung-Hui Cho gunned down 32 before committing suicide.

The spate of school shootings carried out by adolescent males during the late 1990s was, to a large extent, unprecedented. To be sure, there were mass murders that had taken place in schools prior to 1997. Andrew Kehoe killed 43 victims, most of them children, with explosives in Bath, Michigan, in 1927; school principal Verling Spencer fatally shot five colleagues in Pasadena, California, in 1940; Paul Harold Orgeron killed six victims with a bomb on a Houston schoolyard in 1959; Charles Whitman claimed the lives of 16 victims, 14 at the University of Texas at Austin in 1966; Edward Allaway murdered seven victims at the Cal State-Fullerton campus in 1976; Patrick Purdy killed five at a Stockton, California, schoolyard in 1989; and Gang Lu murdered five on the University of Iowa campus in 1991.

None of these incidents, however, were committed by juveniles. Of 828 mass killings that took place between 1900 and 1996, there were 47 incidents (6 percent) that involved 65 juveniles as offenders. Not one of these incidents, however, was a mass public shooting, which, prior to 1997, had been committed exclusively by adult males. Instead, juvenile mass murderers are more likely to either kill their parents and siblings in a familicide or to be involved in a felony-related massacre.

The series of school massacres that began in 1997 was thus, to a large extent, a historically new phenomenon. But the identification of juvenile mass killers as a new problem is also a microcosm of mass murder in general. Recall, for example, that even though there was a mass murder wave in the 1920s and 1930s, which was comprised mainly of familicides and felony-related massacres, mass murder was not constructed as a new crime problem until the mid–1960s, when the incidence of mass public shootings began to accelerate. Similarly, prior to 1997, juvenile mass murderers were not recognized as a problem because they, for the most part, committed familicides and felony-related massacres, which are the least newsworthy mass murders. But when juveniles began using guns to kill large numbers of innocent victims in public locations — factors that increase the newsworthiness of a mass murder — it was only then that they were identified as a new problem.

Why mass murder never developed into a full-blown moral panic

Although claimsmakers achieved some success in constructing mass murder, there are several reasons why it did not develop into a full-blown moral panic. First, unlike other crime problems such as serial murder, for example, wherein claimsmakers grossly exaggerated its incidence, scholars like Fox and Levin noted that even though mass murder was on the rise, it was still rare. As a result, this may have tempered the urgency to do something about the mass murder problem.

Second, although Fox and Levin established ownership of mass murder, there were never any claimsmakers who had a vested interest in promoting the problem. If anything, the news media promoted the mass murder problem by presenting feature stories and editorials in response to high-profile cases. As Best (1991) points out, however, problems constructed by the press are often short-lived because media attention is ephemeral. Although there are, on average, two mass murders a month, which, given the seriousness of the crime would be enough to sustain interest, only a small minority gain widespread publicity. Consequently, because there are only about four or five high-profile cases per year, the supply of incidents is usually too low to attract and maintain prolonged media coverage. However, during the late 1980s and early 1990s, there were several times when high-profile cases clustered together, prompting the news media to run feature stories on the growing problem of mass murder.

Finally, claimsmakers limited their chances for success by framing mass murder as a gun problem. To be sure, claimsmakers effectively used high-profile mass murders to bring about a federal assault weapon ban in 1994. However, some of the more ambitious proposals to control mass murder, such as a ban on handguns, were met with resistance due to the entrenched debate over gun control.

Conclusion

This study has shown that, contrary to popular belief, the mid–1960s did not mark the onset of an unprecedented and ever-growing mass murder wave. Rather, mass murder was nearly as common during the 1920s and 1930s as it has been since the mid–'60s. The increase in mass murder during the '20s and '30s may have been due to the agricultural depression and rising divorce and unemployment rates, for most of the mass killings were familicides and felony-related massacres. However, because these are among the least newsworthy mass killings, mass murder failed to attract much attention, not only at that time but also later on when claimsmakers began to make historical claims about it.

Following a period of low mass murder rates during the 1940s and '50s, mass murder began to increase sharply in the mid–'60s. This increase paralleled the rise in general homicide, and indeed crime as a whole. Although mass murder rates fluctuated wildly, they stayed relatively high for the rest of the century. While the most recent mass murder wave has been marked by the emergence of the drug-related massacre, it eventually attracted the attention of claimsmakers because of the rise in mass public shootings — the most newsworthy mass murders.

After mass murder was redefined in the early 1980s, claimsmakers adduced the surge in high-profile cases since the mid–1960s as evidence of an unprecedented mass murder wave. Drawing upon the high-profile cases, claimsmakers typified mass murder by characterizing it as a gun and, to a lesser extent, as a workplace and school violence problem. Claimsmakers were modestly successful in constructing mass murder, as they were able to use high-profile cases to bring about a federal ban on assault weapons and changes in policy concerning workplace and school violence.

Although the news media have had a decisive influence on the social construction of mass murder, this influence has produced a number of distorted claims. The distortion emanates from the news media's financial imperative to attract as many consumers as possible in order to turn a profit, which involves selecting informative yet entertaining stories for presentation. With respect to crime news, the emphasis on the unusual and the melodramatic has led to an overrepresentation of violent, interpersonal crimes and to an underrepresentation of the far more prevalent property and white-collar crime. But with mass murder, the distortion results not so much from whether incidents get reported — since almost all receive at least local coverage — but from the extent to which they get reported. As shown earlier, the cases that garner widespread attention are perhaps the least representative examples of mass murder. What makes this significant is that the news media have been the primary, if not the sole, source of information on mass killings not just for the general public, but also for scholars and other claimsmakers. But those making claims about mass murder have not demonstrated an awareness of the biases associated with using national news coverage as a source of data. Therefore, by uncritically using the atypical high-profile cases, claimsmakers have made a number of questionable assertions, not only about long-term trends in the prevalence of mass murder but also about the characteristics of the typical mass killing. And the news media have been the chief means through which these claims have been promulgated, thus completing the circle of distortion.

But considering that news organizations must be profitable in order to survive, perhaps it is too much to expect the news media to deliver news that depicts the social reality of mass murder — or crime for that matter — nearly as accurately as government statistics or social science research. After all, journalists are not trained as criminologists and are bound by a different set of constraints; most notably, the tight deadlines under which they operate. Moreover, given that the news media have to attract as many consumers as possible, news organizations are compelled — to a large extent — to give the public what it wants. And since the inception of the penny press in the early nineteenth century, the public has shown that it wants news not only about crime, but about unusual, dramatic, violent crimes.

In light of the seller-buyer relationship between the news media and the public, the news media will probably always present a distorted image of crime. This is not to say, however, that news coverage cannot or should not be used as a source of information on mass murder or on other crimes for which data are not readily available. On the contrary, news accounts have constituted a vital source of information not just for previous research on mass murder, but for this study as well. In addition, newspaper articles have been an important source of data in studies on serial murder (Hickey, 1990; Jenkins, 1989), lynching (Tolnay and Beck, 1995) and homicide (Eckberg, 2001). More important, though, considering that most crime news is obtained directly from the police, the distortion lies not so much in what gets reported, but in what does not get reported. As a result, the distortion seemingly inherent to crime news simply places a greater responsibility on researchers to recognize and take into account the limitations of using news coverage as a source of data, much as they do with official crime data like the Uniform Crime Reports.

In addition to highlighting the limitations of the news media, this study has also illustrated the advantages of utilizing both the objectivist and social constructionist approaches in delineating the history of mass murder in twentieth-century America. There are still some, however, who might criticize this research on the grounds that it did not focus exclusively on claimsmaking but examined the social conditions of mass murder as well. Best (1995) has argued, for example, that the objective conditions of a social problem should never be the focus of constructionist analyses. To evaluate the validity of claims made about a social problem, constructionist studies typically use government statistics to describe the conditions of the problem. The use of such data is, to be sure, largely a function of the emphasis placed on examining the claimsmaking process. But it also has another effect: it helps obscure the objectivist assumptions on which constructionist analyses rely. Although the means by which the data are acquired may differ between previous constructionist studies and this research, the purpose, or end, remains the same — to describe the objective conditions of the social problem. Scholars should, therefore, not have to limit their inquiries to problems on which data have already been collected. Nor should they ignore issues central to social constructionist analyses simply because it might be construed as objectivist.

On the contrary, by using both the objectivist and social constructionist perspectives, this study has provided a richer, more penetrating level of analysis. For example, had I concentrated only on delineating the patterns and prevalence of mass murder, I would not have been able to explain why and how it was constructed as a new crime problem in the 1980s. Conversely, had I focused exclusively on the claimsmaking process, I would not have been able to show that the mid–1960s marked the beginning of the second, rather than the first, mass murder wave in the twentieth century. Nor would I have been able to show that in typifying mass murder, claimsmakers used the most celebrated and least representative instances of mass murder.

Although this study has attempted to provide a better understanding of mass murder in twentieth-century America, there are still a number of promising possibilities for future research. For example, previous studies have not systematically examined mass murder in the U.S. prior to 1900. In an earlier study, Cohen (1995) looked at seven familicides that occurred in the U.S. during the late eighteenth and early nineteenth centuries. Of the seven cases, only five would be classified as mass killings according to the definition used here since two of the familicides did not meet the four fatal victim requirement. Nevertheless, the killers Cohen studied were, similar to the familicides examined here, depressed and, in a few instances, psychotic males who murdered their families out of either delusional jealousy or a warped sense of altruism. The inner turmoil that plagued these offenders, Cohen argues, was both engendered and exacerbated by the rapid social change that occurred during the early republic, not least the expansion of individual autonomy.

While the cases examined by Cohen suggest that little has changed with familicides in the U.S. over the last few centuries, they almost certainly represent a small portion of the mass murders that occurred prior to 1900. Before the twentieth century, the conflict between Native Americans and white settlers produced a litany of mass killings, many of which were committed in retaliation for property theft or previous acts of violence. In Gnadenhutten, Ohio, in 1782, Pennsylvania militiamen murdered 106 Native American men, women and children to avenge the kidnappings and deaths of a few white pioneers. In 1824, six white settlers murdered six Seneca and Miami Indians in the Fall Creek massacre that took place in Madison County, Indiana. Eight years later, between 800 and 1,000 Native Americans were killed by U.S. troops in Bad Axe, Wisconsin. The massacre was carried out in response to the massacre of four white families earlier that year in Dekalb County, Illinois.

Following the discovery of gold at Sutter's Mill in 1848, California was the site of a large influx of white settlers hoping to "strike it rich." It was also the site of a spate of mass killings, as the settlers, who were generally uprooted young males, clashed with the local Indian tribes. In 1850, approximately 150 Pomo Indians were killed in the Clear Lake massacre and at least 150 members of the Wintu tribe were murdered in the 1852 Bridge Gulch massacre. The following year, several hundred Tolowa

Indians were murdered by white settlers during their harvest dance at Yontoket, and 13 Indians were killed to avenge theft of livestock near Sacramento (Osborn, 2000). And in 1860, at least 80 Wiyot were murdered by locals in Eureka, California.

The violence committed by whites against the California Indians eventually subsided by the early 1860s, but it still continued in other parts of the country. In 1863, for example, roughly 250 Shoshone were slaughtered in the Bear River massacre in the state of Washington, and 150 Cheyennes and Arapahos were murdered by U.S. troops in the 1864 Sand Creek massacre. The following decade, 118 Apaches—eight men and 110 women—were killed by white settlers in the 1871 Camp Grant massacre in Arizona, and 17 Modoc Indians were murdered by Oregon volunteers in 1873 (Osborn, 2000). Finally, approximately 300 Sioux were murdered by U.S. troops in the 1890 Wounded Knee massacre in South Dakota.

The genocide of Native Americans perpetrated, in large part, by the U.S. government represents one of the darkest chapters in American history. Of course, the violence was hardly one-sided, however, as whites were the victims in a score of mass killings, some of which involved torture and cannibalism. In New York in 1778, nearly 40 whites were killed and eaten by Seneca and Mohawk Indians in the Cherry Valley massacre (Osborn, 2000). Seven years later, four members of the Scott family were murdered by Indians in Virginia. In 1813, seven families were killed by Chickasaw Indians in Pulaski County, Illinois. And in 1847, 11 whites were murdered by five Cayuse Indians in the Oregon territory.

Dr. Marcus Whitman, after whom this massacre was named, headed West in 1836 to set up a mission for the American Board of Commissioners for Foreign Missions. Like other Indian tribes, the Cayuse were ravaged by disease after coming into contact with white settlers. In the two months leading up to the massacre, almost half the tribe died from measles and smallpox. Because the medicine Whitman had been giving to the Cayuse had done little to stem the epidemic and, in fact, seemed to make it worse, they thought he was trying to poison them. Thus, on November 29, five Cayuse murdered Whitman and 10 others, a crime for which they were hanged in 1850.

The hostilities between Native Americans and whites provided a disturbing number of mass killings carried out, or at least sanctioned, by the U.S. government. The 1838 Haun's Mill massacre offers another example; this time, however, the mass murder was committed not for the sake of American imperialism, but for religious persecution. In 1829, Joseph Smith completed the Book of Mormon and the following year established the Church of Jesus Christ of Latter-day Saints in New York. Facing heated opposition, members of the church moved to Ohio and then again to Missouri in 1836. Shortly after their arrival, however, the Mormon community came into conflict with the local residents in Caldwell County. On October 27, after a series of violent incidents, Missouri governor Lilburn Boggs issued an order that called for the extermination or forcible removal of all Mormons in the state. Three days later, 250 militiamen carried out the order, killing 18 and wounding 13 at Haun's Mill. Within days, the Mormons moved from Missouri, eventually settling in Utah seven years later.

Just as the Indian Wars produced occasions in which military fighting mutated into mass murder, so, too, did the Civil War. Most of these massacres occurred near the Kansas-Missouri border, where bitter fighting had raged since the passage of the Kansas-Nebraska Act in 1854. In 1858, for example, 11 free-state men were murdered by proslavery forces in the Marais des Cygnes massacre in Kansas. But with the start of the Civil War, the fighting only intensified, as dramatically illustrated by the 1863 massacre in Lawrence, Kansas. In August of that year, Union troops arrested a number of women suspected of providing aid to William C. Quantrill and his band of Border Ruffians, who terrorized Kansas border towns since the start of the war. On August 14th, the dilapidated jail in which the women were being kept collapsed, killing four and seriously injuring many others. For Quantrill and his men, who had already for months been planning an attack on Lawrence, this added further grist to the mill. A week later, they invaded Lawrence and killed nearly all its male inhabitants, which numbered a little over 150. Sparing the women and children, who nevertheless witnessed the murders of their husbands and fathers, Quantrill and his men burned and pillaged Lawrence before fleeing back across the border to Missouri.

As mentioned earlier in Chapter 2, a number of mass killings occurred in the late 1800s in connection with the labor movement. For example, on May 5, 1886, just one day after the much better known Haymarket Square Riot, the Bay View massacre took place in Milwaukee. As with the Haymarket tragedy in Chicago, workers in Milwaukee organized a parade in support of the eight-hour workday. After several days of demonstrations, approximately 10,000 workers went on strike. At the behest of employers in the city, Wisconsin governor Jeremiah Rusk called out the state militia to try to enforce order. When roughly 1,500 marchers approached the Bay View Rolling Mill, the militia fired into the crowd, killing seven. No one was ever indicted for these killings.

The following year, at least 30 black sugar cane workers were murdered in the Thibodaux massacre in Louisiana. Like the Ludlow massacre discussed in Chapter 2, these workers had virtually every aspect of their lives controlled by their employers, the planters. They lived in homes owned by the planters, and were paid about a half dollar per day in coupons redeemable only at the company store, which had grossly inflated prices and was, of course, run by the planters. As a result, sugar cane workers often went into debt and, according to Louisiana state law, could not move off the land until it was paid off.

Shortly after establishing a local Knights of Labor chapter in Thibodaux, workers presented a list of demands to the Louisiana Sugar Producers Association (LSPA) in late October 1887. After the LSPA summarily rejected their request for increased pay, the elimination of coupons, and the receipt of a paycheck every two weeks, the workers struck on November 1, the start of "rolling" season. Concerned that they would lose money due to frozen crops, the planters asked Governor McEnery, himself a former planter, to send in the state militia to evict the workers from their homes and to provide protection for the strikebreakers. With no place to live, the black workers began to congregate in Thibodaux, where rumors started circulating that they were going to burn the city down. After two white citizens were fired upon, vigilantes reacted by killing as many as 30 blacks on the morning of November 23, 1887 (Rodrigue, 2001).

Although extreme, the Thibodaux massacre was unfortunately an all-too-common occurrence in the post–Civil War South. To be sure, the surrender at Appomattox brought about an end to slavery, but it did little to alter the racial caste system in the South. Shortly after the end of the war, state legislatures created laws (i.e., "Black Codes") designed to preserve white dominance. Although unsuccessful due to active Northern intervention during Reconstruction, legal efforts to maintain the subjugation of blacks later became a reality with the passage of Jim Crow laws.

Violence was another popular form of social control, as evidenced most dramatically by the Ku Klux Klan and other similar white supremacist organizations that focused on terrorizing the black population. Indeed, the end of the war unleashed a wave of violence in the South, directed mostly against blacks but also against "northern carpetbaggers" and "southern scalawags." During Reconstruction, for example, there were at least ten deadly race riots in the South that claimed hundreds of black lives

(Tolnay and Beck, 1995). In addition to riots, lynching was another violent method used by Southern whites to scare and intimidate blacks. As noted earlier, Tolnay and Beck (1995) estimate that almost 2,500 blacks were the victims of lynchings from 1882–1930. And along with the aforementioned Thibodaux massacre, there were a number of mass killings, of which at least four took place in Louisiana. In 1866, for example, at least 48 blacks were murdered in the New Orleans massacre over voting rights; approximately 200 blacks lost their lives in the 1868 Opelousas massacre; nearly 60 blacks were killed in the 1873 Colfax massacre; and at least 20 more were murdered in the 1878 Caldonia massacre. Outside Louisiana, four blacks were murdered in the 1883 Danville, Virginia, mass killing; 20 more lives were lost in the 1886 Carrollton massacre in Mississippi; and at least 14 were killed in the 1898 Wilmington, North Carolina, massacre.

Although far from a complete inventory, the above discussion nevertheless indicates there were more than a few mass murders that took place in the U.S. prior to 1900. Previous historical research on murder in the U.S. suggests that homicide rates were as high or possibly even higher in the nineteenth century (Lane, 1997, 1999; McGrath, 1984; McKanna, 1997; Monkkonen, 2001). Thus, the U.S. homicide rates for the first two-thirds of the twentieth century may reflect a long-term decline in the prevalence of murder in America. The surge in homicide rates since the early 1960s, then, merely represents a return to previous levels of violence. Given that the findings in this study suggest that trends in the mass murder rate tend to parallel those for homicide, mass murder rates may have been higher in the nineteenth century than they were in the twentieth century.

By examining cases that took place prior to 1900, researchers could not only determine whether mass murder rates were higher in the eighteenth and nineteenth centuries, but they could also address important questions about the history of mass murder in the U.S. For example, perhaps the most striking feature about the pre–1900 cases discussed above is the apparent overrepresentation of Native Americans, blacks, and union workers — who were frequently recent immigrants — among the victims. Most of these cases were, therefore, mass killings committed by the powerful (i.e., the military, police, or whites) against the powerless. Given that the creation and enforcement of criminal laws often benefits those in power, it should come as little surprise that no one was ever indicted for most of the mass murders listed above. And the few times the offenders were charged and convicted (or killed in retaliation) were usually when whites were the victims.

At the very least, the occurrence of these incidents prior to 1900, and their relative absence since the 1930s, constitutes a shift in the patterns of mass murder in U.S. history. During the twentieth century, for example, mass murders were usually carried out by a lone offender who felt helpless and ineffectual, either in providing for his family or in holding on to his wife or job. The twentieth-century massacres, then, were generally not instances in which the "haves" murdered the "have-nots." What remains to be seen, however, is whether this shift was a substantial one; that is, were these cases representative of mass murder prior to 1900?

Research on mass murder before the twentieth century could also shed light on several other questions concerning the history of mass killings in America. For example, were familicides still the modal mass murder before 1900? Are mass public shootings and, more narrowly, workplace massacres a relatively new historical phenomenon? If so, is the emergence of these incidents due to the urbanization of America or to other social forces? Moreover, were guns used as frequently in mass killings as they have been in the twentieth century? Were the demographic characteristics of mass killers significantly different prior to 1900? And were they more or less suicidal?

Another promising avenue for future research is the study of mass murder in other countries besides the U.S. The academic and popular literature has suggested that mass murder is a uniquely American phenomenon, or is at least much more prevalent in the States. But the origin of terms such as "running amok" and "berserk" implies that mass murder is clearly not isolated to the U.S. For example, "amok," a Malayan word, refers to a form of psychosis characterized by a brief, sudden outburst of homicidal violence (Arboleda-Florenz, 1979, p. 289; Macdonald, 1986, p. 140). The incidence of amok in Malaysia dates back to at least the sixteenth century, although some reports indicate that amok has prevailed since the beginning of recorded history (Arboleda-Florenz, 1979, p. 291; Macdonald, 1986, p. 140). Research indicates that cases of amok generally follow a similar pattern in which the amok runner — armed with a curved knife (kris), chopper (parang), rifle, or grenades — indiscriminately kills everyone in his path — friends, family, or strangers — until he is killed or is safely restrained (Arboleda-Florenz, 1979, p. 289; Macdonald, 1986, p. 140; Schmidt, Hill, and Guthrie, 1977, p. 264). Further, studies suggest that amok runners generally experience a precipitating event, frequently suffer from personality disorders, and are often under the influence of alcohol. Moreover, amok runners usually commit suicide after the attack, which is typically carried out in a crowded location with the most destructive weapon available (Arboleda-Florenz, 1979, p. 289; Schmidt et al., 1977, p. 264; Westermeyer, 1972, p. 707).

The term "berserk," on the other hand, is derived from a type of killer that disrupted the Viking community between A.D. 870 and 1030 (Macdonald, 1986, p. 139). On occasion, a man would become seized by a wild fury (I. e. "berserksgang") that would culminate in the death of everyone who happened to cross his path (Macdonald, 1986, p. 140). Afterwards, the berserker was often overcome by a great dulling of the mind and feebleness that could last for one or several days (Macdonald, 1986, p. 140).

More recently, a number of well-publicized mass killings have occurred outside the U.S. For example, Michael Ryan killed 16 in Hungerford, England, in 1987; Marc Lepine fatally shot 14 in Montreal, Canada, in 1989; Thomas Hamilton killed 17, all but one of them children, in Dunblane, Scotland, in 1996; and Martin Bryant gunned down 35 in Australia in 1996. As these incidents suggest, even for massacres that occur outside the U.S., the most newsworthy cases tend to be public shootings with high body counts. But in light of the findings reported earlier, it is reasonable to infer that the high-profile cases may not be valid indicators of the patterns and prevalence of mass murder for countries outside the U.S. In particular, the apparent infrequency with which high-profile cases have occurred abroad does not necessarily mean that mass murder is much more prevalent in the U.S. After all, the results reported here showed that there was a mass murder wave in the 1920s and '30s despite the relative paucity of celebrated cases prior to the mid–1960s.

Because previous research has not systematically examined mass murder in other countries besides the U.S, especially in other high-violence nations, conducting cross-national research may yield important insights about the patterns and prevalence of mass murder. For example, are trends in the prevalence of mass murder in other countries similar to those in the U.S.? What is the most common form of mass murder — terrorism, familicides or some other type? Are the incident, victim, and offender characteristics for non–U.S. massacres significantly different than those in the U.S.? In particular, are guns used as frequently in mass killings that occur abroad? And how does their level of availability affect the mass murder rate?

Given that previous studies have been largely descriptive, future research should also look at what causes mass murder. There have been a few studies that have speculated on the etiology of mass murder. Hall (1989) suggests, for example, that biochemical imbalances may play a role in the development of the mass murderer after he found significantly elevated lead and cadmium levels in a hair trace analysis of Patrick Sherrill, who killed 14 and wounded 6 during a shooting spree at an Edmond, Oklahoma, post office in 1986. Hempel and colleagues (1999) posit that mental illness is an important etiological factor. In their study of 30 mass killers, they found that half had a documented psychiatric history in which the most common diagnoses were paranoid schizophrenia and major depression. In addition, a few studies have noted that mass murderers are loners who often experience precipitating events such as the loss of a job or a relationship (Fox and Levin, 1994; Hempel et al., 1999). It is unclear, however, whether mass killers are more likely than others to have biochemical imbalances, to suffer from mental illness, or to experience these types of precipitating events. Future research should therefore examine comparison groups from offending and non-offending populations to determine whether the backgrounds of mass killers are significantly different.

Considering that accurate annual data on mass murder are available since 1976, it is also possible to look at what, if anything, affects the incidence of mass killings. Fox and Levin (1994), for example, have offered an explanation for why mass murder has become much more prevalent since the mid–1960s. Drawing upon the descriptive characteristics of mass murder, they assert that rising divorce and unemployment rates, increased social isolation, greater residential mobility, a growing percentage of middle-aged men, and easy access to firearms have had an impact on recent trends in the incidence of mass killings. And in this study, I have suggested that other factors such as religiosity may have had an effect on trends in the prevalence of mass murder. Using annual data since 1976, it would be possible to conduct a macro-level analysis by examining whether factors such as divorce, unemployment, social isolation or religiosity have had an impact on the incidence of mass murder.

There still remains much to be studied about mass murder. But there is also much to gain from obtaining a clearer understanding of its causes and correlates. Although mass murder is an extreme and, fortunately, rare form of violence, examining the exceptions can sometimes lead to a better grasp of the factors that make up the rule. This study has elucidated, for example, not only the nature and incidence of mass murder across the twentieth century, but also the news media's presentation of crime, the social construction of crime problems, and other issues such as the copy-cat effect. By studying mass murder, then, we may be able to deepen our understanding of what causes it. But in doing so, we may also be able to increase our understanding of the causal factors related to homicide and perhaps even crime in general.

Appendix:
Data and Methods

Data and Search Methodology

Two main sources supplied data on mass killings that took place between 1900 and 1999: the FBI's Supplementary Homicide Reports (SHR) data and newspaper accounts. Because the SHR contain incident, victim, and offender information on most homicides reported to the police, they are invaluable source of data on mass murder. Nevertheless, there are several limitations to using the SHR. Most notably, although introduced in 1961, the SHR did not become a valuable source of data until it underwent a major revision in 1976 (Riedel, 1999, p. 38–9). As a result, for the 1976–1999 period, I used both the SHR and newspaper articles as sources of data. For the 1900–1975 period, however, I relied on news accounts from the *New York Times*.

The decision to use the *Times* was based on its availability, its reputation for offering readers a national coverage of the news, and its being perhaps the most thoroughly indexed newspaper in this country, especially for the earlier decades of the twentieth century. There are two main problems, however, with using this source for data on cases that occurred before 1976. First, it is likely that the *Times* underreported the incidence of mass murder from 1900 through 1975 due to limitations on time and space. Indeed, only 45 percent of the mass killings that occurred between 1976 and 1999 were reported by the *Times*. Second, it is likely that the *Times* will provide a somewhat distorted image of mass murder because the news media prefer to report crimes that are sensational and out of the ordinary. As discussed shortly, I attempted to address these shortcomings by using data from the 1976–1999 period.

1900–1975

To find news accounts on mass killings that occurred before 1976, I searched the *Times* index for the years 1900–1975. I located articles by examining the description of each story listed in the following index categories: murders and attempted murders, shootings (this category was introduced in 1948), arson, fires, bomb explosions (changed to "bomb explosions, plots, and warnings" in 1930 and then to "bombs and bomb plots" in 1957), and mass murder (introduced in 1982). The story descriptions in the *Times* index often provided enough information to identify the cases that were mass killings. For some cases, however, it was not as readily apparent whether they were mass murders because their story descriptions were either too vague or too brief. I gathered news reports on any case that might be a mass murder to increase the chances of locating every mass killing reported by the *Times*.

The search identified 403 cases that were potential mass murders. After reading the news accounts on these cases, I determined that 259 met the criteria for mass murder classification. The other 144 cases were excluded because the news reports indicated that they were spree or serial murders, they did not meet the four fatal victim requirement, or they occurred outside the U.S. There was at least one instance in which the *Times* failed to index a story on a mass killing. When reading the *Times'* coverage of the murders committed by Richard Speck, I found an article on the familicide committed by Elias Vargas in Newark, New Jersey, on July 22, 1966. The *Times* reported that Vargas killed himself after murdering his common-law wife and three children. Short of poring over every page of the *Times* from 1900 through 1975, it is difficult to know with certainty how many articles on mass killings were missed because they were not listed in the index. It is worth noting, however, that I did not find any additional unlisted cases when I conducted a similar search of the *Times'* index for stories on mass killings from 1976 through 1999.

After including the Vargas case, the search revealed 875 articles on 260 mass killings that occurred between 1900 and 1975. I recorded the number of stories the *Times* presented on each of the 260 incidents. In addition, I examined the articles to record data on the same variables used for the 1976–1999 period.[1] The *Times* articles usually provided enough detail to record data on most of these variables. However, determining the race of victims and offenders was often difficult because the *Times* seldom identified the race of persons involved in mass killings. And when race was mentioned, it was almost always in reference to minorities. For example, when Julian Carlston killed six and wounded four in Chicago in 1914, the *Times* referred to him as a "wild negro." Likewise, Julian Marcelino was called a "mad Filipino" after he killed six and wounded fifteen with a bolo knife in Seattle in 1932. In contrast, the *Times* never described a mass murderer as a "crazed white man" or as a "white gunman who went berserk." In fact, the only instances where the *Times* mentioned the race of white victims and offenders were when they were involved in interracial massacres. In 1946, the *Times* instituted a policy that prohibited mentioning the race of minorities, especially in crime stories, unless it was "germane" (Tifft and Jones, 1999, p. 275).

Given the *Times'* practice of selectively identifying the race of minorities, at least until 1946, it is reasonable to infer that many of the victims and offenders whose race was not mentioned were white. Rather than recording these cases as missing, I coded victims and offenders as white when race was not identified. Although this probably provides a more accurate representation of the racial distribution among victims and offenders, it will still inflate the percentages of white victims and offenders. Consequently, the results pertaining to race should be interpreted with a great deal of caution, especially from 1947 to 1975.

1976–1999

SHR data revealed there were 775 homicide incidents involving four or more victims that occurred between 1976 and 1999. Although the SHR contain incident, victim, and offender data on the homicides that are reported, they do not include important information such as the specific location where the homicide took place (e.g., residential location, public setting, etc.) or the outcome of the case (e.g., offender(s) were arrested, offender committed suicide, etc.). Still, because the SHR include data on the reporting law enforcement agency and the month and year in which each recorded homicide took place, they provide an excellent means by which to locate more detailed news accounts on mass killings. Using the SHR data to determine when and where the 775 incidents took place, I conducted an exhaustive search of the newspaper databases in Lexis-Nexis, Dialog@CARL, and CD Newsbank in an effort to locate every news account on each mass murder reported to the SHR. Aside from their availability, I used these databases because they collectively offer a relatively large number of news sources, including major newspapers such as the *New York Times*, newspapers with smaller circulations that are more regional in coverage, and articles from newswires such as the Associated Press (AP) and United Press International (UPI).

To find newspaper articles in the databases, I used connected search terms including the name of the city or county in which the massacre took place along with a descriptive word like "murder," although I used other terms such as "homicide," "shot," "shooting," "stabbed," "slayings," "killed," "dead," "fire," and "arson."[2] Depending on the database, I initially placed limits on the search in terms of the dates covered (i.e., month and year in which the incident occurred) in order to cut down on the number of items returned. For the cases that could not be found with the initial pair of search terms, I broadened the investigation so that the state name was used in place of the city or county name, while the time frame was extended to approximately five years after the crime took place.

If the database search for an SHR-recorded incident was unsuccessful, I examined indexes from the *New York Times, Chicago Tribune, Washington Post, Atlanta Journal-Constitution*, and *Los Angeles Times* to locate cases that might have been missed by the search terms used in the databases. For the few incidents found by inspecting these five newspaper indexes, I conducted a follow-up database search to more easily account for these cases. Once a case was located, I used the offender's or victims' names (most often the offender) in a succession of follow-up searches to uncover all additional news reports that may have been missed by the previous search terms. The newspaper articles found on each mass murder were examined to record additional information not provided by the SHR.[3]

The following case, which is a fairly typical example, illustrates the search methodology. As indicated by the SHR, the New Mexico state police reported that a massacre took place in January 1991 in which a 28-year-old white male killed seven white victims (three females and four males) whose victim-offender relationship was classified as "other known." The weapon the offender used was a rifle and the circumstance listed was "other." In the initial database search, I used the terms "murder" and "New Mexico" (the city or county name was unavailable since the state police agency reported the homicides), while the search was limited to the dates between January 1, 1991, and February 5, 1991, in order to reduce the number of articles returned. This search returned 11 items, all of which were news reports on the incident. I compared the newspaper data to that provided by the SHR and determined that there was a match between the two data sources. The news reports indicated that the seven homicides took place in Chimayo, New Mexico, on January 26 and that the offender's name was Ricky Abeyta. The newspaper accounts further revealed that Abeyta fled after murdering his ex-girlfriend, four of her relatives, and two law enforcement officers who attempted to intervene. Abeyta was the subject of a 24-hour manhunt before he surrendered to police.

In the initial follow-up inquiry, I used the terms "Abeyta" and "murder" and found five news reports, whereas the search with the term "Ricky Abeyta" returned 20 articles. I did not find any additional news reports when I used different search terms or when I inspected the newspaper indexes. The newspaper data found in the later stages of the search process indicated that the murders committed by Abeyta were the culmination of a tumultuous relationship with his girlfriend, Ignacita Sandoval, after she terminated their relationship and attempted to move her belongings from his home. Abeyta was convicted and later sentenced to 146 years in prison.

During the database search for the 775 incidents, I found news accounts on 55 mass killings not reported to the SHR.[4] In addition, I removed 71 cases that were not mass murders, 64 because they were inaccurately recorded by the SHR and 7 because they were either spree or serial murders. To address concerns that murderous intent is absent in the vast majority of SHR-reported homicides involving the use of fire (Fox and Levin, 1998), I included fire-related cases only if one of the offenders was convicted of murder (felony murder or murder in the first or second degree) or was found to have committed suicide.[5] I also used this criterion for the 1900–1975 period. Of the 193 SHR-reported cases involving the use of fire, 83 met the criteria for mass murder classification.[6]

Overall, I found newspaper accounts on 576 of the 649 cases (89 percent) from 1976 through 1999. Of the 73 incidents that were not located through the newspaper search, more than one-third (26) took place in 1976 and 1977, which is likely because most news sources did not fully cover the 1976 to 1999 time frame. That is, there were often no data for most of the news sources for the beginning years of the 1976–1999 period. It is highly probable that most, if not all, of the unlocated cases were reported at least locally by the news media and that the failure to account for these cases stems from this deficiency of resources. But it is also possible that at least some were not found due to undetected reporting errors; that is, they might not have been mass murders. Nevertheless, the 73 cases on which news accounts were not found were included in the analyses, resulting in a total of 649 mass killings for the 1976–1999 period and a total of 909 for the full 1900–1999 period.

By attempting to locate news accounts on each mass murder reported to the SHR from 1976 through 1999, I was able to address several short-comings associated with these data. First, because the SHR is a voluntary program involving law enforcement agencies nationwide, an estimated 8 percent of all homicides are not reported (Fox, 2000, p. 291). I greatly min-imized the underreporting problem by locating 55 cases not reported to the SHR. Given that my sample from 1976 through 1999 consists of 649 cases, this figure is consistent with the 8 percent estimate reported by Fox. Second, previous research has noted that the SHR contain a number of reporting errors (Wiersema, Loftin, and McDowall, 2000). I significantly reduced this source of measurement error by removing 64 miscoded cases that were not mass murders. Finally, instead of excluding every fire-related case, as Fox and Levin (1998) have done, I obtained a more accurate meas-ure of mass murder by including the 83 fire-related cases where it was evi-dent that murder was the predominant motive.

Estimating the Prevalence of Mass Murder from 1900 through 1999

To determine whether the mid–1960s marked the onset of an unprece-dented mass murder wave, I calculated estimates of the mass murder rate from 1900 through 1999. For the 1976–1999 period, I obtained annual rates by counting the number of massacres that occurred within a given year and then determining the rate per 100,000 people. A different approach is needed to calculate annual rates for the 1900–1975 period because it is almost certain that the *Times* underreports the frequency of mass killings. However, even though the *Times* reported only 45 percent of the massacres that took place between 1976 and 1999, there is, perhaps somewhat surprisingly, a fairly high correlation (r = .74) between the annual number of *Times*-reported cases and the total yearly number of mass killings for the 24-year period. Because the *Times* appears to be a decent indicator of trends in the overall mass murder rate, I used information from the 1976–1999 period to estimate the *Times'* underreporting of mass killings from 1900 through 1975. More specifically, I attempted to address the underreporting problem by using a regression-based technique to estimate the mass murder rate from 1900 through 1975.

First, I counted the number of mass killings reported by the *Times* for each year during the 1900–1999 period and then calculated annual rates per 100,000 people. Next, I regressed the rates derived from the *Times* data for 1976–1999 (independent variable) on the overall mass murder rates from the same 24-year period (dependent variable) to yield the following equation

Annual Mass Murder Rate = a + (b × Annual *Times* Rate)

where a is the intercept and b is the slope. I used this equation, which measures the extent to which the *Times* underreported mass killings during 1976–1999, and the annual rates of the *Times*-reported cases during 1900–1975 to obtain estimates of the overall mass murder rate for the 1900–1975 period.

To illustrate, the *Times* rate for 1928 was .005809 because the *Times* reported seven mass murders that occurred in 1928 and the U.S. population for that year was 120,590,000. Inserting the 1928 *Times* rate into the regression equation yields the following point estimate for the 1928 mass murder rate

.01243 = .004775 + (1.3132 × .005809)

This estimation procedure is based, of course, on the assumption that the *Times*' presentation of mass murder did not change substantially over the 100-year period. A review of the literature on the history of the *Times* reveals that there have been a number of changes over the years (Berger, 1951; Faber, 1963; Goulden, 1988; Stevens, 1991; Tifft and Jones, 1999). For example, in response to the advent of television, the *Times* began to provide greater depth and detail to compete for consumers (Goulden, 1988). In the 1960s, the editorial page became more strident and liberal, and there was an increased emphasis on investigative journalism. In the 1970s, the *Times* expanded from a two- to a four-section paper, and there was a surge in advocacy reporting. There is nothing from the literature, however, that indicates the *Times* was any more or less likely to report mass killings in the 1920s or 1930s, for example, than in the 1980s or 1990s (Goulden, 1988).

Analyzing the News Media's Coverage of Mass Murder

News reports undoubtedly provide a more detailed portrait of the incident, victim, and offender characteristics of mass murder during the twentieth century. But the use of news accounts as a source of data also yields an opportunity to examine the news media's presentation of mass murder. To this end, I performed analyses on the *Times'* coverage of 540 mass killings from 1900 through 1999 as well as on newspaper, network television news, and weekly newsmagazine coverage of 495 mass murders from 1976 through 1996. The following sections describe the methodology used for these analyses.

New York Times, 1900–1999

Two different types of analyses were performed on the *Times* data. The first type analyzed which characteristics affected whether a mass murder was reported by the *Times* during the 1976–1999 period, whereas the second type examined which characteristics influenced the number of stories the *Times* presented on the mass killings it reported from 1900 through 1999. Of the 649 mass killings that took place between 1976 and 1999, 280 were reported by the *Times*. A logistic regression model was estimated to assess the extent to which 22 predictors, which described the mass murder incidents, influenced the *Times* in its selection of mass killings for presentation.

To determine which characteristics affected the amount of attention the *Times* gave to the 540 incidents from 1900 through 1999, I first recorded the number of stories per incidents. The average number of stories presented per mass murder was 4.5, with a minimum of 1 and a maximum of 500. Next, I estimated an ordinary least squares (OLS) regression model in which 22 incident, victim, and offender variables, which described the mass murders, were regressed on a variable that measured the number of stories per incident. Because the SHR data were available only for the 1976–1999 period, I estimated OLS regression models for three different periods: 1900–1975, 1976–1999, and 1900–1999.

Newspapers, 1976–1996

To provide a broader perspective on the news media's presentation of mass murder, I analyzed newspaper coverage of 495 mass killings that took place between 1976 and 1996. During the newspaper search, I located 30,027 articles from 117 newspapers on the 495 incidents. The 117 newspapers were published in 41 of the 50 states, providing a national representation of newspaper coverage.

I began my analysis of the newspaper coverage by giving each mass murder located through the database search a newspaper score that measured the extent to which it was reported. The newspaper score derived from a scale developed on the premise that national public perceptions of mass murder are more likely to be influenced by cases that receive prominent and widespread news coverage. As such, I gave greater weight to articles in newspapers with larger circulations and to reports by news outlets that were geographically distant from the site where the massacre took place. The reasoning behind placing greater emphasis on these aspects of news coverage was to offset the bias that might be produced by simply measuring the newspaper score as the total number of news reports on a given mass murder. For instance, under such a scoring system a mass killing that garnered strictly local yet heavy media coverage might have a newspaper score greater than a more widely reported massacre that had fewer news reports, but had a more even distribution of local and non-local coverage.

I assigned each newspaper article on a given mass murder a value ranging from 1 to 7, with higher scores indicating greater prominence and visibility of news coverage. The values were based on both the circulation of the news source and the geographical relationship between the locations of the mass killing and the news source. On the basis of circulation, I placed newspapers in three categories: national, major, and non-major. The *New York Times, Chicago Tribune, Washington Post, Los Angeles Times,* and *USA Today* were placed in the national category because of their large circulation, their reputations for offering readers a national coverage of the news and because together they contribute to a sense of geographic representation. Newspapers other than these five were assigned to the major category if their circulation figures were among the top fifty daily newspapers according to *Editor & Publisher Yearbook* (1985–1997). I placed all remaining newspapers in the non-major or regional category. Greater importance was given to the newspapers in the national category because of the large readership and national prominence associated with these newspapers, whereas newspapers in the non-major category were weighted less than those in the major category because of their smaller circulation.

A news report was considered local if the location of the news source was within a 100-mile radius from the site where the mass murder took place. Thus, local news reports generally encompassed incidents occurring within the town, city, county, or metropolitan area of the reporting news source while massacres occurring outside this territory were regarded as non-local. I gave greater weight to non-local news reports because they tend to increase public awareness of a mass murder more than articles from local news sources.

As shown in Table 27, I assigned a value of 7 to articles by any of the newspapers in the national category on non-locally occurring mass murders. For example, if the *Washington Post* reported a mass killing that occurred in Chicago or Kansas City, the article was given a value of 7. I gave values of 6 and 5 to reports from newspapers in the major and non-major newspapers, respectively, when the mass murder occurred non-locally. I assigned a value of 4 to reports on locally-covered incidents by any of the newspapers in the national category. I gave values of 3 and 2 to articles on locally-occurring murders from newspapers in the major and non-major categories, respectively. If a massacre took place in Chicago, for example, and was reported by the *Chicago Tribune*, a value of 4 was given to the article, whereas a value of 3 was assigned to an article from the *San Diego Union-Tribune* on a mass murder occurring in San Diego. Finally, I gave a value of 1 to news reports from the major newswires found in the Lexis-Nexis and Dialog@CARL databases. Although this type of source was used to account for cases that did not receive newspaper coverage, the value given to newswire reports was also recorded for the incidents that were reported by newspapers.

Again, I use the Ricky Abeyta case to illustrate the scoring of the data and the calculation of the newspaper score since it is a fairly typical example. I found a total of 36 news reports on the Abeyta massacre. I gave values of 7 to each of the three articles reported by the *Los Angeles Times*, two articles apiece by the *New York Times* and *USA Today*, and one article apiece by the *Washington Post* and *Chicago Tribune*. The two articles from both the *Louisville Courier-Journal* and *Newsday* (New York), and the articles from the *St. Louis Post-Dispatch* and *Orlando Sentinel Tribune* were each given a value of 6. I gave values of 5 to the two articles from the *Record*

Table 27.
Newspaper Score

Score	Type of Coverage
1	Newswire Only
2	Non-major paper, local story
3	Major paper, local story
4	National paper, local story
5	Non-major paper, non-local story
6	Major paper, non-local story
7	National paper, non-local story

(Hackensack, NJ) and to articles reported by the *Memphis Commercial Appeal* and the *Washington Times*. The two articles from the *Santa Fe New Mexican* and the article from the *Albuquerque Journal* were given values of 2 (since both cities are within a 100-mile radius of Chimayo, New Mexico), while the 13 wire service reports were each assigned a value of 1. Adding up the values for each news report yielded a total newspaper score of 144 for the Abeyta case, which was close to the average for the 495 cases.

I analyzed newspaper coverage by conducting multiple regression analyses in which newspaper score was the dependent variable. The predictors, on the other hand, were 23 incident-, victim-, and offender-level variables. These variables, which describe the mass murder incidents, were derived from both the SHR and newspaper data. Because newspaper score was an incident-level measure, I converted the victim- and offender-level variables into incident-level measures to properly account for these variables in the regression analyses.

Network Television News, 1976–1996

I examined network television news coverage of mass murder by searching Vanderbilt University's Television News Archive, which has an electronic database containing transcribed evening newscasts from the three major television networks: ABC, NBC, and CBS. As in the newspaper search, I located television news reports by using a variety of search terms pertaining to characteristics such as date (e.g. month and year), location (e.g. city or state), and names of the victims and offenders. I created a dichotomous variable, TVNEWS, by assigning a value of "1" to the 104 cases that were presented by ABC, NBC, or CBS in their evening newscasts, and a value of "0" to the 391 massacres that did not receive coverage. I analyzed network television news coverage by conducting a multivariate logistic regression analysis in which TVNEWS was the dependent variable while the independent variables were the incident-, victim-, and offender-level variables provided by the SHR and newspaper data.

Weekly Newsmagazines

I examined weekly newsmagazine coverage by searching the *Reader's Guide to Periodical Literature* for the years 1976–1998. After locating weekly newsmagazine accounts by examining the articles listed in the "murder" category, I created a dichotomous variable, WEEKLY, by giving a value of "1" to the 23 massacres reported by either *Time*, *Newsweek*, or *U.S. News & World Report*, and a value of "0" to the incidents that did not receive coverage. To assess newsweekly magazine coverage, I conducted a logistic regression analysis in which WEEKLY was the dependent variable while the predictors were those derived from the SHR and newspaper data.

Chapter Notes

Introduction

1. A third type, spree murder, was also identified. Although it was originally conceptualized as a category that comprised multiple murders committed, mostly one at a time, over the span of a few days or a week, the spree murder type has often been used as a residual grouping for cases that do not easily fit into the other two categories.

Chapter 1

1. As discussed in the Appendix, news coverage constitutes an important source of data for this study. Supplementary Homicide Report data of 1976–1999 reveal, for example, that a three-victim criterion would yield more than three times as many cases as a four-victim requirement. However, a three-victim criterion would increase the risk of underreporting because incidents with smaller body counts are not only more numerous, they are also less newsworthy, which is an important consideration given the reliance on news coverage as a source of data. Indeed, previous research has shown that the number of fatal victims has a significant positive effect on the newsworthiness of a murder (Duwe, 2000; Johnstone, Hawkins, and Michener, 1994, p. 865–6; Wilbanks, 1984, p. 111). Therefore, even though triple homicides often receive news coverage, these cases are still more likely to go unreported than those involving four or more victims.

Chapter 3

1. I used *In Cold Blood* (Capote, 1965) as the source for material on the Clutter case.

Chapter 6

1. Some of the cities included Atlanta, Chicago, Cicero (IL), Lincolnshire (IL), Niles (IL), East Chicago (IN), Gary (IN), Boston, Albany (NY), New York City, Rochester (NY), Cincinnati, Cleveland, Columbus (OH), Dayton (OH), and Philadelphia (Tartaro, 1995).

Appendix

1. The incident data contained the following information: date (e.g., day, month, and year in which the murders occurred), city and state in which the homicides took place, the number of fatal and wounded victims, the number of offenders, weapon type, victim-offender relationship, location (e.g. public or residential setting), circumstance (e.g. robbery, drug-related, gang-related, etc.); as well as whether the incident was an interracial massacre, whether it involved assault weapon use, and whether it involved workplace violence. Both the victim and offender data contained variables on age, sex, and race, whereas the offender data also included information on whether the offender was arrested, killed by police, or had committed suicide.

2. Though it might seem more prudent to use "mass murder" as a search term, the vast majority of cases could not be located with this phrase in either the databases or the newspaper indexes because this term was often reserved for the heavily publicized incidents.

3. Specifically, the location of the offense (public or residential setting), the number of wounded victims, the offender outcome (arrested, killed by police, suicide, attempted suicide), the use of an assault weapon, whether the incident was a workplace massacre, and whether the offenders were motivated by profit were all recorded for each mass murder found through the newspaper search.

4. Because the SHR is a voluntary program involving law enforcement agencies nationwide, there is a small amount of underreporting. Fox (2000) has estimated that 8 percent of all homicides are not reported to the SHR.

5. This criterion includes cases in which the offender(s) intended to kill one person, but unintentionally killed others as well.

6. Newspaper accounts were found on 157 of the 193 cases. However, I was unable to locate offender outcome data for 46 of the 157 cases, leaving 111 in which there was sufficient information to determine whether these incidents were mass murders. Of the 111 cases, 83 (75 percent) were mass killings; 7 of these incidents were mass murder-suicides, whereas the remaining 76 involved offenders who were convicted of murder. The data obtained on the remaining 28 cases (25 percent) indicated that they were not mass murders because the offender was either acquitted or convicted of manslaughter or because the fire was later ruled to be an accident.

References

Adler, Jeffrey S. 1996. "The making of a moral panic in 19th-century America: the Boston garroting hysteria." *Deviant Behavior: An Interdisciplinary Journal* 17: 259–278.

Agnew, Robert. 1985. "A revised strain theory of delinquency." *Social Forces* 64 (1): 151–167.

_____. 1992. "Foundation for a general strain theory of crime and delinquency." *Criminology* 30 (1): 47–87.

Andrews, Reid. 1984. "Handgun Control Inc.'s exploitation of the McDonald's massacre." *Guns & Ammo* 28: 8.

Anfuso, Dawn. 1994. "Deflecting workplace violence." *Personnel Journal* 73: 66–78.

Antunes, George E., and Patricia A. Hurley. 1977. "The representation of criminal events in Houston's two daily newspapers." *Journalism Quarterly*, 54, 756–760.

Arboleda-Florez, J. 1979. "Amok." *Bulletin of the Academy of Psychiatry Law*, 7: 286–295.

Banay, Ralph S. 1956. "Psychology of a mass murderer." *Journal of Forensic Sciences* 1: 1–6.

Ben-Yehuda, Nachman. 1986. "The sociology of moral panics: Toward a new synthesis." *The Sociological Quarterly* 27: 495–513.

Berger, Meyer. 1951. *The Story of The New York Times, 1851–1951*. New York: Simon and Schuster.

Berne, E. 1950. "Cultural aspects of multiple murder." *Psychiatric Quarterly* 24: 250.

Best, Joel. 1987. "Rhetoric in claims-making: constructing the missing children problem." *Social Problems* 34: 101–121.

_____. 1990. *Threatened Children*. Chicago: University of Chicago Press.

_____. 1991. "'Road warriors'" on 'hair-trigger highways': Cultural resources and the media's construction of the 1987 freeway shooting problem." *Sociological Inquiry* 61: 327–45.

_____. 1999. *Random Violence: How We Talk About New Crimes and New Victims*. Los Angeles: University of California Press.

Blum, John Morton. 1991. *Years of Discord: American Politics and Society, 1961–1974*. New York: Norton.

Bruch, Hilde. 1967. "Mass murder: the Wagner case." *American Journal of Psychiatry* 124: 693–698.

Bureau of Labor Statistics. 1994. "National census of fatal occupational injuries, 1993." Washington, DC: U.S. Department of Labor.

_____. 1995. "National census of fatal occupational injuries, 1994." Washington, DC: U.S. Department of Labor.

Busch, Katie A., and James L. Cavanaugh Jr. 1986. "The study of multiple murder: preliminary examination of the interface between epistemology and methodology." *Journal of Interpersonal Violence* 1: 5–23.

Capote, Truman. 1965. *In Cold Blood.* New York: Vintage Books.

Cawood, James S. 1991. "On the edge: assessing the violent employee." *Security Management* 35: 131–136.

Chermak, Steven M. 1994. "Crime in the news media: a refined understanding of how crimes become news." Pp. 95–129 in Greg Barak (ed.) *Media, Process, and the Social Construction of Crime.* New York: Garland.

_____. 1995. *Victims in the News: Crime and the American News Media.* Boulder, CO: Westview Press.

_____. 1997. "The presentation of drugs in the news media: The news sources involved in the construction of social problems." *Justice Quarterly,* 14, 4, 687–719.

_____. 1998. "Predicting crime story salience: The effects of crime, victim, and defendant characteristics." *Journal of Criminal Justice,* 26, 1, 61–70.

Chester, Graham. 1993. *Berserk! Motiveless Random Massacres.* New York: St. Martin's Press.

Chiricos, Theodore G. 1996. "Moral panic as ideology: drugs, violence, race and punishment in America." Pp. 19–48 in Michael J. Lynch and E. Britt Patterson, eds. *Justice with Prejudice: Race and Criminal Justice in America.* Guilderland, NY: Harrow and Heston.

Chiricos, Theodore, with Sarah Eschholz and Marc Gertz. 1997. "Crime, news and fear of crime: Toward an identification of audience effects." *Social Problems,* 44, 3, 342–357.

Cohen, Daniel A. 1995. "Homicidal compulsion and the conditions of freedom: the social and psychological origins of familicide in America's early republic." *Journal of Social History* summer: 725–764.

Cohen, Stanley. 1972. *Folk Devils and Moral Panics.* London: McGibbon and Kee.

Cooper, John Milton. 1990. *Pivotal Decades: The United States, 1900–1920.* New York: Norton.

Courtwright, David T. 1996. *Violent Land.* Cambridge, MA: Harvard University Press.

Daly, Kathleen. 1995. "Celebrated crime cases and the public's imagination: From bad press to bad policy?" *Australian and New Zealand Journal of Criminology,* 28, special issue, 6–22.

Davis, F. James. 1952. "Crime news in Colorado newspapers." *American Journal of Sociology,* 57, June, 325–330.

de Becker, Gavin. 1988. "Damage control: managing the violent employee." *Security Management* 135: 138–144.

Dietz, Park E. 1986. "Mass, serial, and sensational homicides." *Bulletin of the New York Academy of Medicine* 62: 477–490.

DiLorenzo, Louis P., and Darren J. Carroll. 1995. "The growing menace: violence in the workplace." *New York State Bar Journal* January 1995: 24–30.

Ditton, Jason, and James Duffy. 1983. "Bias in the newspaper reporting of crime news." *British Journal of Criminology* 23: 159–65.

Douglas, John, and Mark Olshaker. 1995. *Mindhunter*. New York: Scribner.

Durkheim, Emile. [1897] 1966. *Suicide: A Study in Sociology*. New York: Free Press.

Duwe, Grant. 2000. "Body count journalism: The presentation of mass murder in the news media." *Homicide Studies* 4: 364–399.

_____. 2004. "The patterns and prevalence of mass murder in twentieth-century America." *Justice Quarterly* 21: 729–761.

_____. 2005. "A circle of distortion: The social construction of mass murder in the United States." *Western Criminology Review* 6: 59–78.

Duwe, Grant, with Tomislav Kovandzic and Carlisle Moody. 2002. "The impact of right-to-carry concealed firearms laws on mass public shootings." *Homicide Studies* 6: 271–296.

Eckberg, Douglas. 1995. "Estimates of early twentieth-century U.S. homicide rates: An econometric forecasting approach." *Demography* 32: 1–16.

_____. 2001. "Stalking the elusive homicide: A capture-recapture approach to the estimation of post–Reconstruction South Carolina killings." *Social Science History* 25: 67–91.

Editor & Publisher Yearbook. 1985–1997. New York: Editor & Publisher.

Egger, Steven A. 1984. "A working definition of serial murder and the reduction of linkage blindness." *Journal of Police Science and Administration* 12: 348–357.

Ericson, Richard V., with Patricia M. Baranek and Janet B.L. Chan. 1987. *Visualizing Deviance: A Study of News Organizations*. Toronto: University of Toronto Press.

_____. 1989. *Negotiating Control: A Study of News Sources*. Toronto: University of Toronto Press.

_____. 1991. *Representing Order: Crime, Law, and Justice in the News Media*. Toronto: University of Toronto Press.

Evseef, G.S., and E.M. Wisniewski. 1972. "A psychiatric study of a violent mass murderer." *Journal of Forensic Sciences* 17: 371–376.

Faber, Doris. 1963. *Printer's Devil to Publisher: Adolph S. Ochs of The New York Times*. New York: Messner.

Falk, Gerhard. 1990. *Murder: an Analysis of its Forms, Conditions, and Causes*. Jefferson, NC: McFarland.

Fishman, Mark. 1978. Crime waves as ideology. *Social Problems* 25: 531–43.

Fox, James Alan. 1996. *Uniform Crime Reports (United States): Supplementary Homicide Reports, 1976–1994* (computer file). ICPSR version. Boston: Northeastern University, College of Criminal Justice (producer), 1996. Ann Arbor, MI: Inter-university Consortium for Political and Social Research (distributor), 1996.

_____. 2000. "Demographics and U.S. homicide." Pp. 288–317 in Alfred Blumstein and Joel Wallman, eds. *The Crime Drop in America*. New York: Cambridge University Press.

Fox, James Alan, and Jack Levin. 1994. *Overkill: Mass and Serial Killing Exposed*. New York: Plenum Press.

_____. 1998. "Multiple homicide: Patterns of serial and mass murder." Pp. 407–455 in Michael Tonry, ed., *Crime and Justice: A Review of Research* (volume 23). Chicago: University of Chicago Press.

Friedman, Lawrence M. 1993. *Crime and Punishment in American History.* New York: Basic Books.

Gallemore Jr., Johnnie L., and James A. Panton. 1976. "Motiveless public assassins." *Bulletin of the American Academy of Psychiatry Law* 4: 51–57.

Galvin, James A.V., and John H. Macdonald. 1959. "Psychiatric study of a mass murderer." *The American Journal of Psychiatry* 115: 1057–1061.

Gamson, William A., David Croteau, William Hoynes, and Theodore Sasson. 1992. "Media images and the social construction of reality." *Annual Review of Sociology* 18: 373–393.

Garofalo, James. 1981. "Crime and the mass media: A selective review of research." *Journal of Research in Crime and Delinquency* 18: 319–350.

Goldberg, David J. 1999. *Discontented America: The United States in the 1920s.* Baltimore: Johns Hopkins University Press.

Goldstein, Paul J. 1985. "The drugs/violence nexus: A tripartite conceptual framework." *Journal of Drug Issues* 39: 143–174.

_____. 1998. "Drugs, violence, and federal funding: A research odyssey." *Substance Use and Misuse* 33: 1915–1936.

Goode, Erich, and Nachman Ben-Yehuda. 1994. "Moral panics: Culture, politics, and social construction." *Annual Review of Sociology* 20: 149–171.

Goulden, Joseph C. 1988. *Fit to Print: A.M. Rosenthal and His Times.* Secaucus, NJ: Lyle Stuart.

Graber, Doris. 1980. *Crime News and the Public.* New York: Praeger.

Gresswell, David M., and Clive R. Hollin. 1994. "Multiple murder: A review." *The British Journal of Criminology* 34: 1–14.

Gusfield, Joseph R. 1981. *The Culture of Public Problems.* Chicago: University of Chicago Press.

Hall, Stuart, Chas Critcher, Tony Jefferson, John Clarke, and Brian Roberts. 1978. *Policing the Crisis: Mugging, the State, and Law and Order.* London: Macmillan.

Harris, Frank. 1932. *Presentation of Crime in Newspapers.* Minneapolis: Sociological Press.

Heath, Linda. 1984. "Impact of newspaper crime reports on fear of crime: Multimethodological investigation." *Journal of Personality and Social Psychology* 47: 263–276.

Hempel, Anthony G., with J. Reid Meloy, and Thomas C. Richards. 1999. "Offender and offense characteristics of a nonrandom sample of mass murderers." *Journal of the American Academy of Psychiatry and the Law* 27 (2): 213–225.

Hilgartner, Stephen, and Charles L. Bosk. 1988. "The rise and fall of social problems: A public arenas model." *American Journal of Sociology* 94: 53–78.

Hirschi, Travis. 1969. *Causes of Delinquency.* Berkeley: University of California Press.

_____, and Rodney Stark. 1969. "Hellfire and delinquency." *Social Problems* 17: 202–213.

Holmes, Ronald M., and Stephen T. Holmes. 1992. "Understanding mass murder: a starting point." *Federal Probation* 56: 53–60.

_____. 1994. *Murder in America*. Thousand Oaks, CA: Sage.

Humphries, Drew. 1981. "Serious crime, news coverage, and ideology: A content analysis of crime coverage in a metropolitan paper." *Crime and Delinquency* 27, 2, 191–205.

Inciardi, James A. 1990. "The crack-violence connection within a population of hard-core adolescent offenders." *Drugs and Violence: Causes, Correlates, and Consequences*. National Institute on Drug Abuse Research Monograph 103.

Inter-university Consortium for Political and Social Research (ICPSR). 2002. *Uniform Crime Reports (United States): Supplementary Homicide Reports, 1995–1999*. Ann Arbor, MI: ICPSR.

Jacobs, James B., and Jessica S. Henry. 1995. "The social construction of a hate crime epidemic." *The Journal of Criminal Law and Criminology* 86: 366–391.

Jang, Joon Sung, and Byron R. Johnson. 2001. "Neighborhood disorder, individual religiosity, and adolescent use of illicit drugs: A test of the multilevel hypothesis." *Criminology* 39: 109–143.

Jenkins, Philip. 1988. "Myth and murder: the serial killer panic of 1983–5." *Criminal Justice Research Bulletin* 3: 1–7.

_____. 1989. "Serial murder in the United States 1900–1940: A historical perspective." *Journal of Criminal Justice* 17: 377–392.

_____. 1994. *Using Murder: The Social Construction of Serial Homicide*. Hawthorne, NY: Aldine De Gruyter.

Johnson, Byron R., with Soon Jung Jang, David B. Larson, and Spencer De Li. 2001. "Does adolescent religious commitment matter? A reexamination of the effects of religiosity on delinquency." *Journal of Research in Crime and Delinquency* 38: 22–44.

_____. 2000. "The 'invisible institution' and black youth crime: The church as an agency of local social control." *Journal of Youth and Adolescence* 29: 479–498.

_____. 2000. "Escaping from the crime of inner cities: Church attendance and religious salience among disadvantaged youth." *Justice Quarterly* 17: 379–391.

Johnson, Dennis L., with John G. Kurutz and John B. Kiehlbauch. 1994. "Break the cycle of violence." *Security Management* 38: 24–28.

Johnstone, John W.C., with Darnell F. Hawkins and Arthur Michener. 1994. "Homicide reporting in Chicago dailies." *Journalism Quarterly*, 71, 4, 860–872.

Kahn, Marvin W. 1960. "Psychological test study of a mass murderer." *Journal of Projective Techniques* 24: 148–160.

Kappeler, Victor, Mark Blumberg, and Gary W. Potter. 1996. *The Mythology of Crime and Criminal Justice*. Prospect Heights, IL: Waveland Press.

Karpman, Ben. 1955. "Multiple murders." *Archives of Criminal Psychodynamics* 1(3): 713–721.

Kelleher, Michael. 1997. *Flashpoint: the American Mass Murderer*. Westport, CT: Praeger.

Kleck, Gary. 1991. *Point Blank: Guns and Violence in America*. Hawthorne, NY: Aldine DeGruyter.

_____. 1997. *Targeting Guns: Firearms and Their Control*. Hawthorne, NY: Aldine DeGruyter.

Krajicek, David J. 1998. *Scooped! Media Miss Real Story on Crime While Chasing Sex, Sleaze, and Celebrities.* New York: Columbia University Press.

Lane, Roger. 1997. *Murder in America: A History.* Columbus: Ohio State University Press.

_____. 1999. *Violent Death in the City: Suicide, Accident, and Murder in Nineteenth-Century Philadelphia.* Columbus: Ohio State University Press.

Larson, Erik. 1994. "A false crisis: how workplace violence became a hot issue." *Wall Street Journal* October 13.

Lavergne, Gary. 1997. *A Sniper in the Tower: The Charles Whitman Murders.* Denton: University of North Texas Press.

Levin, Jack, and James Alan Fox. 1985. *Mass Murder: America's Growing Menace.* New York: Berkley Books.

_____. 1996. "A Psycho-social analysis of Mass Murder." Pp. 55–76 in Thomas O'Reilly-Fleming, ed., *Serial and Mass Murder: Theory, Research, and Policy.* Toronto: Canadian Scholars Press.

Liska, A. E., and W. Baccaglini. 1990. "Feeling safe by comparison: Crime in the newspapers." *Social Problems,* 37, 3, 360–374.

Loseke, Donileen R. 1989. "Violence is 'violence' ... or is it? The social construction of 'wife abuse' and public policy." Pp. 191–205 in Joel Best, ed., *Images of Issues: Typifying Contemporary Social Problems.* New York: Aldine DeGruyter.

Lotz, Roy E. 1991. *Crime and the American Press.* New York: Praeger.

Lowney, Kathleen S., and Joel Best. 1995. "Stalking strangers and lovers: Changing media typifications of a new crime problem." Pp. 33–57 in Joel Best, ed., *Images of Issues: Typifying Contemporary Social Problems.* New York: Aldine DeGruyter.

MacDonald, John M. 1986. *The Murderer and His Victim.* Springfield, IL: Thomas.

Malmquist, Carl P. 1980. "Psychiatric aspects of familicide." *Bulletin of the American Academy of Psychology* 8: 298–304.

Marsh, Harry L. 1989. "Newspaper crime coverage in the U.S.: 1893–1988." *Criminal Justice Abstracts* 21: 506–514.

McCorkle, Richard C., and Terance D. Miethe. 1998. "The political and organizational response to gangs: An examination of a 'moral panic' in Nevada." *Justice Quarterly* 15 (1).

McCully, Robert S. 1978. "The laugh of Satan: a study of a familial murderer." *Journal of Personality Assessment* 42: 81–91.

McElvaine, Robert S. 1993. *The Great Depression: America, 1929–1941.* New York: Times Books.

McGrath, Roger. 1984. *Gunfighters, Highwaymen, and Vigilantes: Violence on the Frontier.* Berkeley: University of California Press.

McKanna, Clare. 1997. *Homicide, Race, and Justice in the American West, 1880–1920.* Tucson: University of Arizona Press.

Merton, Robert K. 1938. "Social structure and anomie." *American Sociological Review* 3: 672–682.

Messner, Steven F., and Richard Rosenfeld. 1994. *Crime and the American Dream.* Belmont, CA: Wadsworth.

Minor, Marianne. 1995. *Preventing Workplace Violence: Positive Management Strategies.* Menlo Park, CA: Crisp.

Monkkonen, Eric H. 2001. *Murder in New York City*. Los Angeles: University of California Press.

Newton, Michael. 1988. *Mass Murder: an Annotated Bibliography*. New York: Garland.

Nichols, Lawrence T. 1997. "Social problems as landmark narratives: Bank of Boston, mass media and 'money laundering.'" *Social Problems*, 44, 3, 324–341.

Osborn, William M. 2000. *The Wild Frontier*. New York: Random House.

Palermo, George B. 1997. "The berserk syndrome: A review of mass murder." *Aggression and Violent Behavior*, 2, 1, 1–8.

_____, and Lee E. Ross. 1999. "Mass murder, suicide, and moral development: Can we separate the adults from the juveniles?" *International Journal of Offender Therapy and Comparative Criminology*, 43, 1, 8–20.

Petee, Thomas A., Kathy G. Padgett, and Thomas S. York. 1997. "Debunking the stereotype: an examination of mass murder in public places." *Homicide Studies* 1: 317–337.

Pfohl, Stephen J. 1977. "The 'discovery' of child abuse." *Social Problems* 24: 310–323.

Pritchard, David, and Karen D. Hughes. 1997. "Patterns of deviance in crime news." *Journal of Communication* 47 (3): 49–67.

Rappaport, Richard G. 1988. "The serial and mass murderer: patterns, differentiation, pathology." *American Journal of Forensic Psychiatry* 9: 39–48.

Reader's Guide to Periodical Literature. 1976–1998. New York: Wilson.

Reeves, Thomas C. 2000. *Twentieth Century America: A Brief History*. New York: Oxford University Press.

Ressler, Robert K., Ann W. Burgess, and John E. Douglas. 1988. *Sexual Homicide: Patterns and Motives*. New York: Lexington Books.

Riedel, Marc. 1999. "Sources of Homicide Data." Pp. 31–48 in M. Dwayne Smith and Margaret A. Zahn, eds., *Studying and Preventing Homicide: Issues and Challenges*. Thousand Oaks, CA: Sage.

Rodrigue, John C. 2001. *Reconstruction in the Corn Field: From Slavery to Free Labor in Louisiana Sugar Parishes 1862–1880*. Baton Rouge: Louisiana State University Press.

Roth, Jeffrey A., and Christopher S. Koper. 1997. "Appendix A: Assault weapons and mass murder." *Impact Evaluation of the Public Safety and Recreational Firearms Use Protection Act of 1994*. Washington, DC: The Urban Institute.

Rowlands, M. 1990. "Multiple murder: a review of the international literature." *Journal of the College of Prison Medicine* 1: 3–7.

Sacco, Vincent F. 1995. "Media constructions of crime." *The Annals of the American Academy of Political and Social Sciences* 539: 141–154.

Schmidt, Karl, Lee Hill, and George Guthrie. 1977. "Running amok." *International Journal of Social Psychiatry*, 23: 264–274.

Schneider Denenberg, Tia, Richard V. Denenberg, Mark Braverman, and Susan Braverman. 1996. "Dispute resolution & workplace violence." *Dispute Resolution Journal* January-March: 6–17.

Schwartz, Martin D., and Walter S. DeKeseredy. 1993. "The return of the 'battered husband syndrome' through the typification of women as violent." *Crime, Law, and Social Change* 20: 249–65.

Sheley, Joseph F., and Cindy D. Ashkins. 1981. "Crime, crime news, and crime views." *Public Opinion Quarterly*, 45, 4, 492–506.

Sherizen, Sanford. 1978. "Social creation of crime news: All the news fitted to print." Pp. 203–224 in C. Winick, ed., *Deviance and Mass Media*. Beverly Hills, CA: Sage.

Slora, Karen B., with Dennis S. Joy and William Terris. 1991. "Personnel selection to control employee violence." *Journal of Business and Psychology* 5: 417–426.

Smith, Susan J. 1984. "Crime in the news." *British Journal of Criminology*, 24, 3, 289–295.

Spector, Malcolm, and John I. Kitsuse. 1977. *Constructing Social Problems*. Menlo Park, CA: Cummings.

Stack, Steven. 1997. "Homicide followed by suicide: An analysis of Chicago data." *Criminology*, 35, 3, 435–453.

Stevens, John D. 1991. *Sensationalism and the New York Press*. New York: Columbia University Press.

Stuart, Peggy. 1992. "Murder on the job." *Personnel Journal* 71: 72–84.

Tartaro, Joseph P. 1995. "Symposium: Violent Crime Control and Law Enforcement Act of 1994: the great assault weapon hoax." *Dayton Law Review*.

Tierney, Kathleen J. 1982. "The battered women movement and the creation of the wife beating problem." *Social Problems* 29: 207–219.

Tifft, Susan E., and Alex S. Jones. 1999. *The Trust: The Private and Powerful Family Behind The New York Times*. New York: Little, Brown.

Tolnay, Stewart, and E.M. Beck. 1995. *A Festival of Violence: An Analysis of Southern Lynchings, 1882–1930*. Champaign: University of Illinois Press.

United States House of Representatives Committee on Post Office and Civil Service. 1987. "Events of August 20, 1986, in Edmond, Oklahoma; joint hearing before the Subcommittee on Postal Operations and Services and the Subcommittee on Postal Personnel and Modernization of the Committee on Post Office and Civil Service." Washington, DC: U.S. Government Printing Office.

_____. 1992. "A Post Office tragedy: the shooting at Royal Oak." Washington, DC: U.S. Government Printing Office.

Westermeyer, Joseph. 1972. "A comparison of amok and other homicide in Laos." *The American Journal of Psychiatry* 129: 703–709.

Wiersema, Brian, Colin Loftin, and David McDowall. 2000. "A comparison of Supplementary Homicide Reports and National Vital Statistics System homicide estimates for U.S. counties." *Homicide Studies* 4: 317–340.

Wilbanks, William. 1984. *Murder in Miami: An Analysis of Homicide Patterns and Trends in Dade County (Miami) Florida, 1917–1983*. Lanham, MD: University Press of America.

Windau, Janice, and Guy Toscano. 1994. "Workplace homicides in 1992. Compensation and working conditions, February 1994." Washington, DC: Department of Labor, Bureau of Labor Statistics.

Windhauser, John W., with Jennifer Seiter and L. Thomas Winfree. 1990. "Crime news in the Louisiana Press, 1980 v. 1985." *Journalism Quarterly*, 67, 72–78.

Woolgar, Steve, and Dorothy Pawluch. 1985. "Ontological gerrymandering: the anatomy of social problems explanations." *Social Problems* 32: 214–227.

Zahn, Margaret A., and Patricia L. McCall. 1999. "Homicide in the 20th-Century United States: Trends and patterns." Pp. 10–30 in M. Dwayne Smith and Margaret A. Zahn, eds., *Studying and Preventing Homicide: Issues and Challenges*. Thousand Oaks, CA: Sage.

Index